THE PATIENT
FLOW

How Hardwiring
Hospital-Wide
Flow Drives
Competitive
Performance

ADVANTAGE

Kirk Jensen, MD, MBA, FACEP
and Thom Mayer, MD, FACEP, FAAP

Foreword by Tom Peters

Published by:
Fire Starter Publishing
350 W. Cedar Street
Pensacola, FL 32502
Phone: 866-354-3473
Fax: 850-332-5117
www.firestarterpublishing.com

ISBN: 978-1-622-18018-9

Library of Congress Control Number: 2014956829

Printed in the United States of America

To my beautiful, brilliant and always inspiring wife, Maureen-you are and will always be the most amazing person in the world.

To our sons, Kevin, Greg and Josh-your humor, kindness and courage have made me a better man and I love you deeply.

To Josh's wife Valerie and their wonderful daughters, Eve and Audra, who are wonderful, gracious and generous additions to our lives and who are the future we hope to affect.

To the memory of my parents, affectionately known as Grandpa Jim and Grandma Bette, your wisdom, I hope and pray, is somehow reflected, however imperfectly, in these pages.

To the memory of Maureen's Father, John B. Henry, MD, who was a scientist, physician and man filled with intellectual curiosity, integrity, and energy. And to Maureen's elegant mother, Georgette, who gave me the greatest gift in my life-her daughter.

—Thom Mayer, MD

To my wonderful parents, Earl and Naomi, who as the parents of eight children first introduced me to the importance of process, management, and organization.

To my sons Christopher and Michael, you are constant reminders of what is truly important in my life.

And finally, to my wife Karen, thank you for your ongoing support, judgment, wisdom, and humor.

—Kirk Jensen, MD, MBA

TABLE OF CONTENTS

Section 2 — Advanced Flow Concepts

- A Unified, Overall Approach
- The Beginning and The End
- Culture and Leadership
- Benefits of Successful Hospitalist Programs
- The Hospitalist's Critical Role

- The Process: A Four-Step Sequence and Refinement
- Predicting Capacity
- Predicting Demand
- Plan For Mismatches
- Evaluate The Plan
- Getting Results

Section 3 — Frontiers of Flow

- How The Use of Flow Bundles Enhances Flow
- Principles of Demand-Capacity Management in The ICU
- Reliably Forecasting Demand
- Real-Time Monitoring of Flow
- Queuing Theory in the ICU
- Managing Variation to Maximize Value and Eliminate Waste
- Eliminating Constraints and Bottlenecks to Improve Access to Critical Care Units
- Flow as a Complex, Adaptive System

- Natural Variation
- Artificial Variation
- Know Who is Coming—And When
- Segment Patient Flow
- Optimize Management of The Start Time
- Using Variation to Add Value
- Coordinating Overall Flow
- Bringing The Surgeon On Board

FOREWORD

I suspect that ninety percent of the people who read this book will have technical and scientific backgrounds. (Like me, an engineer-MBA.) Hence I am very loathe to begin with: I love this book.

But I do.

Books like this are rarely well written. (Understatement.) This one, dare I say it, flows. It is clear and predicates follow subjects, etc. A terrific piece of prose.

The prescriptions described are doable (with a lot of hard work—an incredible amount of hard work in fact) and clear and free of jargon and gobble-dygook and circular thinking. C follows B follows A. It adds up.

Though implementation will take enormous effort that is not because the steps are complex—it is because you will be dramatically rewiring the way in which hundreds of exceptionally well-trained professionals will be living and working together.

This is *not* rocket science. Healthcare delivery is enormously complex to be sure, and much data is required here to make various bits of the system and sub-systems work together effectively. Yet the pieces of the puzzle are astonishingly straightforward in terms of their underlying logic and construction.

This *is* rocket science. The process is clearly specified and the steps are brilliantly articulated. But the *will* to make it work and construct a new structure for doing the work must be there. Quite simply (to state), full-value implementation requires a redistribution of power. You won't get more than a small fraction of the potential yield unless you can introduce and achieve, to use an overused term, true teamwork, i.e., people from different bits of the organization, with ranks from high to "low," working across traditional boundaries as a coherent organism to deliver a very high-quality, relatively low cost product.

(I must repeat myself: the *willpower* and *passion* to reconceive the delivery of "product" in your institutions must be in place to do this right.)

The opportunity represented herein is staggering. The opportunity to deliver the highest quality care on an unprecedented scale. The opportunity to remove unimaginable quantities of waste—time and other scarce resources—that attend the mismatched, frequently non-communicative sub-systems generally in place today.

This is a book, though the formula is clear, about revolution. The delivery of care, if this is done right, will barely be recognizable if the implementation is more or less complete.

Yes, I do love this book; because it has the potential to make miracles. Operations that work seamlessly—"seamless" in its literal sense is a term of awe-inspiring power. The aim is sky high. But, as the authors imply and sometimes say directly, in actual fact you have no option. To operate (to survive!) in an exponentially changing environment requires an exponentially different way of doing business than is normally the fact today. Between these covers lies a guide that is truly priceless.

(Following a nasty car accident this past winter, I wrote a paper I titled "Excellence. NO EXCUSES" that ran over 500 pages. As always, choosing the appropriate epigraph for the monster was almost the most difficult part of the exercise. But I ended up with this one, from the physicist Albert Bartlett: "The greatest shortcoming of the human race is our inability to understand the exponential function." Healthcare, and many other parts of our gargantuan economy, are flying in exponentially changing turbulence. The rewards for "getting it right" are gasp worthy; the costs of dawdling or getting it wrong are, make no mistake, institutional collapse.)

Tom Peters

Acknowledgments

When it comes to gratitude, it is always difficult to know where to begin…and where to end.

Having worked this soil for a very long period of time with the best and the most generous people in the profession, we have so many to thank that writing "Acknowledgments" is in many ways as big a challenge as writing this book—and equally as satisfying. The chance to recognize so many to whom we owe so much is both humbling and gratifying.

Sir Winston Churchill once said of a contemporary, "He is a humble man…with much to be humble about." We have much to be humble about when it comes to the kind words our colleagues, friends, and mentors have uttered about our work, and in their innate willingness to share in advancing the future of flow and its dramatic impact on the changing and evolving healthcare environment. Our first debt of gratitude is therefore to the healthcare caregivers and their leaders and managers who have read and adopted these principles in service to their patients. Our friend, colleague, and mentor, Harry Rhoads, Jr. is the founder of the Washington Speakers Bureau, arguably the most prestigious and successful such group in the world. He constantly reminds us, "The only reason to give a speech is to help someone." Our deepest hope is that the words and insights in this book help someone make their job easier and their patients' burdens lighter.

This book is not our work alone, but rather reflects the collective wisdom and experience of those with whom we have come into contact while developing and implementing the emerging concepts that flow's many insights can create in increasing value and eliminating waste in healthcare. Thus we would like to thank all of our colleagues at our physician group, BestPractices, including Doctors Robert Cates, Glenn Druckenbrod, John Howell, Rick Place,

Dan Hanfling, John Maguire, Dan Avstreih, Alan Lo, Alice Gouvenayre, Praveen Kache, and Peter Jacoby.

Medicine is by its very nature a team endeavor. The most important members of that team are the dedicated nursing professionals who tirelessly and against difficult odds provide the best possible care to hundreds of millions of patients each year one at a time. They are not only our trusted colleagues, but true co-creators of the flow solutions embodied in this book. Among the many humbling facts we encounter in our work, none is more so than the nursing heroes with whom we work every day.

The authors of the chapters were truly a joy with which to work. Their insights make this a book which encompasses a broad swath of flow concepts across the entire healthcare system. To Drs. Jason Vourlekis, John Jones, Francisco Loya, Michael Hicks, Nathan Goldfein, and Mr. Mark Hamm goes our deep thanks and appreciation.

Without visionary leadership, flow can be a sterile concept. With such leadership, flow accelerates at a breathtaking pace in the best of organizations, who are fortunate to have leaders like Knox Singleton, Mark Stauder, and Patrick Christiansen at Inova Health Services; Michael Burnette at Piedmont Health Services; Tony Ardabell at Bon Secours Health System; Charles Barnett at Seton Health; Marvin Pember, Frank Lopez, Karla Perez, and Dr. Lynda Smirz at United Health Services; and Chad Wable at St. Mary's Health System in Connecticut. Without their support of the concepts of hardwiring flow in their hospitals, none of this work could have succeeded.

Our friend and mentor Tom Peters has not only been consistently supportive of this work, he has been a constant source of insights and inspiration. To have such an internationally recognized thought leader in our court is fortune beyond belief.

Leonard Berry's work on service and the intersection of business and healthcare has been an important and ongoing influence on us, and we are grateful for the assistance he has lent.

Two legendary leaders in healthcare serve both as mentors and friends, Dr. Don Berwick and Quint Studer. These insightful, kind, and generous men have truly changed the landscape of healthcare and how it is delivered—and they have dramatically influenced our work.

Since our group's merger with EmCare and Envison Healthcare, their leaders have not only sustained their commitment to our work, but indeed ac-

Acknowledgments

celerated it. Todd Zimmerman, Bill Sanger, Ron Williams, and Drs. Dighton Packard, Terry Meadows, Brian Erling, Russ Harris and Angel Iscovich have been particularly supportive.

Linda Cooper and Cyndra Fye are quite simply the finest administrative support people in the world and are emblematic of the positive and creative spirit that flow requires. Robert Milks was of great help in organizing and facilitating the development of the manuscript. The leaders at Fire Starting Publishing were responsible for taking these ideas and turning them into the polished format in which it currently occupies. Bekki Kennedy, Jamie Stewart, and Chris Roman contributed their combined professionalism over a sustained period of time to make this a book that, while taxing in the many hours it took to complete, was absolutely enjoyable to produce.

B.G. Porter, the President of Studer Group, has not only supported our work over the years, but immediately approved our moving forward with Fire Starter Publishing to expedite its publication. His kind heart and wisdom are as constant as they are appreciated.

While we have many friends and mentors in healthcare, we would like to specifically thank Dr. Rob Strauss, whose thoughts and insights are countless. He is truly a national treasure.

We have had the chance to work personally over the years with numerous leaders and advocates in healthcare, all of whom have contributed to our understanding of healthcare, process improvement, and change management. For this we will always be grateful.

Many individuals and organizations have contributed to our evolving understanding of how to improve patient flow operations and management. The Institute for Healthcare Improvement (IHI), the American College of Emergency Physicians (ACEP), the Emergency Nurses Association, Martin Gottlieb and Associates, Associates in Process Improvement (API), X32 Healthcare, and Studer Group have all provided opportunities to learn, grow, share, and implement positive and productive change.

We would like to specifically acknowledge a number of people who have supported and stimulated us in our intellectual and professional endeavors and who are passionately committed to improving healthcare delivery and care: Kevin Nolan, Jody Crane, MD, MBA, Chuck Noon, PhD, Roger Resar, MD, Carol Haraden, PhD, Dan Kirkpatrick, MHA, Marilyn Rudolph, RN, Deb Kaczynski, RN, Maureen Bisognano and Eugene Litvak, PhD.

Our colleagues at Studer Group, Stephanie Baker, RN, Lynne Cunningham, and Dan Smith, MD, have been passionate about this subject and generous in sharing their wisdom and experience.

For their sustained patience, forbearance, and humor, I (Thom) thank my always inspiring wife, Maureen, and our sons, Greg, Kevin, and Josh. The warmth of their love fuels my work always.

I (Kirk) would like to acknowledge my parents, Earl and Naomi, who as the parents of eight children first introduced me to the importance of process, management and organization. My sons Christopher and Michael are constant reminders of what is truly important in my life. To my wife Karen, thank you for your ongoing support, judgment, wisdom, and humor.

If we have unintentionally neglected to mention the many others who have contributed to our lives and our thinking about flow and its essential contributions to healthcare, it is only because of space limitations and does not reflect the depth of our appreciation and gratitude. Any errors or omissions are ours alone.

CHAPTER 1

WHY FLOW MATTERS

by Kirk Jensen, MD, and Thom Mayer, MD

"May you live in interesting times."

—*Ancient Chinese Curse*

"Only connect! That was the whole of her sermon.
Only connect the prose and the passion, and both will be exalted,
And human love will be seen at its height.
Live in fragments no longer.
Only connect…"

—*E. M. Forster,* Howards End

In healthcare, we live in interesting times, both for better and for worse. In the not so distant past, change in healthcare seemed less frequent, less cataclysmic, and interspersed with stretches of time in which we could avoid change and merely focus on operations. When change did occur it seemed to engulf us, in the same way that Class V whitewater rapids do to a kayaker… It was exhilarating, stimulating, but also a bit dangerous if not handled with consummate skill and technique.

But at least there were some calm, placid stretches of water between the changes where we could relax, get our wits about us, and take in the view, to gain some semblance of perspective until the next set of rapids. Today, all of us in healthcare find ourselves in what we call "the perpetual whitewater of change." In fact, it seems the only constant is…change!

For the remainder of our careers, each of us will operate in highly capacity-constrained environments, which will require us to find creative and sustainable ways to become *the high-quality, low-cost providers of healthcare*, while simultaneously assuring stakeholders that reliability, patient safety, service excellence, and risk reduction are not only maintained but improved over time.

It is a daunting challenge and one that is increasing—not diminishing—in both importance and complexity. Fundamentally, we are perpetually being asked to do "more with less" (IHI, 2005). Indeed, Quint Studer's recent book (Studer, 2014) sums up our core challenge in the title: *A Culture of High Performance: Achieving Higher Quality at a Lower Cost.*

FLOW IS NON-NEGOTIABLE

Creating a smoother hospital operation by increasing flow is a critical imperative for our healthcare facilities. It delivers a better experience for patients and staff, with improvements in safety, service, and outcomes. In fact, hardwiring flow offers all of the following benefits to our healthcare systems:

- improves financial return by increasing capacity;
- shortens time intervals by decreasing or eliminating waste;
- identifies and removes bottlenecks;
- reduces stress for patients, families, and caregivers by driving simplicity and increasing reliability;
- increases safety by reducing non-value-added variation;
- improves service and the perception of service by tying flow and service together;
- increases the number of positive clinical outcomes through the use of evidence-based approaches; and
- reduces costs by decreasing steps that don't add value.

E. M. Forster's quote earlier guides us in our understanding that flow matters precisely because it connects the pieces of the healthcare system and its processes in deeply important ways. Further, our patients come to the healthcare system with a reasonable expectation that "connection" and meaningful interrelatedness fundamentally drive our design of such processes, only to be surprised and disappointed to learn that they are not nearly as connected as they might think.

As Nobel Prize–winning novelist Saul Bellow pointed out, "Reality greets these ideas the way a cement floor greets a dropping light bulb" (Bellow, 1965). Despite that observation—which definitely holds true for changing systems and process in this case—flow matters. It is the best tool for assuring that hospitals and healthcare systems are not only "connected," but "interconnected," to add value and decrease waste. Flow is thus the primary "connected-ness tool."

THE IMPLICATIONS OF CROWDING

A fundamental problem facing nearly every healthcare system is crowding. Reports by the federal government and medical organizations over the past decade have consistently found that crowding in emergency departments is a serious problem (See, e.g., GAO, 2009). And usually, where there is crowding in the emergency department (ED), there is crowding in the hospital as a whole, or at least problems with processes and performance. The situation is likely only to worsen; consider these facts about the underlying conditions behind ED crowding (as well as crowding in the hospital at large) in the years to come:

- The American population is aging. As baby boomers move into old age, their health problems are increasing and becoming more complex, and they will continue to do so. Because of the size of that baby boomer generation, more and more patients will be coming into our EDs as emergency patients and our hospitals as inpatients. And that's not to mention their parents, the "greatest generation." More people are alive in their late 80s and 90s (or even older) than ever in human history, forming for the first time a cohort at that age level. (See Figure 1.1).

- Contrary to popular belief, increases in ED patient volume come primarily from critical care patients and not from non-urgent patients. Critical care patient volume rose 50 percent in the first years of this century, while non-urgent volume remained about the same (CDC, 2006; EDBA, 2013). And as baby boomers age, more of their problems will fall into that critical care and urgent care category.

- Visits to the ED increased by 23 percent between 1997 and 2007, a report by the Centers for Disease Control and Prevention (CDC) indicated, and 2008 saw a record high in the number of those visits (ACEP, 2010).

- National studies in the early years of this century revealed that 91 percent of ED directors reported crowding as a problem, with 40 percent reporting crowding daily (Schneider et al., 2003).

- The impact of the Affordable Care Act, while emerging in precise detail, already means that there are fewer primary care physicians, as more internal medicine doctors, family practice physicians, and even pediatricians abandon their practices for "Concierge Medicine" (Mayer, 2014).

The Baby Boomers are Here...

Demographics growth is driven by the elderly:
- The 65 and older age cohort will experience a 28% growth in the next decade
  - One baby-boomer turns 50 every 18 seconds and one baby-boomer turns 60 every 7 seconds (10,000 a day)
  - This will continue for the next 18 years

- This cohort will comprise 15% of the total population by 2016

- A higher proportion of patients in this cohort, in comparison to other age groups, are triaged with an emergent condition

- One-quarter of Medicare beneficiaries have five or more chronic conditions, sees an average of 13 physicians per years, and fills 50 prescriptions per year

Figure 1.1 The aging of our population makes flow matter even more, as demands by the increasing number of "Baby Boomers" impact healthcare.

Crowding in the ED will cause problems for the hospital as a whole, frequently reflecting patient flow problems (process and capacity) in the hospital as a whole as well. One study of the effects of crowding noted, "When the bed capacity of an ED is routinely reduced by boarders, it signifies a critical problem elsewhere in the system. A boarding problem most likely reflects a resource constraint (i.e., inadequate inpatient bed capacity) or a policy constraint (e.g., bed management policies, financial incentives to prioritize elective admissions over emergency ones)" (McCarthy et al., 2009). The study also reported that length of stay in the ED correlates with hospital occupancy rate and number of emergency admissions. In the context of the input-throughput-output model of movement through the ED, another study observed that a "common barrier to output is high inpatient occupancy, resulting in patients boarding in the ED while waiting for an available hospital bed" (Sun et al., 2013).

While non-urgent patients are not the cause of increasing crowding, volumes from this patient cohort are unlikely to cease. Discussing the CDC report in 2010, the president of the American College of Emergency Physicians (ACEP), Dr. Angela Gardner, noted that the report:

"made the excellent point that non-urgent does not imply unnecessary…Our patients are in the [ED] because that's where they need to be…Most doctors' offices are open for around 45 hours a week, as opposed to the 168 hours a week emergency departments are open. That nearly two-thirds of emergency patients come to the [ED] between 5 pm and 8 am during the week or on weekends highlights the unpredictable nature of health emergencies. When you are the one who has a sick child, the last thing you want is a 'closed' sign or after-hours message" (ACEP, 2010).

Consider this:
Every **emergency department** is a 24/7/365 operation, meeting demand 8,760 hours per year. And it's attached to a **hospital,** which typically operates at maximum peak **capacity** for only 12 to 18 hours per day five days per week (3,000–4,500 hours per year). It's also attached to an **outpatient healthcare system,** which typically operates 9 am to 5 pm 250 days per year (or 2,000 hours per year). Clearly this is a **demand-capacity mismatch,** requiring the tools and strategies to hardwire efficient flow.

Combining that constant volume with the increasing number of patients who require more complicated and critical care ensures continued demand for emergency care and services in the future. One other factor guarantees that the patients will keep coming. It results from what we might call the "paradox of full capacity." Primarily because of financial and operational pressures, hospitals have limited their capacity and tried to operate at near 100 percent of that capacity.

Such operations often lead to a "factory model," one in which "everybody is busy all the time and there is seldom unused capacity" (Jensen and Kirkpatrick, 2014). The paradox lies in the effects of this model in action. Benjamin Sun and his colleagues pointed out in their recent study that "attempts to maximize inpatient bed occupancy have reduced the ability of hospitals to absorb new patients and increased the prevalence of admitted patients boarding in the ED" (Sun, 2013).

A system with the unscheduled arrival of people, such as a hospital, that operates near 100 percent, in fact, generates backups for itself and therefore delays, which should not surprise anyone; queuing theory predicts such an outcome. Further illustrating this paradox is a training course called "Friday Night at the ER" that Peter Senge and his colleagues (who pioneered systems theory concepts) utilize. The course is designed to educate leaders and managers *outside of healthcare* in the intricacies and vagaries of systems thinking (Kim, 2006; Senge, 2006).

The familiar lines in stores at checkout are queues; any system with unscheduled arrivals is susceptible to queues. Queuing theory is based on mathematical and management operations principles that such systems follow. Once the principles were understood, the theory was developed to address how a system with a fixed amount of resources could meet unscheduled demand.

Queuing theorists have learned that the optimal operational capacity of a system with unscheduled demand is about 80 to 85 percent. (In fact, above 60 percent, the chances of backup begin to accelerate more quickly.) Because 50 to 75 percent of patients admitted to hospitals go through the ED (CDC, 2006), when hospitals are operating at close to capacity and admissions start to back up, the crowding in the ED is likely to compound quickly. As we indicate in Chapter 2, meaningful changes at these maximum demand-capacity mismatches have logarithmic, geometric impacts, not simply arithmetic ones, and therefore have dramatic effects.

WHAT CROWDING IMPLIES

When we talk about crowding, what we mean may seem obvious. Defining it, though, makes the problems associated with crowding clearer. ACEP has provided a clear definition, in a report of its Crowding Resources Task Force in 2002: "[Crowding] is a situation in which the identified need for emergency services outstrips available resources in the ED…[which] occurs in hospital EDs when there are more patients than staffed ED treatment beds and wait times exceed a reasonable period.

"Crowding typically involves patients being monitored in non-treatment areas (e.g., hallways) awaiting ED treatment beds or inpatient beds. Crowding may also involve an inability to appropriately triage patients, with large numbers of patients in the ED waiting area of any triage assessment category" (Case et al., 2004).

Or, to put it more succinctly, crowding is when an ED lacks the capacity to meet "the demands of the next patient who needs emergency care" (Asplin et al., 2008). Stated from a systems viewpoint, it is not simply the "next patient," but the "next *group* of patients" who must be considered in the equation of why flow matters.

Crowding doesn't just entail delays; it brings costs of various sorts. These range from tangible financial losses to decreases in patient safety, patient satisfaction, physician productivity, and staff satisfaction. These costs are why implementing the principles of flow in the ED and the rest of the hospital is not just an agreeable theoretical concept; it is an urgent and essential requirement.

THE REPUTATIONAL COST OF CROWDING

One of the most devastating yet least obvious costs of crowding is the loss of the institution's reputation that occurs when we squander flow opportunities. Each of us spends countless hours and hundreds of thousands, if not millions, of dollars in our marketing budgets to attract patients. Yet if we waste the opportunity to hardwire flow, we allow our patients to experience us at either our worst or, at a minimum, less than our best. We work so hard to *gain our patients' trust*, and then we fail to *re-earn their trust through the course of their experience.*

Consider this example from the emergency department: What is the single most important piece of data that drives the reputation of the ED? There are many answers to this important question, including:

- total length of stay (LOS);
- door to doc;
- door to room;
- room to doc; and
- doc to decision.

But by far, the most important risk to reputation is none of these—as important as they all are—but rather the *percentage of patients who left without treatment (LWOTs)*. Think about it. These patients have:

- identified a perceived need to seek ED treatment;
- decided that the need requires immediate treatment that cannot wait;
- had their lives (and in many cases, those of their family's) disrupted sufficiently to seek ED care; and
- chosen—in most cases, among *several different options*—to seek care in *our* ED.

In spite of all of this, if we have, through the failure of our systems, not allowed the patient to *actually* be seen in a timely manner by the emergency physician, that patient will turn away. If the LWOT rate in your ED is above 1 percent, you are turning away patients who have already chosen your hospital for care. You are systematically telling them, "No, you can't come here!" Or, at a minimum, "We *might* be able to see you if you are willing to wait…"

> If the LWOT rate in your ED is above 1 percent, you are turning away patients who have already chosen your hospital for care.

This is a huge reputational cost to our healthcare systems, particularly because patients who leave without treatment overwhelmingly have insurance, compared to those who wait hour after hour for care, since they don't have a legitimate alternative (New York Times, 2008). It is as if the patient is saying, tacitly if not explicitly, "I *want* to give you my money. I have *chosen* to give you my money. But you are saying, by your actions and by the failure of your processes, that *you don't want my money!"*

While the analogy is perhaps most dramatic in the ED setting, there are countless examples in hospital and healthcare-wide system flow in which we are telling our patients, "If you came here expecting connectedness, hardwired flow, and a clear sense that we value your time, energy, and input—*you came to the wrong place!"* Any time a registrar sees an outpatient surgery patient and fails to say, "Good morning, Mr. Smith. We were *expecting* to see you! Thanks for choosing our hospital for your care," he or she is jeopardizing the reputation of your healthcare system.

Any time a nurse or doctor accepts a transfer from another unit without saying, "Mrs. Jones, we heard you were coming to us and we are so happy to have a chance to care for you," he or she is putting your reputation at risk for failing to hardwire flow into the system. The point is simple, but simply and consistently underrated: At a fundamental level, there is a huge reputational cost for failing to hardwire flow.

THE FINANCIAL COSTS OF CROWDING

Treating healthcare as a business is perhaps an uncomfortable notion to many in the field, so here is a useful perspective for viewing this subject: Healthcare facilities provide services to people who are customers as well as patients. If a hospital does not provide those services well, those patients may choose to go somewhere else, and usually today they have that choice. If they do, that hospital will not generate the financial returns it needs to continue to provide high-quality patient care and services. Current conditions, as we've described, present obstacles to good service and good care. Thus, the importance of improving flow.

On the most basic level, crowding incurs costs for a facility that it could have avoided. Sun and colleagues found that significant crowding led to a 1 percent increase in costs per admission. That may not sound like much, but in their study of 995,379 admissions at 187 hospitals in California, that increase amounted to $17 million in additional costs in a year (Sun, 2013). Boarding patients for long periods in EDs or inpatient hallways, for example, adds costs that could have been reduced if they had been treated and discharged promptly, particularly if their conditions worsen.

Aside from increased costs, hospitals sacrifice potential revenue when they are crowded. When patients are diverted to other facilities or leave without being seen, the hospital loses revenue it could have had from those patients and it forfeits the opportunity to add potential revenue from new patients that might have resulted from a smoother stream of patients. When patients are boarded in the ED or operating room, they are preventing treatment of new patients and thus reducing potential revenue.

Another aspect of the cost of crowding is that it results in longer waits, which reduce patient satisfaction; hospitals thereby sacrifice potential revenues they might have gained, not only from those dissatisfied patients, but from others as well. Patricia Weber, an author and trainer in customer service for business, cited a commonly used statistical formula based on research, which found that one dissatisfied customer who complains represents six others who don't complain (Weber, 2013). Each dissatisfied customer, according to the formula, tells an average of nine other people, for a total of 63 who have heard of those negative impressions. An estimated 25 percent of those people, or 16, will choose not to use a service they've received negative information on.

In the context of the ED, if you multiply the average revenue (let's say $400 for the average visit) from one patient who chooses not to use its services by 16, the department has just lost $6,600 in potential revenue. If you then multiply that amount by the average number of visits a patient would make during his or her life—estimate that at five—the financial loss is now $33,000. That is the average ramification of one complaint! And that's just for visits to the ED; those dissatisfied patients may also choose other facilities for elective or emergent admissions that would generate considerably more revenue. If an average ED admission generates $5,000 or more in contribution margin, the lost dollars quickly add up.

The converse side of this equation is even more powerful. While there is an understandable tendency to focus on the "negative" aspects of patient complaints and failing to meet expectations—and the costs thereof—there is also the positive side of this equation. While dissatisfied patients may tell nine people about their poor service, our research and that of others has shown that loyal patients—those whose expectations we have not only met but exceeded—will tell 40–50 people (Mayer and Cates, 2014)! This is in many ways a non-intuitive or even counterintuitive insight. We expect complainers to tell a lot of people; that seems like the fundamental unfairness of life. But to hear that a patient whose expectations we have exceeded will tell five times as many people doesn't fit our mental models quite as easily. Thus, while there is a clear downside to the failure to hardwire flow, there is also an even larger upside to exceeding expectations and creating loyal patients.

THE COST TO PATIENT SAFETY

To put it simply, when crowding increases, patient safety decreases (Watts, Sikka, and Kulstad, 2010). In general, increased time in the emergency department equates to decreasing quality of care. One study concluded that patients who had to wait more than eight hours for a bed received inferior care to those who waited less than four hours (Hollander and Pines, 2007). This finding has ominous implications when linked to that of another study, by Melissa McCarthy and colleagues, which found that even high-acuity level 2 patients and level 3 patients, using the Emergency Severity Index five-level triage scale, suffered significant delays in their treatment in crowded conditions (McCarthy et al., 2009). The level 2 patients waited up to 29 percent longer when the patient capacity rose from 50 to 90 percent, while level 3 patients waited up to 68 percent longer.

Increased crowding also leads to less safe hospitals. A striking illustration of this conclusion is the finding in the Sun study that high ED crowding is correlated with a 5 percent greater chance of inpatient death; again, in that study of California hospitals, that meant 300 more deaths of patients in the hospital in a year. In applying another metric, Sun and colleagues found that the odds of death in the hospital were 9 percent greater within three days.

They phrased the implication bluntly: "Patients admitted through the ED during periods of high ED crowding died more often than similar patients admitted to the same hospital when the ED was less crowded… Our findings support the perception of ED crowding as a marker of poor quality of care… [including] worse care for all ED patients who might require hospital admission" (Sun, 2013).

Another, more subtle manifestation of the threat of ED and hospital-wide crowding to the safety of patients occurs beyond the walls of the hospital. Crowding affects public health because diversions of patients from crowded EDs to other facilities hamper the ability of paramedics to transport emergency patients by ambulance, because their ambulances are tied up with diversion patients.

Commenting in a letter to the editor of the *Annals of Emergency Medicine* on the study that addressed this issue (Eckstein and Chan, 2004), Raphael Barishansky and Katherine O'Connor (2004) pointed out that: "the ability for ambulances to deliver emergency patients to a 911-receiving facility, complete transfer of care to the hospital staff, and return to service in a relatively short… time is vital to emergency medical services (EMS) operations. This is true of not only large metropolitan systems with high volumes but also in rural areas where EMS resources are limited and transport times extended as a result of wide coverage areas."

They also noted that the city of Memphis had banned diversions because of their impact on the fire department's provision of emergency medical care.

THE COST TO PHYSICIAN PRODUCTIVITY

Plenty of research has established that frequent interruptions increase mistakes in the workplace, something that is clear to most people from abundant experience. Physicians and other providers are no different; when the ED or hospital is crowded, medical errors rise. So does the frustration of the providers—physicians, nurses, and support staff. If this is repeated often enough, burnout can often ensue.

Aside from decreasing productivity and contributing to medical errors, burnout degrades the health of providers and lessens the quality of care their patients are receiving. Lower physician productivity in turn leads to longer waits for treatment, more boarding, and thus, even more crowding. The effect tends to multiply itself. Simply stated, multitasking makes you stupid (Jensen, 2012; Mayer, 2014)! And yet, as eminent emergency medicine educator Dr. Steven Davidson has noted, multitasking is an essential skill for emergency physicians, yet one we are neither selecting for nor training our students and residents in (Davidson, 2011).

The seriousness and widespread extent of this problem should not be underestimated. Studies have shown high levels of burnout among physicians nationally. Researchers at the Mayo Clinic studying quality of life and job satisfaction among 7,288 physicians, for instance, found that 46 percent demonstrated one or more symptoms of burnout (Schattner, 2012).

We have previously noted that "burnout" may be a less accurate way of describing the problem than "rust" (Mayer and Jensen, 2009). "Burnout" carries the connotation of an immediate, incendiary event. We believe the effect on clinicians occurs over a longer period of time, and more closely approximates atrophy of skills as opposed to a fire burning. Indeed, we recently had someone describe to us how some members of their staff had "compassion fatigue." One of the key ways in which this can be combated is by unleashing capacity to improve flow, which makes our jobs easier over time.

The cost of physician productivity is in itself a bottleneck in that it is an example of wasting time for, arguably, the most expensive and highly trained resource in the healthcare system. Distracting that resource from being able to add value to the patient, family, and team is simply not a good business model. In those systems where flow has been accentuated, the impact on the system has been dramatic (Mayer and Jensen, 2009; Touissaint and Berry, 2013).

BOARDING: THE BIGGEST BARRIER

As noted earlier, not only has the percentage of non-urgent patients remained steady, studies in recent years have demonstrated that the numbers of non-urgent patients have almost no effect on crowding. These studies increasingly have singled out boarding patients in the ED and the shortage of inpatient beds in the hospital as the primary causes of crowding.

The 2010 CDC report, for instance, identified the main issue in overcrowding as "delays in moving the sickest patients to inpatient beds" (ACEP, 2010). A more recent study found that the greatest threat to patient safety was boarding rather than general crowding in the ED (Sun et al., 2012). Other studies have suggested that "prolonged boarding time may delay definitive testing and increase short-term mortality, length of stay, and associated costs" (Sun et al., 2013).

These two factors are interrelated. Increasing the number of beds in the ED does not significantly affect crowding. What does affect it is improving the rate at which patients leave the ED, either by discharge or admission to the hospital. Improving that rate, increasing effective inpatient capacity, and reducing boarding are among the most effective steps a hospital can take to improve flow as well as its service to its patients and community. An increasing number of authorities—both political and medical—are noticing these connections.

We believe that all language has meaning, and the language of boarding must be clear and precise. "Boarders" who wait in the ED for an inpatient bed are not "ED boarders," but rather are "hospital boarders" (Druckenbrod, 2004). While patients may be physically in the ED, the system problem that forces them to wait is a problem with poor management of hospital bed capacity. The Institute of Medicine has called on hospitals to end boarding as well as diversion (Asplin and Magid, 2007).

In addition to local initiatives such as Memphis's ban on diversion, national governments have acted as well. The United Kingdom adopted a "Four-Hour Rule" in 2005, in which EDs had to limit the length of stay of patients to four hours, either treating and discharging them or admitting them to the hospital within that time frame, with hospital chief executives held accountable for meeting the requirement. By 2010, the policy had led to 96 percent of British patients meeting that criterion. The government, however, recently rescinded the rule, and studies have not assessed its effect on outcomes (Sun et al., 2013).

THE SOLUTION

For all the reasons outlined here, improving hospital-wide flow as a whole is the most effective response to the challenges we face in healthcare now and those we will face in the coming years. That requires not only a fundamental and widely understood definition of flow but also use of strategies and tools to hardwire flow to effect these changes and sustain them over time. These efforts result in increased capacity, improved performance, and a reduction in healthcare provider frustration.

Improving flow requires an integrated, hospital-wide approach; ED management cannot achieve this goal alone. Inpatient services have an important stake in this work as well. The report of an ACEP task force on boarding in 2008 focused on patient flow in hospitals as the solution to ED crowding, recommending various actions by both EDs and hospitals as a whole (Asplin et al., 2008).

These included actions in the ED such as:

- bedside registration;
- limiting triage to critical cases;
- using scribes for documentation; and
- establishing a fast track for quick treatment of less acute patients.

For hospital-wide actions, the report called for:

- promoting institutional awareness;
- establishing a "24/7" operational culture;
- coordinating scheduling of elective and surgical patients; and
- addressing delays in admitting patients from the ED due to waiting for nursing reports.

Crowding may seem a problem primarily for the ED, but only because the signs and the symptoms manifest themselves here. McCarthy and colleagues make an important point: "The ED is the front door of the hospital to almost half of all patients admitted… During the waiting room time… ED patients and their families form their first impressions of the facility. A number of studies have found that prolonged wait time is associated with patient dissatisfaction and an unwillingness to return to the same facility or recommend it to others. Thus, it is critical that EDs keep waiting room times to a minimum… and develop strategies… to make patients' waiting room time as short and pleasant as possible" (McCarthy et al., 2009).

Indeed, the ED is the facility's front door, and when the passage from front door to back door is smooth, the hospital opens itself to the community as an institution that can serve its needs effectively and provide better medical care to more patients more efficiently. None of this is easy, but it is clearly essential.

We often hear this question: "This is going to take a lot of work and a lot of change—do we really have time for this now?"

Our answer is simple: "If you don't have time to add value and eliminate waste, what *do* you have time for? And how will you *compete* with those hospitals and healthcare systems that master hardwiring flow?"

Or, as the Talmud advises, "If not us, who? If not now, when?"

HARDWIRING FLOW™ FOCUS: WHY FLOW MATTERS

Flow matters precisely because it connects the elements of the healthcare system and its processes in critically important ways. Hardwiring flow has all of the following effects:

- improves financial return by increasing capacity;
- shortens time intervals by decreasing or eliminating waste;
- identifies and removes bottlenecks;
- reduces stress for patients, families, and caregivers by driving simplicity and increasing reliability;
- improves safety by reducing non-value-added variation;
- improves service and the perception of service by tying flow and service together;
- improves outcomes through evidence-based approaches; and
- reduces costs by decreasing steps that don't add value.

Conversely, an inability to hardwire flow:

- results in crowding and boarding of patients; (This presents a substantial threat to flow and must be addressed by using the tools to hardwire flow.)
- imposes a reputational cost to the institution due to patients who leave without being seen because of crowding and boarding;
- sends the message that there is essentially "no room at the inn" to patients who choose the hospital for care;
- exacts expensive financial costs due to decreased capacity, patients leaving, longer waits, and decreased patient satisfaction, all of which are important in the value-based payment era; and
- additionally imposes costs due to lost patient loyalty, compromised patient safety, physician productivity, and physician satisfaction. Physicians preferentially choose hospitals that have hardwired flow.

16

CHAPTER 2

DEFINING FLOW: ESTABLISHING THE FOUNDATIONS OF FLOW

by Thom Mayer, MD, and Kirk Jensen, MD

"It was the best of times. It was the worst of times."

—*Charles Dickens,* A Tale of Two Cities

"Example is not the main thing in influencing others, it is the only thing."

—*Albert Schweitzer, MD,* Out of My Life and Thought

DELIVERING THE RESULTS THAT MATTER

One of the best ways to address the perpetual whitewater of change is to use Evidence-Based Leadership[SM] (EBL) to guide us (Studer, 2004; 2013). As medical directors for Studer Group, we believe that Evidence-Based Leadership is just as important to the success of healthcare as evidence-based medicine (EBM). Both rely on application of the principles of scientific leadership and clinical evidence to guide the right choices in healthcare. EBL comprises 3 fundamental components, each with core elements:

1. **Aligned Goals**
   - Objective Evaluation System
   - Leader Development

2. **Aligned Behavior**
   - "Must Haves"
   - Performance Management

3. **Aligned Processes**
   - Standardization
   - Accelerators

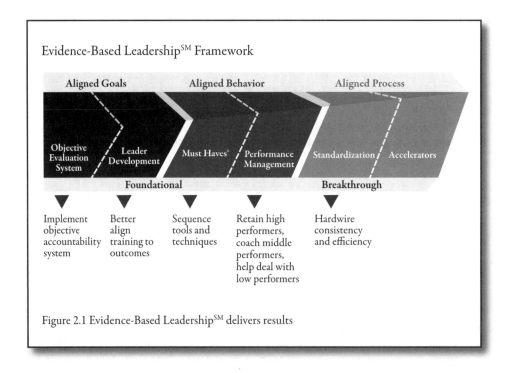

Figure 2.1 Evidence-Based Leadership^SM delivers results

Traditional approaches to leadership (and medicine) were "eminence-based" instead of evidence-based, in that they relied on a fundamental principle from logic and theology known as "the argument from authority." Basically this meant that healthcare leaders (and even some medical school professors) relied on the authority of their position to assure that their dictums were followed. "Do it because the boss says so" played an important role in healthcare leadership for decades.

EBL and EBM rely much more heavily on clearly-demonstrated approaches that are supported by evidence from leadership and clinical settings, respectively, to drive decisions. In addition, everyone on the healthcare team must be accountable in a metrics-based way to "deliver the results that matter," as the motto of our physician group, BestPractices, states it. Metrics not only matter; they are the foundation of how we measure progress. For over 20 years, we have been driven by a commitment to specificity: "**Some** is not a number. **Soon** is not a time. **Somehow** is not a strategy" (Mayer, 1991).

"**Some** is not a number. **Soon** is not a time.
Somehow is not a strategy"

The central mental model for us is to assure that a highly specific vision is backed by specific strategies in service of our patients. Here's the vision for BestPractices—the reason our organization exists. It has also been adopted by our parent company, EmCare, Inc., which provides integrated physician services to over 12 million patients per year in emergency medicine, hospital medicine, anesthesia, radiology, and acute care surgery.

To Create an New, Integrated Model of Physician Services through the:

Science of Clinical Excellence

Art of Customer Service

Business of Execution

Figure 2.2 The Vision

This vision begins with a commitment to **innovation**, a fundamental belief that the *status quo ante* is simply not good enough for either a present full of challenge or a future brimming with potential. Without question, a core feature that will distinguish great healthcare systems is the ability to effectively, efficiently, and reliably innovate. Without innovation, there is little hope for healthcare.

To demonstrate this, simply ask your staff: "How many of you would like to continue to work precisely where you are, doing the same things you are doing, and getting the same results in healthcare? How many of you would rather poke your eyes out and run the other way?"

Trust us: Your staff inherently understands the need for innovation to relieve them from the often-flawed processes and systems in which they currently work. Moreover, in addition to innovation, we believe that the present circumstances and the future challenges of healthcare require integration of all healthcare services, but especially physician services. For too many years, we have operated in functional silos, in that there have been too few seamless transitions across services in healthcare.

In a word, there has been too little **flow.** Diagnosing the presence of functional silos in your system can be done in several ways, but we suggest one of the best ways is to listen carefully to see if you hear these kinds of responses to problems identified in your hospital:
- "That's not a *doctor* problem, that's a *nurse* problem."
- "That's not a *nurse* problem, it's a *doctor* problem."
- "That's not *our* problem; it's a *lab/x-ray, environmental services, bed board, etc.* problem."

If you hear these kinds of statements, the team is working in functional silos. It will be necessary to employ the principles of hardwiring flow to correct the situation. Perhaps the most dramatic example of siloing is when you hear, "You've got a problem? Take it up with the folks upstairs." And of course, "the folks upstairs" are the leadership team of the hospital or healthcare system.

A simple way to help illustrate our focus on hardwiring flow and teamwork, is reflected in a simple motto: "If it's a problem for the patient, it's a problem for everyone on the team!" One of the best examples of the critical nature of eliminating silos and assuring there are seamless transitions of care comes from the 2008 Beijing Olympics.

The United States mens' 4 X 100 meter relay team came into the Olympic Games heavily favored to take the Gold Medal. In fact, they were prohibitive favorites, and were even expected to set a World Record on their journey to the medal podium. But, did they win the Gold Medal? Most decidedly, they did not. Why? Take a look at this photograph and see if you can discover why…

Figure 2.3 Passing the baton is key to success in healthcare

As you can see, they "dropped the baton." Without question the runners were:
- highly-motivated,
- well-trained,
- the best athletes in the world in their event, and
- motivated by clear metrics.

Unfortunately, at least on that day, they didn't function as a team, which focused not just on speed, but also on **transitions**. Far too often, that's what we do in healthcare. We have highly-motivated, well-trained "athletes" (our leaders and clinicians) who are motivated by clear and compelling metrics…

and yet we "drop the baton" because of our failure to provide an integrated model of care in which we focus not just on excellence, but on transitions as well. As the famed 17th century philosopher Baruch Spinoza noted, "Excellence is what we strive for, but consistency is what we demand." Hardwiring flow requires a focus on transitions of care, an evidence-based approach to teamwork, and a fanatic dedication to reliability and consistency.

Hardwiring flow requires a focus on transitions of care, an evidence-based approach to teamwork, and a fanatic dedication to reliability and consistency.

---

3 KEYS TO INNOVATION AND INTEGRATION

Innovation and integration, in our view, must occur in three areas: the **science** of clinical excellence, the **art** of customer service, and the business of **execution**. "Science" refers to our deep belief in the universal use of evidence-based practices, continuously refined to produce ever-improving results. "Art" reflects the fact that far too few healthcare institutions have embraced the need for effective hiring, training and systems of accountability in fundamental service principles.

Indeed, we have noted on many occasions that perhaps the greatest enemy of customer service excellence in medicine are the 167 medical schools in this country which have systematically ignored the opportunity to select medical students based upon their commitment to and potential for service skills. They have also failed to provide systematic training to hone and nurture the ability for such students to become "servant leaders" (Greenleaf, 2010).

We know of two dramatic exceptions to this. The first is Duke University School of Medicine, which has for years had service excellence training as a part of their "Capstone Course" for graduating medical students. (For full disclosure, one of us—Thom Mayer— teaches that course.) The other is the recently-created Virginia Tech medical school, which requires prospective students to interview with at least 10 current or former patients to assess their interpersonal skills before they are cleared for presentation to the Admissions Committee.

Perhaps the best sign of healthcare's increased commitment to the art of service is that, beginning in 2015, the American Association of Medical Colleges (AAMC), which designs and administers the Medical College Admission Test—or MCAT—will include elements designed to test prospective medical students' interpersonal skills. Finally, "execution" is a reflection of the deep need to eschew any lofty goal which can't be put into practical and pragmatic use and measured regularly to assure accountability.

There is no shortage of great ideas to improve healthcare service and outcomes. What distinguishes great from merely good hospitals and healthcare systems is their ability to execute those great ideas in ways that benefit the patient and those who care for the patient.

Execution is not *just* about getting things done; it is very much about understanding the things that are *necessary* in order to get those things done. Execution requires a disciplined cultural change so that leaders and managers at every level of the organization are passionate, not just about great ideas, but rather about how great ideas can be put to work in meaningful and measurable ways.

EXECUTING TO ADD VALUE AND AGILITY

At a minimum, this means that all of us in healthcare have three jobs:
- your job,
- finding innovative ways to improve the job, and
- leaving a legacy.

Obviously, all of us are hired into the organization to do a specific job, almost always described in a job description, with specific delineated responsibilities and reporting relationships. However, fewer organizations hire with the discrete intention that everyone at every level of the organization is expected, as a part of the job itself, to find innovative ways to improve the job by adding value and eliminating waste.

We should be expected to not only execute in ways that add value, but also to have the agility to find innovative ways to eliminate waste at every step of our processes. Finally, as we will discuss in more detail later, all of us should seek to leave a legacy by performing our work as servant leaders.

One step towards assuring that we leave a legacy is to put the patient first in all of our efforts to improve healthcare, especially with regard to flow. BestPractices' mission statement (what we are trying to accomplish) is summarized by three rules:

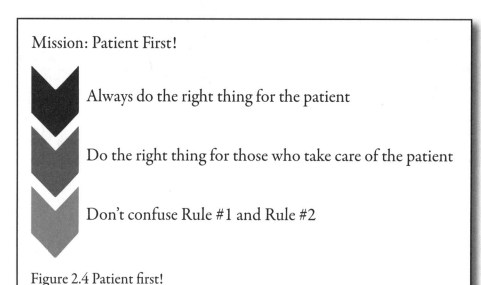

Mission: Patient First!

Always do the right thing for the patient

Do the right thing for those who take care of the patient

Don't confuse Rule #1 and Rule #2

Figure 2.4 Patient first!

Rule # 1 is to assure that we *always* do the right thing for the patient. The Mayo Clinic focuses, as we do, on a "Patient First" mantra (Berry and Seltmann, 2008). In any given effort to improve flow, the first question must always be, "Is this the right thing for the patient?" If the answer is no, there is no reason to go any further, despite the fact it might be good for other reasons. If it doesn't work for the patient, it can't work for us.

Rule # 2 is to do the right thing for those who take care of the patient— our healthcare team. In other words, we have stressed that the number one reason to get customer service (or any other aspect of healthcare) "right" is that it makes our jobs easier. So after assuring that our improvement efforts are good for the patient, the second question is, "Does this make things easier for the team caring for the patient?"

Rule # 3 of course is not to confuse Rule # 1 and Rule # 2. If you look carefully at many of our processes in healthcare, it seems we often confuse

Rule # 1 and Rule # 2. We focus on ourselves when we design processes instead of the patient. By way of simple example, any time we try to make the waiting room more comfortable instead of trying to get the patients out of the waiting room, we are probably confusing Rule #1 (eliminate waits and delays) and Rule #2 ("It's OK to wait. That's part of healthcare") (Mayer and Cates, 2014).

A LEAN DEFINITION OF FLOW

Justice John Potter Stewart, who in a famous ruling, said: "I may not be able to define it, but I know what it is when I see it". Many people feel the same way about flow. We know it when we see it, even if we can't precisely define it.

Our definition of flow is: "Flow exists to the extent that we *add value and decrease waste* by increasing benefits and decreasing burdens (or both) as our patients move through the service transitions and queues of healthcare." Because of its focus on adding value and eliminating waste, we clearly have a *lean focus* in how we define flow, and we do so to lock leaders and bedside clinicians into finding creative ways to increase value and eliminate anything that doesn't add value (waste).

DEFINING VALUE

Defining healthcare value can be done on the macroeconomic level or at the level of bedside providers. At the macroeconomic level of healthcare planning, Michael Porter and others (Porter and Teisberg, 2004; Porter and Lee, 2013) have defined value as a ratio of healthcare outcomes divided by the cost to provide those outcomes:

$$\text{Value} = \frac{\text{Outcomes}}{\text{Cost}}$$

While this definition is important in the broad debate on value, it is of limited help to clinicians and leaders as they deal with patients. Porter himself noted: "Value measurement in healthcare today is limited and highly imperfect. Not only is outcome data lacking, but understanding of the true costs of care is virtually absent". Don Berwick, MD, the founder and former CEO of The Institute for Healthcare Improvement (IHI) added, "When it comes to healthcare value, we are in measurement adolescence" (Berwick and Hackbarth, 2012).

In an effort to make the definition of flow more practical and actionable to healthcare providers, we have worked with our friend and colleague Len Berry (Berry, 1999) to define value for bedside providers in a more pragmatic way by this calculus:

$$\text{Value} = \frac{\text{Benefits Received}}{\text{Burdens Endured}}$$

We have found that this definition is one that physicians, nurses, leaders and the entire healthcare team understand intuitively and embrace enthusiastically. Anything that doesn't add value is *waste*. Simply stated, increasing value can occur by:

- increasing or improving the benefits received,
- decreasing the burdens endured in the course of delivering those benefits, or
- some combination of both increasing benefits and decreasing burdens.

As we'll see below, this is a calculus which is far from theoretical and can be understood and put into action at all levels of healthcare.

The Value-Added Equation

- What are the **benefits received**?
  Obvious? - re-affirm them
  Non-obvious? - Inform them

- What are the **burdens endured**?
  Necessary? - Explain them
  Unnecessary ?- Eliminate them

Would you tolerate this ratio?

Figure 2.5 Defining Value: The Benefit-Burden Ratio

The final litmus test in adding value by increasing the benefits received and decreasing the burdens endured is to ask this question: "If this were a member of your family, would **you** tolerate this ratio?" If the answer is no, it is time to get innovative and integrative in the process of adding value and eliminating waste.

AN EMERGENCY DEPARTMENT EXAMPLE OF DEFINING FLOW

Here's a simple example from the emergency department (ED) that shows how this definition can be put to work. The most common presenting symptom in every ED is abdominal pain. How do we add value and eliminate waste by increasing benefits and decreasing burdens for such patients? Some of the *benefits received* for these patients are:
- pain relief,
- hydration,
- treatment of nausea,

- providing an accurate diagnosis, and
- reassurance that "it's not serious".

The *burdens endured* for these patients include:
- time required to administer,
- time to complete imaging and laboratory studies,
- pain from blood draws or IV starts,
- potential side effects of medicines, and
- inconvenience of drinking oral contrast solutions.

If we can increase benefits *and* decrease burdens, we will have added value and diminished waste. How does that work? Using our abdominal pain example, here are some ways to add value by increasing benefits:

Category	Flow Action
Pain relief	Pain protocols, rapid acting agents
Hydration	Rapid IV access, fluid bolus, use of IV and PO routes
Treating nausea	Rapid IV medications with fewer side effects
Accurate diagnosis	Imaging protocols, EBM-guided work-up
Reassurance	Rapid results communicated clearly, e.g., "Good news! Your tests show no signs of cancer."

Similarly, we can improve flow by decreasing the burdens for abdominal pain patients by decreasing necessary burdens or eliminating unnecessary burdens:

Category	Flow Action
Time to studies/medication	Immediate pain/nausea treatment
Pain from blood draws/IVs	Topical anesthetics, IV & blood draw together
Side effects	EBM protocols, asking patients about side effects
Oral contrast	Eliminate routine use of oral contrast

THE VALUE OF FLOW

The elimination of oral contrast has several flow effects, in that it decreases the burden of drinking the liquid, decreases length of stay by two to three hours on average, and creates (or preserves) additional capacity for other patients by eliminating the time to drink the liquid. When teams hardwire flow, one of their key insights is that in healthcare, capacity cannot be *stored*. Capacity is not a commodity we can store on the shelf and pull out when it is needed. *Capacity neglected is capacity lost*!

Capacity neglected is capacity lost!

For example, an ED with 40,000 visits in which 9,000 abdominal CTs per year are obtained (the national average) (EDBA, 2013), eliminating the routine use of oral contrast that takes 3 hours on average creates 27,000 hours of additional capacity for the ED. If the average length of stay for the ED is 2.5 hours, this flow effort results in creating the capacity to see an additional 10,800 patients per year. If the net collected revenue per ED patient is $100 for the emergency physician and $400 for the hospital, the revenue impact of these additional patients is $1,080,000 and $4,320,000, respectively. So the financial impact of flow is considerable, as shown graphically here in Figure 2.6.

40,000 annual visits	No routine oral contrast
9,000 abdominal CTs per year	3 hours x 9,000 patients = 27,000 hours of
All with oral contrast	additional capacity
3 hours needed for oral contrast	27,000 hours/2.5 hour LOS = 10,800
27,000 hours of waste	additional patient volume
2.5 hour average ED LOS	ED Doc revenue @ $100/pt = $1,080,000
	Hospital Revenue @ $400/pt = $4,320,000
Typical ED	Hardwiring Flow ED

Figure 2.6 The Value of Flow: ED Example

IMPROVING FLOW BY DECREASING WASTE

The example in the previous figure shows how adding value (shorter length of stay for patients) and eliminating waste (both the time required and the inconvenience of oral contrast, which doesn't add value) hardwire flow. Anything that doesn't add value is not just the *absence* of value, but the *diversion* of resources from the value stream. Because our resources are so severely capacity-constrained, waste is no less than the *destruction of possibility,* since it distracts time, energy, effort and capacity away from where it is so desperately needed. Taiichi Ohno, one of the earliest proponents of the use of lean, said, "Waste is any expenditure of time, money, or other resources that doesn't add value" (Black and Miller, 2008).

But burdens and waste are decidedly not the same thing. Burdens are necessary, though inconvenient, parts of healthcare processes which nonetheless contribute to the value stream. For example, a necessary burden of cardiac catheterization is obtaining access to the femoral vessels in order to thread the catheter into the heart. Femoral cannulation is uncomfortable, carries the risk of bleeding and infection, and requires hemostatic measures following the procedure: all burdens, but ones which must be endured to perform a procedure which demonstrably *adds value* in determining the presence and degree of cardiac disease.

It also *adds value* because the diagnostic information from the cardiac catheterization is necessary to guide appropriate evidence-based therapies for these patients. (That said, many cardiac centers, in an effort to decrease burdens, now perform elective cardiac catheterizations from a radial or brachial artery approach.) This illustrates a key point of hardwiring flow: All waste is burden, but not all burden is waste.

All waste is burden, but not all burden is waste.

THE PARADOX OF VARIATION

An important corollary involves understanding the role that variation plays in healthcare systems and processes. While reducing variation is a common tactic to improve flow, developing consistent value-added processes does not *necessarily* mean reducing variation. To be sure, reducing variation *that doesn't add value* is an important part of hardwiring flow. Yet there are many situations in which *increasing variation can simultaneously add value.* Let's look at some of the emergency department flow solutions which we will delineate in much more detail in Chapter 4:

Triage Bypass or Direct to Room—When ED rooms are available, patients are taken directly to the room after a basic "name, demographics, and chief complaint" at triage, which speeds care.

Advanced Triage/ Advanced Initiatives (AT/AI) Guidelines for Nurses—When all rooms are full, nurses begin testing and care through standing physician orders (e.g., ankle x-rays for sports injuries, leukocyte esterase tests or urinalysis for urinary frequency, point-of-care (POC) pregnancy tests for vaginal bleeding) (Kokiko and Mayer, 1997).

Team Triage (physician or mid-level in triage)—When all rooms are full and are likely to be so for extended periods of time, or when the number of patients predictably exceeds the number of available beds, a team comprising a physician (or mid-level provider), nurse, tech, scribe and registrar are deployed to the triage area where patients are evaluated and treated (Mayer, 2004). This is a classic example of "front-loading flow" by putting the patient and the doctor together as fast as possible (Mayer and Jensen et al., 2014).

Results Waiting Room—Patients are kept in ED rooms only as long as the room is needed; then moved to a comfortable waiting area to await their results and subsequent discharge.

Fast Track—Patients with low acuity are triaged to a specific area with specific staff to care for their needs according to evidence-based protocols.

Level 3 Fast Track—Those patients with higher acuity than Fast Track who are unlikely to require admission are treated in an area designated for their care.

All of these programs represent opportunities *to increase variability to add value* by creating and adapting processes to the changing situation of the number and acuity of ED patients arriving, the beds and staff available to care for them, and the need to change processes to meet the patient demand and our capacity to care for them.

Thus, understanding how much and what type of variation is the <u>right variation to add value</u> is an essential leadership skill. In developing this skill, two points deserve great emphasis. First, successfully leading flow requires creatively assessing which of the many ways of delivering processes and services leads to value creation and waste reduction.

Thus, understanding how much and what type
of variation is the *right* variation to add value is
an essential leadership skill.

This requires skill in experimentation, since if variation is blindly eliminated, experimentation is stifled and potential improvements in flow are lost. Second, if leaders state that elimination of variation (rather than adding value and eliminating waste) is the primary driver of success, there is no room for diversity, which is a key value in healthcare. Creativity, successful experimentation, and diversity of opinion are necessary in determining how much and what type of variation best creates value. We will discuss managing variation to increase value in more detail in Chapter 3, since it is one of the 7 core strategies of hardwiring flow.

THE 6 "RIGHTS" OF HARDWIRING

Applying all of these insights are essential to make sure we deliver "The 6 Rights of Hardwiring Flow:"
1. the Right Resources
2. **to the Right Patients**
3. **in the Right Environment**
4. **for the Right (Evidence-Based) Reasons**
5. **with the Right Team**
6. **at the Right Time—*Every time!***

To determine what is "right," we simply use the flow equation of adding value and eliminating waste by increasing benefits and decreasing burdens across the resources, patients, environment, reasons, team, and time that comprise our service.

BECOMING A FLOW DETECTIVE

Leaders, managers, and healthcare providers must all be a part of a culture that makes them "flow detectives," who prowl their units in search of processes and people who do not provide benefits or cause unnecessary burdens. When value is added, those processes and people need to be celebrated, accentuated, and standardized by making sure they are hardwired into the organization. But they must also identify processes which produce waste (non-value-added). Becoming a flow detective means putting this insight to work:

A continuous **Treasure Hunt** to add value

A continuous **Bounty Hunt** to eliminate anything which doesn't add value (waste)

Figure 2.7 Becoming a "Flow Detective"

Hospitals and healthcare systems which have liberated their staffs to discover the treasure that value-added systems and processes represent not only better care for the patient, but provide a better work environment, one in which it is far easier to leave a legacy…one patient at a time. The other side of the coin is being on a bounty hunt to eliminate the many wasteful steps which are buried within the typical processes of healthcare.

This leads to a new culture in which leaders, managers, and team members are empowered to act aggressively in processes which are constantly being redefined. Quint Studer has said many times, "Culture outperforms strategy every time and culture plus strategy is unbeatable" (Studer, 2013). A culture which empowers all staff at all levels to engage in this "treasure hunt, bounty hunt" approach to increasing value and eliminating waste is on the path to sustainable success. Adding the hardwiring flow strategies to the mix makes for an "unbeatable" prescription for success.

PHYSICIANS AND FLOW

We can't state it any more clearly or concisely: Physicians must not only be involved in hardwiring flow; they must be at the core of flow improvement efforts. As the adage goes, "If they are not with you on the take-off, they won't be with you on the landing". Physicians are simply too valuable a resource *not* to have them as champions of flow, as opposed to being dragged along for the ride.

Similarly, once processes have been redesigned to add value and eliminate waste, physicians must be held accountable for following those processes to deliver the results that matter. Conversely, it is difficult, if not impossible, to hold physicians accountable if the system is broken and opportunities to hardwire flow are not being implemented.

Here are some key elements required for holding physicians accountable for flow:

- common goals,
- transparent expectations,
- aligned strategic incentives,
- clear measures and metrics,
- deep commitment to success, and
- a focus on progress, not perfection.

It starts with clearly-stated attainable goals, tied to the success of the entire team to deliver better patient care. It is impossible to attain success if we haven't defined success prospectively. As the great Coach John Wooden said, "Failing to prepare is preparing to fail." In addition, the expectations we have for physicians must not only be understood, but completely transparent, even intuitive. If delineating expectations requires an arcane set of explanations, physicians will be reluctant to commit to the effort.

It is impossible to attain success if we
haven't defined success prospectively.

One extremely common source of failure in hardwiring flow is an inability to assure that there are aligned strategic incentives across the service transitions the patient experiences. Physician, nursing, and hospital incentives must be aligned, with appropriate financial incentives and disincentives for success and failure, respectively. Aligning these incentives helps assure that "the baton is never dropped" during the course of patient care.

Physicians are highly motivated in most cases, both by nature and training. Motivating them for measurable team success helps assure they will be fully committed to the effort. That said, it is important to make sure the initial goals in hardwiring flow are attainable, since success breeds further success. Progress is thus the initial goal, not perfection…and progress should be rewarded at each step along the way.

Several other factors are important in motivating and sustaining physician progress in flow objectives:

- assure that there are evidence-based clinical and operational practices,
- report results transparently with a "Show me the data!" mantra,
- use peer comparisons and benchmarking data, as physicians innately like peer comparisons,
- assure there is frequent feedback and a culture of coaching and mentoring, and
- focus on moving the bell-shaped curve and a commitment to the "highest, not the lowest common denominator".

Training physicians in evidence-based medicine is a rapidly accelerating trend. Their ability to translate evidence-based medicine into evidence-based leadership can be dramatic, if presented in a data-driven way. A recommendation: Identify physicians who are likely sources of resistance to the change effort and put them on the planning team.

This may seem counterintuitive, but it is wise to recall Lyndon Baines Johnson's wisdom (paraphrased for political correctness): "I'd rather have that SOB on the inside of the tent urinating out, than outside of the tent urinating in." That isn't quite the language LBJ used, but you get the point. Get them involved early and they will be among the strongest proponents of hardwiring flow because they feel the "pride of authorship".

Doctors love data. Use that insight by making the data transparent, meaningful, and frequently reported. Physicians are usually competitive as well; we want to be among the best when the data is reported. So make your team's mantra, "Show me the data!" Share the specific means by which high-performing physicians are attaining their results (adding value), as well as changing the behaviors which are not producing effective results (eliminating waste).

In addition to peer comparisons within the teams, use benchmarking data from other areas in the hospital or healthcare system, as well as data from across the country, to guide the way towards success. While coaching and mentoring are fundamental to the process of medical school education and residency training programs, too few healthcare institutions have formal coaching and mentoring programs.

Use high-performing A-Team physicians as formally-assigned mentors to new physicians. Make sure there is a formal coaching and mentoring program, including regular meetings during the orientation period, and for the first year new physicians that are on staff. All of this will assure that the entire team is motivated to move the entire bell-shaped curve towards better performance, both for the individual physician and for the entire team. Again, we seek progress, not perfection. Another way to look at this is that we are continuously raising the bar, so we are helping everyone to rise to the highest common denominator, rather than accepting the lowest common denominator.

Finally, remember Pareto's Paradox, named for Italian economist Vilfredo Pareto. He noted that 80 percent of a leader's time is spent dealing with 20 percent of the "problem" people (ie., B-Team members) in the organization. You know, or should know, who the problem people are, including physicians. If you continue to tolerate the problem behavior of those physicians, you not only waste a great deal of you time, you also demoralize the staff by failing to effectively deal with a known problem. What you permit, you promote. Hold physicians accountable for adding value and eliminating waste and your teams' flow efforts will flourish.

FLOW AS A FUNDAMENTAL LEADERSHIP TEST

In closing this initial chapter, we point out a somewhat sobering, and yet ultimately liberating, insight. We are at a critical inflection point in healthcare as we seek to go from good to great and become a high-quality, low-cost provider of care. *By putting value and waste under the microscope and in the forefront of our innovation and improvement efforts, we unintentionally but unavoidably place the focus on whether we have the leadership skills requisite to fix what is now clearly defined as a problem.*

That's the sobering insight: Hardwiring flow is ultimately a test of our leadership and the ability to execute. It's not a theoretical exercise. Focusing on flow is focusing on the core issue for all of us in healthcare: how to add value and eliminate waste. We can't survive in today's market if we don't. No one *intends* to fail to address flow, but it happens all too frequently, largely because the answer to the question, "Why are we doing it this way?" is "Because we've *always* done it this way".

Clearly, that's not a good enough answer anymore. Hardwiring flow changes the answer to: "Because it adds value and eliminates waste for our patients and for our team." Be prepared for some tough conversations as you lead your hospital-wide flow efforts, because you are cutting across all of the traditional functional silos in the process. Make sure you have the courage of your convictions as you wade through the waste.

It is true we face many challenges as we reach to become the high-quality, low-cost provider of choice, including:

- delivering metrics-based results that matter,
- dealing with a highly capacity-constrained and cost-constrained environment,
- constantly adding value and eliminating waste by increasing benefits
- and reducing burdens, and
- dealing with Nurse Ratchet and Doctor Cranky as a test of our leadership legitimacy.

We could go on, but even a short list is daunting in the extreme. And yet, rising to this challenge can also be very liberating.

The good news is that there is an evidence-based leadership pathway to hardwiring hospital-wide flow, based on extensive experience and bolstered by specific strategies and tools, which we will delineate in the next chapter. We are convinced that the combined experience of the authors, drawn from hundreds of hospitals across the country, will be of immense benefit to you and your team.

Are we up to it? The ancient wisdom of the Talmud serves us well: "If not us, who? And if not now, when?" Now is the time. You and your team are the people who can meet these challenges and change the landscape of healthcare.

It's not a destination but rather the beginning of a journey to an innovative and productive future.

HARDWIRING FLOW™ FOCUS: DEFINING FLOW

- Healthcare is in the perpetual whitewater of change, where change is seemingly the only constant.
- Becoming the "high quality, low cost provider of healthcare" is an essential goal for all hospitals and healthcare systems.
- Addressing these challenges requires us to aggressively employ the precepts of both evidence-based medicine and evidence-based leadership to decrease variation and increase reliability, predictability, safety and service.
- Delivering the results that matter in a metrics-based environment requires specificity of both purpose and plan ("**Some** is not a number, **soon** is not a time, **somehow** is not a strategy" (Mayer, 1991).
- Many, if not most, healthcare systems are plagued by functional silos, where teamwork is a myth, not a reality.
- The tools of hardwiring flow eliminate functional silos by helping us "pass the baton" efficiently and effectively, focusing not just on **speed**, but on **transitions.**
- Hardwiring flow requires a focus on transitions of care, an evidence-based approach to teamwork, and a fanatic dedication to reliability and consistency.
- A clear and succinct vision is necessary to guide healthcare staff. Ours is "To create a new, integrated model of physician services through the **science** of clinical excellence, the **art** of customer service, and the **business** of execution."
- Our definition of flow is: "Flow exists to the extent that we *add value* and *decrease waste* by increasing benefits and decreasing burdens (or both) as our patients move through the service transitions and queues of healthcare."
- While healthcare value is often defined as the ratio of outcomes to cost, we are "in measurement infancy" (Berwick, 2011) when it comes to defining this in a practical fashion.

- A better, more pragmatic way of doing so is to define value as a ratio of benefits received to burdens endured by the patient and the family in the delivery of healthcare, since this can be defined and delivered at the bedside.
- Capacity is not a commodity we can store on the shelf and pull out when it is needed. *Capacity neglected is capacity lost.*
- Improving flow improves capacity and is therefore a core economic driver for hospitals and healthcare systems.
- Waste is anything that doesn't add value. Waste should be decreased or eliminated.
- The paradox of flow variation is that, in some cases, increasing variation can actually increase value.
- Knowing how much and what type of variation is the **right variation to add value** is an essential healthcare leadership skill.
- The "Six Rights of Hardwiring Flow" are getting the right resources to the right patients in the right environment for the right (evidence-based) reasons with the right team at the right time—*every time!*
- Healthcare leaders and managers at all levels must become "flow detectives," who are on a constant treasure hunt to add value and a bounty hunt to reduce waste.
- Because physicians drive many aspects of flow, they must be an integral part of hardwiring flow.
- Involve physicians early and often. "If they aren't with you on the takeoff, they won't be with you on the landing."
- A-Team members make the job easier. B-Team members make the job harder… infinitely harder!
- Recall Pareto's paradox that 80 percent of a leader's time is spent dealing with 20 percent of the B-Team members.
- Accountability is one of the keys to hardwiring flow. There can't be any exceptions for B-Team members.
- Failing to deal with Nurse Ratchet and Doctor Cranky is a threat to leadership legitimacy.

- By putting value and waste under the microscope and in the forefront of our innovation and improvement efforts, we unavoidably place the focus on whether we have the leadership skills requisite to fix what is now clearly defined as a problem.
- "If not us, who? If not now, when?"

CHAPTER 3

STRATEGIES AND TOOLS TO HARDWIRE HOSPITAL-WIDE FLOW

by Thom Mayer, MD, and Kirk Jensen, MD

"Give us the tools and we will finish the job!"

—*Winston Churchill,* BBC Broadcast, February 9, 1941

"Give me a lever long enough and I can move the world."

—*Archimedes, quoted in* Pappus, Synagoge

THE 7 STRATEGIES OF HARDWIRING FLOW

We have defined flow as adding value and eliminating waste by increasing benefits and decreasing burdens as our patients move through the service transitions and queues of healthcare. So how can we take the next steps to ensure that flow is hardwired into our processes and services?

Flow doesn't just happen. It requires hard work: a specific set of strategies and tools that allow us to systematically pursue flow. Fortunately, there are seven core strategies which reliably and consistently produce flow (Mayer and Jensen, 2009). These are:

1. Demand-capacity management
2. Forecasting demand
3. Real-time monitoring of flow data
4. Queuing theory
5. Managing variation
6. Eliminating bottlenecks and constraints
7. Flow as a complex adaptive system

These seven strategies—as well as the tools that support them—form the basis by which we will develop ways in which we can systematically improve hospital-wide flow. Taken together, they will provide you with the intellectual tools and mental models needed to improve flow and thereby improve the system for your patients and for those who care for those patients. We presented these strategies in some detail in a previous book, *Hardwiring Flow: Systems and Processes for Seamless Patient Care*, but we will briefly review them here. Each of these strategies and tools put the patient in the center and are in service to them.

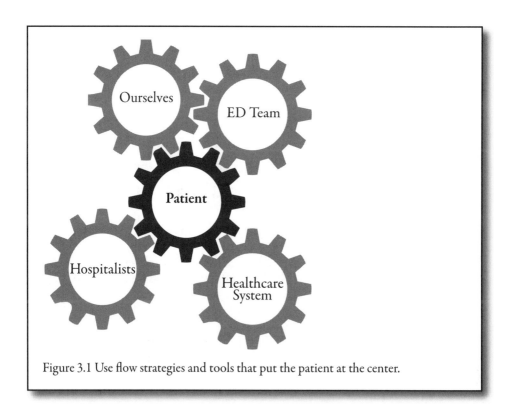

Figure 3.1 Use flow strategies and tools that put the patient at the center.

DEMAND-CAPACITY MANAGEMENT

Healthcare is a service and not a commodity that can be stored on a shelf and retrieved when it is needed. If a period of time goes by when a doctor or a nurse can't deliver care, that service time and opportunity are gone forever, even if the opportunity is missed just by minutes or hours. As we noted in Chapter 1, capacity wasted is lost forever; it can't be recovered. One of the most powerful strategies for improving flow is demand-capacity management.

The most important aim in demand-capacity management is to *establish a measure of patient demand by hour, day, and week and to design a system with sufficient capacity to meet that demand.* This can be accomplished by asking these 5 critical questions:

The Key Questions

Who is coming?

When are they coming ?

What are they going to need?

Is our service capacity going to match patient demand?

What will we do if they don't?

Figure 3.2 The key questions

"Who is coming?"

One of the key concepts of hardwiring flow is, "Don't let life be a surprise to you." And yet many people who lead, manage, and provide healthcare are often surprised at the type and number of patients who come for care, as well as the time they arrive. As emergency physicians by training, we often hear, "Oh, you're an ER doc. That must be exciting…never knowing what is coming through the door."

Well, if we don't know which types of patients we are going to see, we simply haven't been paying attention all these years. One of the fundamental principles of demand-capacity management (and hardwiring flow) is that the answers to these questions are not just predictable, but *highly predictable*. We train our residents in emergency medicine and our fellows in pediatric emergency medicine to say this to their patients: "We knew you were coming. We just didn't know your name!"

The number of patients we are going to be treating should rarely be a surprise to us, regardless of where we practice in the healthcare system…whether in the ED, the ICU, the medical-surgical floors, the outpatient clinic, or the office setting. "Who is coming" tells us *how many* patients we should expect at any given time. That data is or should be readily available with current electronic medical records (EMRs) and healthcare information technology (IT) systems. Insist on it! If you are told the data is not there, persist until you get it. Here is a typical example of how the number of ED patients is plotted by arrival time:

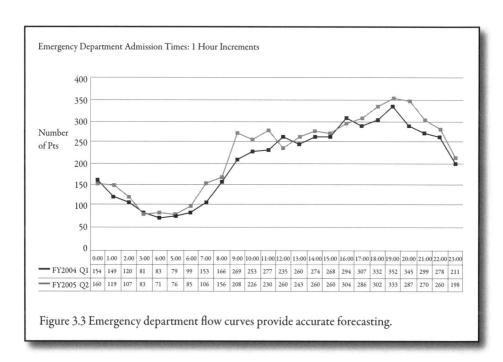

Figure 3.3 Emergency department flow curves provide accurate forecasting.

This graph demonstrates not only "who is coming," but also anticipated arrival times, as we will discuss shortly. The same data is available to plot admissions to the hospital, the number of patients needing critical care beds, and the number of unscheduled appointments for an outpatient practice. As we will discuss in a moment, we should plot not just the *number* of patients arriving, but also the *type* and *acuity* of patients.

"When are they coming?"

Once the number and acuity of patients have been plotted, you should use that data to make clear predictions about *patient demand*: by hour and by day of the week, as shown in the previous graph. These plots are very common for emergency departments, but they can and should be used for every unit in the healthcare system. Again, don't let life be a surprise by not understanding both who is coming and when they are coming.

This needs to be understood not just statistically, but empirically. In other words, does the data with regard to who is coming and when they are coming have "face validity"? Do they make sense to those who provide the service? Does the team feel that, "yes, this makes sense", or does it come as a complete and total surprise to them? We have found that most teams have an "Aha!" moment when they see the data presented graphically. It makes sense to them (at least to the A Team members); they just haven't seen it displayed that way graphically before.

"What are they going to need?"

Now we know the number of patients who are coming and the time they are coming, which are both "mission-critical" to hardwiring flow. So we have begun to establish demand, at least by number and time. But we haven't yet determined what these patients will need. It is one thing to know you should expect five patients to arrive at 10 AM in your ED, or five admissions to your medical-surgical floor during a given eight-hour shift, or three emergency cardiac catheterizations in a 24-hour period, but preparing to care for them requires a deeper understanding of their *acuity*. What are they going to need and when are they going to need it?

You can actually figure out which resources you will need by day, by shift, and even by hour by analyzing patient acuity and what *demands* that creates on the system. Then you can evaluate whether your department is prepared to deliver those resources. You can study the demand for anything and every-thing—staffing, space, essential services, human resources—and then see if, on average, you can meet that demand.

To summarize: Demand comprises, at a minimum, three core elements:

1. How many patients are coming?
2. When (time of day, day of the week, season of the year) are they coming?
3. What are they going to need? (How sick are they and how many and what type of resources will they consume?)

This summarizes the basic concepts of the "demand" side of the De-mand-Capacity equation. Now we need to develop the second half of the equation. What about our capacity to meet this demand?

"Is our service capacity appropriate to meet patient demands?" (Will we have what is needed?)

As we track our data to answer the five demand-capacity questions, match-ing staffing and capacity to patient arrivals and demand is essential for hard-wiring flow. For example, match ED lab and radiology service capacity to the known demand for these services. Remember, we're all part of the system: ED directors and hospital administrators should understand when their EDs are busy, and when they are relatively slow.

In the process of tracking the data, break arrivals down by chief com-plaint, triage, emergency medical-services arrivals, emergency severity index (ESI) level, and ancillary utilization. Last but not least, develop a response plan for times when demand unexpectedly spikes. If demand "unexpectedly" spikes predictably over time, reset the demand-capacity equation to meet the "new reality."

If demand "unexpectedly" spikes predictably over time, reset the demand-capacity equation to meet the "new reality."

Similarly, track discharges from the inpatient units to understand both when patients will be discharged and which resources (capacity) will be need-ed to put the bed of that discharged patient "back in service" for the system. Consider this example of a patient being discharged from inpatient bed 462 at 2 pm:

At 2 pm, a patient is discharged from a med-surg floor at your hospital...

Who puts the bed back in service?

What steps need to be taken to do that?

What are the rate-limiting steps/bottlenecks?

What is the incentive to do so?

Figure 3.4 Medical-surgical demand-capacity management

Your team can do this same exercise. Here are some answers posed to the questions above:

- Staff nurse or charge nurse calls environmental services (EVS) to let them know the bed needs to be cleaned
- EVS assigns and informs a team member to clean bed 462
- EVS team member finishes current task and heads to 462
- EVS team member cleans 462
- EVS team member informs charge nurse or staff nurse that 462 is clean
- Charge or staff nurse informs the bed board that 462 is available

Now, think about this: What happens at 3pm on most medical-surgical floors? Of course, we all know it is "change of shift". Now ask yourself this "flow question": What is the incentive for the staff nurse to get that bed back in service and a new patient into it before 3pm?

Actually, there is a disincentive to do so, since getting a new patient is just "more work." At any good restaurant, the wait staff knows they actually want to "turn the table" as quickly as possible, since it is not only good service, but also a chance to increase income from tips. TGI Fridays and The Cheesecake Factory have "solved" for this by having systems to alert their EVS (the busboys) when tables are "ready to be turned," which means they need to be cleaned and re-set.

Has your hospital put such a system in place? We'll discuss these concepts in more depth throughout the book, but even the simple process of putting a hospital bed back in service is an opportunity to hardwire flow.

What will we do if we don't have the capacity to meet demand?
Demand-capacity management cannot assure that there is always more capacity than demand. The capacity and resource-constrained nature of healthcare drives the need for a fine balance of *matching* capacity with demand. There will always be times when demand exceeds capacity, despite our best efforts to eliminate waste. But the times when demand exceeds capacity should rarely surprise us, since this is highly predictable as well.

There are always disasters and "mini-disasters", but just as we have well-delineated disaster plans, we should also plan in advance to assure we have predictable surge-capacity plans for these times. As we mentioned in the previous chapter and will explore in more detail under "Managing Variation," using variation to create maximum value is the key to understanding what will need to be done when our capacity is insufficient for the demands placed upon us.

As Doctor Paul Batalden wisely noted, "Every system is perfectly designed to get precisely the results it gets". The more we understand demand-capacity management, the more Dr. Batalden's wisdom becomes obvious, because we recognize that matching capacity to demand must be the first step in designing a system to get the results we want.

Matching capacity to demand must be the first step in
designing a system to get the results we want.

FORECASTING DEMAND

We increasingly live in a world where information moves at the speed of electrons. In addition to EMRs and healthcare databases, social media has empowered patients to become more informed than they have ever been in the past. If we tell a patient that we can't accurately forecast patient arrivals and demand in our hospitals, they would likely say, "Don't you have an 'app' for that?"

The fact is that we do have the basic information and tools which—if intelligently applied—can allow us to forecast patient demand, just as we can use an "app" to tell us the weather, flight delays, or what song is playing on the radio. For example, Figure 3.5 shows patient flow for a typical ED, based on simple and readily available data on the number of arrivals by time of day.

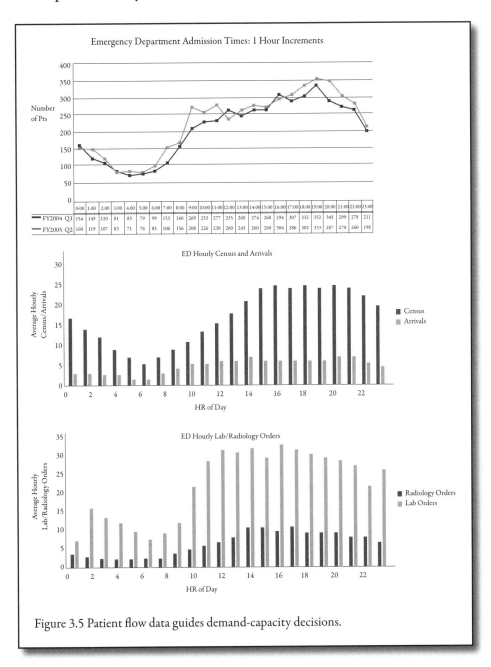

Figure 3.5 Patient flow data guides demand-capacity decisions.

The smaller figures show total ED census and use of laboratory and imaging studies, which is also readily available. While the precise number of patients per hour may vary from ED to ED, the curve is fundamentally the same. To be sure, acuity of those patients will differ in a level I trauma and critical care hospital from a small community hospital. But acuity among hospitals of the same size and services are highly consistent…and predictable. Data from the Emergency Department Benchmarking Alliance clearly demonstrates this, in addition to the phenomenon of "banding," meaning that EDs of certain volumes have highly predictable acuity, demands, and utilization patterns of laboratory and imaging services (EDBA, 2013).

Using these and similar data, you can begin to forecast patient flow, but once you have the data, you can take it a step further. You can similarly track hourly census in the ED, not only the number of arrivals, but also the number of patients actually in your department at particular times. An additional step is to plot lab and radiology orders. Compile these types of data and you can forecast patient flow with a high degree of accuracy.

These same principles apply to every area of the hospital, from medical-surgical admissions to ICU admissions, operating room schedules to outpatient clinic appointments. For minimal delays and high throughput, your team needs to predict admissions for individual units and have the capacity to accept admissions for those units.

They then need to assess, using a designed administrative structure or process, the predicted demand and capacity of each unit to determine whether the unit or the hospital requires a plan to meet the predicted or expected demand if it will be greater than predicted capacity. If so, a plan should go into effect, and the hospital should (at the end of the day or by the morning of the following day) evaluate the success or failure of the defined plan to match capacity to demand. The final step is to revise the plan over time in response to what the evaluation of the plan reveals.

Forecasting Methods

The three most often-used forecasting methods in healthcare rely on historical data as statistical inputs, as well as expert knowledge of the system:

1. Percentage adjustment is the best estimate of what will happen in the future, based on percentage increase or decrease in performance over the previous 12 months.

2. Moving average calculates the average number of patient visits for the previous 12 months and recalculates each month based on the previous 12.

3. A trend line statistically derives a best fit line using regression analysis based on historical data to determine how accurate earlier planning was compared with the actual number of admissions in the previous 12 months.

For more detailed discussion of these forecasting methods, see Jensen, Mayer et al. (2007) and Mayer and Jensen (2009). In summary, the best way to assure that life isn't a surprise to our staff and leaders is to use the tool of forecasting demand, which will become increasingly easier as we effectively use EMRs and our knowledge of the system to improve care.

> The best way to assure that life isn't a surprise
> to our staff and leaders is to use the tool of
> forecasting demand.

REAL-TIME MONITORING OF FLOW DATA

Demand-capacity management and forecasting demand use historical data to tell us what flow is *likely* to be, based on past experience. Real-time monitoring of data uses tracking boards to tell us *what actual demands currently are* for any given unit in the hospital. The best of the current EMRs use flow monitoring capabilities which graphically display information to help us to answer the following questions:

- *How many* patients are we currently caring for?
- *When* do they need *which* services?
- How does our *service capacity match patient demand*?
- What are our *contingency plans*?
- What does this patient need *next*?
- What are the *rate-limiting steps*?

(Note: If you are selecting an EMR, ask potential vendors if their product has this capability, including not just real-time flow displays, but also the ability to extract information to look at historical trends and success factors. If it doesn't have them, select another system.)

As we seek to improve flow, we need to select leaders and managers who are able to use real-time flow data to obtain a clear sense of situational awareness of the current status (based on the questions above). Equally importantly, they must be able to read and react to the situation in ways that deploy resources effectively and efficiently to meet the real-time, dynamic needs. As we will discuss in more detail in Chapters 6 and 7, using this tool for inpatient management will be a critical marker of success for hospitals (Resar et al., 2011).

QUEUING THEORY

Anytime you stand in line—at Starbucks, the grocery store, or the airport—you are in a queue. Queuing theory is the art and science of matching fixed resources to unscheduled (but not unpredictable) demand. One of the key relevant consequences of queuing theory is that when use of the system increases, the response is non-linear, which has important implications.

One of those significant implications is illustrated here:

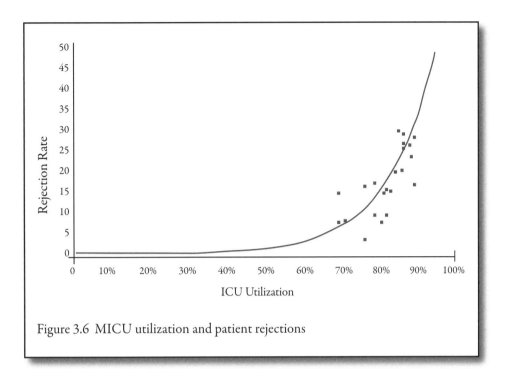

Figure 3.6 MICU utilization and patient rejections

This graph of MICU utilization and patient rejection shows that at 0 percent use of capacity (utilization = 0), the MICU is, as we might expect, empty and the odds of a rejection of a request for an ICU bed ("rejection rate") are zero. If the MICU is full, the odds of being rejected are close to 100 percent.

Notice that as the utilization curves passes 60 percent in the graph, it starts to take off. The reason is because it's not a linear curve. It's a geometric one: a logarithmic curve, meaning that the observed data reflects a sharp increase in rejections as patient utilization increases.

For the patient and the provider, this means that the rejection rates—which represent a system failure to both the user-patient and provider alike—rise dramatically as utilization increases above 60 percent. Utilization of 80 to 85 percent is often the optimal point for a queuing system to operate. Above that rate, it is not only possible, but also highly likely that there will be "no room at the inn" for patients in need of service.

What does this mean from a practical standpoint? If an ED typically sees 150 patients per day and admits 25 percent (37) of them, 10 of whom will need MICU beds, MICU utilization rates over 80 percent at the beginning of the day bode poorly for obtaining MICU beds in a timely fashion, barring a concerted effort to obtain a substantial number of MICU transfers to other units or discharges.

Under these circumstances, we can *forecast* not only our projected MICU needs for the ED, but also the need to use flow tools to address this demand-capacity mismatch. As we'll discuss below, managing variation means having different processes when you start the day at 80 percent MICU utilization than would be used at 60 percent utilization.

The good news is that if you're at 95 percent utilization of your capacity, small changes will lead to a significant difference and reduction in waiting times and rejections. Healthcare systems that have been able to drop to 80 to 85 percent usage of capacity, even 90 percent, have found they can better handle inflows and variation, and as a result, throughput has improved, as have profits and worker satisfaction. Queuing theory is simply the identification of the leverage points needed when queues develop in order to improve capacity.

In healthcare, variation shows up in the difference in diseases and severity in patients and different responses to therapies, as well as in different levels of abilities of providers and different levels of training. There are two kinds of variation: "natural" and "artificial." "Natural variation" is clinical variability in diseases and professional variability in skills, patient-arrival times in the ED, and the duration of surgery. It is random. It is part of flow, and it needs to be managed.

"Artificial variation" is non-random. Such examples include elective surgery, time of discharge, and the schedule of the nuclear-medicine lab for reporting stress-test results. The elements of artificial variation need to be smoothed out so that they are predictable and steady and, in fact, eliminate the high variability often associated with it. Artificial variation often contributes to poor flow.

MANAGING VARIATION

Managing variation that adds value requires a combination of *execution* and *agility*. As we've discussed, execution assures that the value-added systems and processes we've put in place are followed consistently to produce measurable results. But there is also a certain dynamic tension between execution of value-added strategies and the agility required to recognize where waste exists and change the system to improve it. Successfully managing variation requires leaders to have a deep understanding of both the skills and abilities required for execution and agility.

Managing variation that adds value requires
a combination of *execution* and *agility*.

WHY?	WHY NOT?
Why are we doing it **THIS** way?	Why not do it **THAT** way?
EXECUTION	AGILITY
Value-Added	Waste-Reduction

Figure 3.7 The dynamic tension of leadership

ELIMINATING BOTTLENECKS AND CONSTRAINTS

One of the most fundamental concepts in chemistry is that of the "rate-limiting step," which is the phase of a chemical reaction that occurs most slowly and therefore limits the speed of the reaction as a whole. Similarly, bottlenecks and constraints exist throughout healthcare. It is up to us as leaders to identify and eliminate them.

Two fundamental aspects are:

- constraints limit performance, and
- a focus on elimination of constraints is required to improve performance.

A simple definition is that a constraint is anything that significantly limits the performance of an organization or process in moving toward its goal. They fall into two different categories: a weakness in the system or a scarce resource. A physician or lab technician who performs a certain service may be the only one available to do so, for example, and so can easily become a constraint on the system.

This approach to flow operations management, this mental model, was first developed by Dr. Eli Goldratt, an Israeli physicist, who originated the Theory of Constraints model for systems management in his book *The Goal*, a management-oriented novel, and one of the most widely read business books of all time. It was first published in 1984, with revisions in 1992 and 2004.

Theory of Constraints is a management philosophy that focuses an organization's scarce resources on improving the performance of the true constraint(s)—the "bottleneck"—for fluid flow of products or services. Goldratt uses a chain analysis: a focus on "chain strength," that strengthens the weakest link in the chain (i.e., the constraint). Bottlenecks, especially in the healthcare arena, can be fluid, and the journey of a patient into, through, and out of the hospital is actually a journey through a network of queues, each with its own set of constraints or bottlenecks.

When demand for this resource increases beyond its capacity, a bottleneck results. A bottleneck has a precise meaning: It is the part of the process that holds up the flow of the entire system or relevant process; it's more than a constraint that is irritating. Constraints can be internal or external resources, people, equipment, inefficient processes, policies, non-bottlenecks, and market forces.

Here are succinct definitions to distinguish between bottlenecks and non-bottlenecks:

- A bottleneck is any resource whose capacity (ability to serve) is equal to or less than the demand placed upon it.
- A non-bottleneck is any resource whose capacity is greater than the demand placed upon it.

The capacity of the system is thus the capacity of the bottleneck: The slowest process or resource ("rate-limiting") in the service chain governs throughput. Remember that patient care comprises a network of queues and service transitions. A related implication is that you can reduce the time spent at a non-bottleneck, but not reduce time spent within the overall system.

Managing Bottlenecks. To manage bottlenecks, you need to identify the constraints, as well as which of them are the most significant for the system. What processes are causing the longest delays? Look at your staff coverage—physicians, PAs, nurses—and how adequately it matches necessary coverage hours revealed by your tracking of data and use of your real-time dashboard.

Specifically, match the volume of provider hours to peak demand by day of the week. Examine your processing time: For patients entering the ED, how long does it take once they enter to register, to be evaluated by a doctor, to be admitted to a room? How long does it take to gather data? Once you have the data, how long does a decision on treatment require? And finally, how long after treatment begins is the patient discharged?

Is there a fail-safe back-up set up to ensure timely discharge? Identifying constraints is not only a matter of mining your past data; use board rounds and bed huddles to identify them on a daily, ongoing basis. These—board rounds and bed huddles—involve key members of a department who meet at predetermined times, for about 10 minutes, to assess current conditions in the department, anticipate admissions, and analyze patient flow, as well as to make disposition decisions.

Design processes to work most effectively in light of the bottlenecks. Decide what you are trying to accomplish and what interventions are possible in your system, forming both short-term and long-term plans to improve the constraints. Make sure you are carrying out critical steps when you consider what you will do when bottlenecks shift. Then plan your interventions and test them. For long-term interventions, concentrate on identifying chronic causes of demand-capacity mismatches and identifying wasted inpatient capacity.

FLOW AS A COMPLEX ADAPTIVE SYSTEM

Perhaps Peter Drucker said it best: "The hospital is altogether the most complex human organization ever devised!" The concepts of systems thinking are among the most powerful in leveraging the strategies of hardwiring flow. The fact that no less a mind than Peter Drucker's understood the inherent complexity of hospitals and healthcare systems is testament to the highly interrelated nature of the services we provide.

Because healthcare is such a complex system, hardwiring flow must by its very nature of adding value and eliminating waste be focused on becoming a complex but adaptive system. Systems thinking is at the core of the work in hardwiring flow. In fact, the work of great minds like W. Edwards Deming, Peter Senge, Chris Argyris, Russ Ackoff, Tom Peters, and many others all bear upon the way in which we use the mental models of systems thinking to improve healthcare.

> Hardwiring flow must by its very nature of adding
> value and eliminating waste be focused on becoming
> a complex but adaptive system.

In order to optimize the system, everyone working within it must clearly understand the overall aim of the system, since you can't optimize the entire system by separately optimizing each of its parts. Some people may have to give something up or do things differently. Every part of the system can't operate at 100 percent of its potential if the system as a whole is going to operate at its maximum or optimized capacity.

Optimizing flow through an entire system is more difficult than optimizing flow through one department. It requires leaders, a recognized aim for the system, and agreed-upon performance metrics. Peter Senge's insight was that there must be shared mental models that appreciate the fundamental interconnectedness of systems. This is a concept that clearly applies to healthcare, as we hand the patient off from person to person and area to area as they progress through even the simplest of healthcare experiences.

Russ Ackoff cautioned against simply taking the "best practices" of any given area without a deep understanding of how those areas interact. In a simple yet elegant analogy, he notes that taking the suspension system of a BMW, the interior of a Rolls Royce, the engine of a Mercedes, the fuel system of a Maserati, and drive train of a Bentley may seem like an effective way of getting the "best of the best" in luxury automobiles. However, it would be impossible for all of these parts to be assembled together, much less make for a high performance vehicle.

For example, focusing an improvement effort in the ICU that solely looks at decreasing ICO length-of-stay (LOS) may result in the desired results for the ICU, but may produce unfortunate and unwanted consequences for the overall LOS for patients, or even have a negative effect on outcomes. The law of unintended consequences, first described by Robert K. Merton in 1936, offers an important insight in systems thinking, even though its original description predates it.

Chris Argyris of the Harvard Business School has focused attention on the fact that many organizations believe they have a clear aim for the system, known to all within the system. He notes, however, the dichotomy between what he refers to as the "espoused theory" (what leadership teams believe is the commonly understood aim) and the "theory in action" (what actually occurs in the day-to-day operations of the organization). Deming's focus on a clear aim and Argyris' observation that there is often a discrepancy between what we say and what we do must always be kept in mind. Disciplined leader rounding can help pinpoint these discrepancies between plans and reality.

Finally, Abraham Maslow's description of the hierarchy of needs is also an important insight for systems thinking. Maslow ranked his hierarchy of needs beginning with the physiological needs of food, water, and warmth through safety, belonging, self-esteem, and finally to self-actualization at the top of the hierarchy.

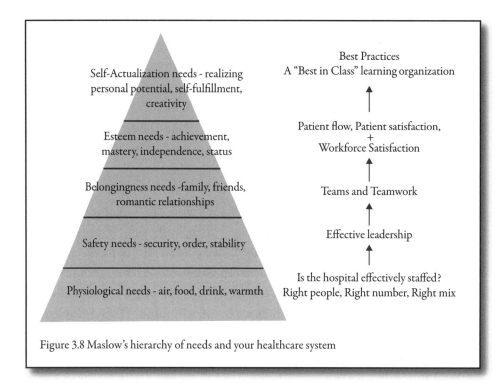

Figure 3.8 Maslow's hierarchy of needs and your healthcare system

However, Maslow had two extraordinarily powerful insights, which are far less commonly known and understood. The first is that you cannot move from one level of the hierarchy to the next until *all* of the needs at the lower level are met. The second is that, if you have moved to a higher level of the hierarchy, but the needs of a lower level are not being met, you *immediately* descend to the level of the unmet needs.

Our experience is that healthcare organizations have a similar hierarchy of needs, beginning with the "physiological" needs of being fully staffed with the right people in the right mix, all the way to the "self-actualization" level of being a "best practices", best-in-class organization. And yet Maslow's insights about being unable to ascend to a higher level until the needs of the lower level are fully met and descending from any higher level to the level at which needs are not met clearly apply at the organizational level as well.

While teams and teamwork are essential to hardwiring flow, if we don't have enough of the right people, we can't hope to focus on effective teams. Similarly, while we can be a world-class healthcare system—and perhaps even have won the Malcolm Baldrige Award for Quality—we can "slide down the hierarchy" on any particular day due to staffing shortages. We will be at the bottom rung of survival, at least until the staffing crisis passes. For those patients and that staff, it will not be a "best in class" day!

The insights of all of these leaders in systems thinking point to the highly interconnected nature of healthcare as a complex, adaptive system and the necessity to take this into account in all flow-related efforts.

THE TOOLS TO HARDWIRE FLOW

Armed with these seven strategies to hardwire flow, let's turn to the tools we have in our armamentarium to address specific means to increase value and eliminate waste as our patients move through the service transitions and queues of healthcare. Each of these tools have utility, depending upon the specific issues being faced. We will give examples of how they can each best be used to leverage flow.

- Demand-Capacity Tools
- Value Stream Mapping
- The 5 "Whys"
- Spaghetti Diagrams
- Huddles and Bed Rounds
- Flow's Team Mates

Figure 3.9 The tools to hardwire flow

DEMAND-CAPACITY MANAGEMENT TOOLS

One of the most powerful tools is the use of software programs to graphically demonstrate and model demand-capacity curves in order to identify and delineate specific changes in how to deploy available capacity to meet demand. At BestPractices and EmCare, we understood how important DCM was to our efforts to improve flow and therefore created such software.

At its essence, demand-capacity software starts by plotting demand by patient arrivals, total census, or acuity-adjusted data for either on the vertical or ordinate axis. Time of arrival by hour of the day is plotted on the horizontal or abscissa, as Figures 3.3 and 3.5 showed.

The first level of demand is the *number* of patients arriving at any given hour of the day. (In more detailed analysis that the software provides, factoring in acuity becomes critical in answering the question "What will the patients need?" not just "Who is coming?" and "When are they coming?") But these plots simply show the *demand* portion of the equation.

To this demand curve must be added the *capacity* of the system at any given time of day (Figure 3.10). The *total capacity* of the system can be a somewhat complex calculus, taking into account not only the *number of providers* of a given type (e.g., nurses, physicians, techs, lab, imaging, EVS), but also the *skill set* of those caregivers. As sophistication with the use of this tool increases, building in historical individual provider or team productivity is a natural outgrowth, since it drives a highly specific prediction of actual capacity.

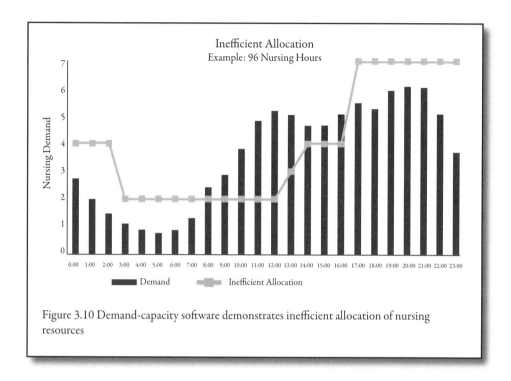

Figure 3.10 Demand-capacity software demonstrates inefficient allocation of nursing resources

Figure 3.10 shows how this software can be used to demonstrate inefficient allocation of resources. The blue bars show the arrival of patients by hour of the day. The gold line overlaying the blue bars shows the number of nurses by hour of the day.

Instead of matching capacity to known patient demand, this staffing pattern (taken from a real example) is highly inefficient, where there are either too many nurses (5 pm to 7 am) or too few (8 am to 4 pm) a majority of hours. Fortunately, demand-capacity tools can model how best to correct these mismatches (as Figure 3.11 shows), using precisely the same number of nursing hours (96 per day) but more efficiently deploying them to match capacity and demand.

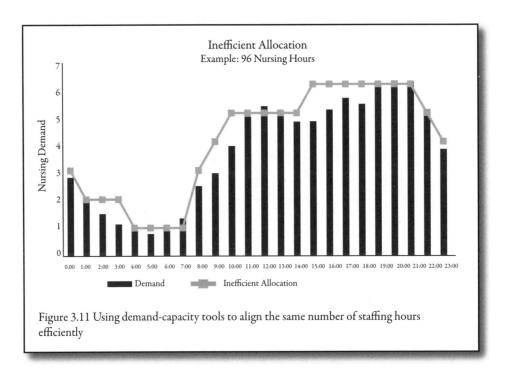

Figure 3.11 Using demand-capacity tools to align the same number of staffing hours efficiently

While this example shows how the tool can be used to match nursing capacity to demand, total team capacity can also be added by including physician and support staff resources. The tool can be used in any area of the hospital or healthcare system and it is an invaluable and essential tool to hardwire hospital-wide flow.

VALUE STREAM MAPPING

While a detailed discussion of value-stream mapping (VSM) is beyond the scope of this book, it is important to have a fundamental understanding of this important tool, which should be used to map the steps in any of the basic processes of healthcare. More detailed information is presented in a number of excellent resources (Graban, 2012; Touissant and Berry, 2013; Crane and Noon 2011).

VSM is a process by which a graphic representation reflecting a deep understanding of patient flow is created by a disciplined, team-based approach to discovering where both value and waste exist in focused healthcare processes. This disciplined approach is usually led by an experienced, lean-trained leader, either form within the organization or a consultant. Here are the steps:

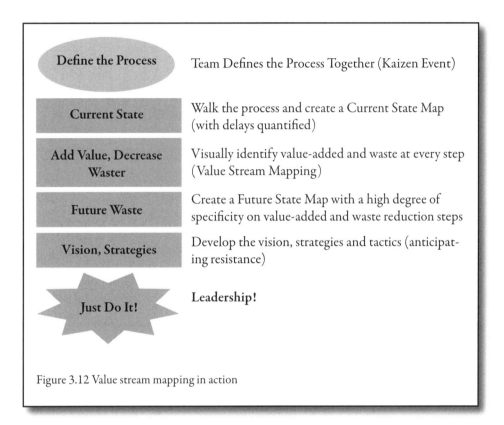

Define the Process	Team Defines the Process Together (Kaizen Event)
Current State	Walk the process and create a Current State Map (with delays quantified)
Add Value, Decrease Waster	Visually identify value-added and waste at every step (Value Stream Mapping)
Future Waste	Create a Future State Map with a high degree of specificity on value-added and waste reduction steps
Vision, Strategies	Develop the vision, strategies and tactics (anticipating resistance)
Just Do It!	Leadership!

Figure 3.12 Value stream mapping in action

It begins with a "kaizen event," which is derived from the Japanese word for "good change." Here, the team invests a considerable amount of time and effort to define the existing process, not as it is thought to be, but as it actually is "discovered" during the course of the event. This is in many ways the most important step, since, almost without exception, the processes studied are actually different than are supposed by the leaders of the team.

Following this investigation, the processes are "walked" and a "current state" map of the existing process is created, using a set of symbols and tools to map the "value stream" itself (Figure 3.13). Although such maps are confusing to read for the uninitiated, once the team is accustomed to the process and the symbols, they are actually easily intelligible.

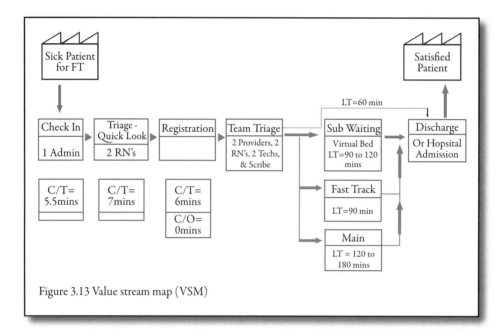

Figure 3.13 Value stream map (VSM)

A key insight in the use of VSM is that 90 percent of the *delays* are in the arrows (which represent steps between the processes) while 90 percent of the *defects and deviations* are in the boxes themselves (which represent the discrete steps within the overall process being studied). Added to this plot of the process and its component sub-processes are the specific areas where value is added or waste exists. This step involves all team members and delivers powerful insights at virtually every level of the organization, since the value-waste ratio becomes abundantly apparent.

At this stage of VSM is when the "Future State Map" is created, where the team designs new processes and sub-processes, each with a view towards increasing value and eliminating waste. Developing and implementing the vision, mission, strategies and tactics necessary to execute these changes by an empowered leadership team is the next step, followed by continuously collecting data to offer feedback on whether the changes are actually improving the value-waste ratio.

Value stream mapping is an excellent flow tool to use when discrete processes are being studied. One important caution is to keep the VSM effort focused on relatively circumscribed processes. VSM works well in focus, but should not be used to "cure world hunger".

THE "5 WHYS"

One of the simplest, yet most effective tools for hardwiring flow is the "5 Whys". Like many good ideas, its parentage is variably attributed, usually to one of two sources: the Toyota Production System and the work of Frederick Reichheld of Bain. In all likelihood, it was first developed by Sakichi Toyoda and refined by Reichheld in his work, "The Loyalty Factor."

Regardless of its precise derivation, the "5 Whys" uses a method of repeatedly asking "Why?" to drill down to the root cause of the problem. It is an iterative process, which is best used to determine primarily human factors involved in processes where problems have occurred and waste is therefore likely to be embedded.

Instead of accepting the natural human tendency to accept the first answer as the definitive answer to the problem, it builds in the discipline of diving deeper into the problem to find the likely root cause. It is sometimes criticized (even within Toyota circles) as lacking a deep basis in data, but it is nonetheless highly effective for identifying problems at a macro or "10,000 feet level," which can then be further studied with other techniques.

Here are two examples:

1. **Why are the Docs and Nurses at odds over the EMR?**

    Because the docs are moving so fast, patients are discharged before the nurses can even get to them

2. **Why are the docs moving so fast?**

    Because there is a huge emphasis on metrics, Docs vs. nurses

3. **Why do metrics concern the nurses?**

    Nurses are concerned about discharge times

4. **Why are the nurses concerned about discharge times?**

    Patients are waiting extended periods after Doc D/C

5. **Why are patients waiting so long after the doc sees them?**

    Because current policy requires the nurses to D/C patients

Figure 3.14 Why are doctors and nurses at odds over the EMR?

1. **Why isn't the lab study back yet?**

    Because the lab didn't run the sample.

2. **Why didn't the lab run the sample?**

    Because the sample wasn't labeled correctly?

3. **Why wasn't the label done correctly?**

    Because the tech who drew the sample didn't know.

4. **Why didn't the tech know how to label it properly?**

    Because he was never trained in the new process.

5. **Why wasn't he trained in the new process?**

    Because the supervisor doesn't believe in "all this training."

Figure 3.15 Why isn't the lab study back yet?

In each of these cases, the problem starts with an answer that focuses on one area, yet ends up focusing on a completely different one. For example, in the last case (Figure 3.15), instead of focusing on the lab not running the sample, the root cause is that the supervisor of the techs (who isn't even in the lab) doesn't believe in training. The "5 Whys" is thus a simple, iterative tool used to identify (but not quantify) root causes of primarily human processes.

SPAGHETTI FLOW DIAGRAMS

Spaghetti flow diagrams are simple graphic representations of primarily physician movement of patients and/or staff during the course of a specific process or sub process. They are designed to be done by actually *observing* the process, not checking a policies and procedures manual, which reflects only what is *supposed* to happen. Thus, this requires direct observation, usually at repeated times and with different providers to see what is *actually happening.*

To create a spaghetti diagram, start with a fairly large scale map of the physical space in which the process occurs. Next, observe the steps taken in the course of the process and plot both "forward" and "backward" movements which occur during the successive course of the process itself. "Forward" movements are plotted in one color and "backward" movements are plotted in another (usually red for "retreat").

Figure 3.16 shows how such graphic flow diagrams can be used to improve flow through a system, eliminating or minimizing "backward" movements (waste), while accentuating forward movements (adding value).

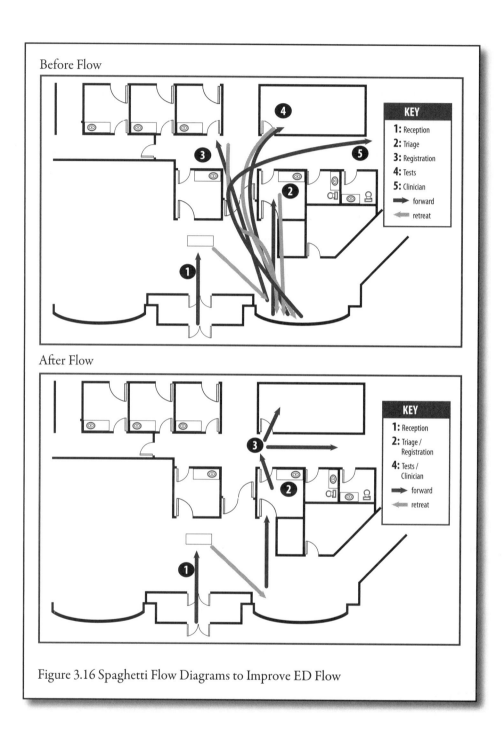

Figure 3.16 Spaghetti Flow Diagrams to Improve ED Flow

HUDDLES AND BED ROUNDS

A huddle in football is designed to get the team together to make sure they all have a common understanding of the current situation, what the team is facing and what the quarterback or defensive signal caller is asking each team member to do. In football, huddles take into account "down and distance," field position, the score, the team members on the field, and the best strategy for success (the play called to "move the chains"). In the same way, team huddles are a consistent feature of high performance healthcare teams that are "hardwired" to ensure consistent communication about critical issues.

To be effective, huddles should be focused, limited to a few crucial elements, and not exceed more than a few minutes. Team members review specific team goals and operational issues that impact the provision of patient care (i.e. staff call-in, CT down, available beds, OR schedules, etc.). Time is also taken to appreciate and recognize team members. Team huddles particularly add value during volume and acuity surges, as these are typically times when a team is most vulnerable to losing situational awareness and control. Team huddles can also help reduce demand capacity mismatches leading to gridlock (i.e. ambulance diversion) because early shared input can both optimize patient flow (i.e. discharge patients, make disposition decisions) and recognize the need for additional resources before it is too late.

Surprisingly, though poor communication skills are frequently cited as the cause of patient error as well as staff discontent, healthcare staff training on such skills is generally limited. High performance teams must continually work to learn critical listening skills and to recognize the importance of proper word selection (including scripting), moderation of tone, awareness of non-verbal communication.

Such teams recognize that patient safety and error prevention are dramatically improved when all team members feel safe to ask or even challenge the approach to the patient's care. High performance teams regularly practice safety communication techniques, such as "order read-back," procedural "time-outs," and multiple "patient identifications" when administering blood, insulin, etc., and double-checks when conducting high-risk tasks. Many hospitals have adopted templates and scripts to standardize the way in which information is communicated, such as SBAR (Situation, Background, Assessment, and Recommendations).

Bed rounds are a variation of the huddle and are used to assess the classic elements of "input, throughput, and output". Each of these areas are assessed to assure that one of the most valuable resources in healthcare—the bed—is managed correctly, depending on demand-capacity curves. Hospital-wide bed rounds pull together leaders from all areas of the hospital to discuss in detail how best to triage those beds to meet incoming patient needs. Bed rounds can also be done on a unit or service-line basis to assure that bed use is maximized. Real-time demand-capacity management of hospital-wide flow is an extremely valuable resource, which is discussed in more detail in Chapter 7.

HARDWIRING FLOW™ FOCUS: STRATEGIES AND TOOLS TO HARDWIRE HOSPITAL-WIDE FLOW

- The 7 strategies to hardwire flow are: demand-capacity management, forecasting demand, real-time monitoring of flow data, queuing theory, managing variation, eliminating constraints and bottlenecks, and flow as a complex adaptive system.

  Align strategic incentives around the patient. (What gets rewarded gets repeated. What you permit, you promote.)

  The 5 questions of demand-capacity management are: Who's coming? When are they coming? What are they going to need? Is our service capacity going to match patient demand? What will we do if it doesn't?

- **Forecasting demand**—Unscheduled arrivals in healthcare can be accurately forecast with an accuracy of 80-85 percent. Forecasting models include a percentage adjustment of previous historical activity, using a 12-month moving average or modeling a trend line.

- **Real-time modeling of flow** data—Healthcare must adopt the concept of dashboards, as used by restaurants and other industries, to better adapt to changing capacity and demand.

- **Queuing theory**—While delays and service failures occur above 80-85% utilization rates, even small changes on this "ascending limb" of the curve result in dramatic improvements.

- **Managing variation**—Reducing variation that reduces waste is positive. Increasing variation that increases value is also positive. (This is the paradox of healthcare variation.) To manage variation: focus on operational efficiency, prioritize available resources, flex scheduling, predict demand, smooth demand, and increase the accuracy of predictions.

- **Eliminating constraints and bottlenecks**—Constraints and bottlenecks are a major performance-limiter in healthcare. Capacity cannot be stored. If it isn't used, it is wasted! To manage bottlenecks, determine what and where the constraints are, which are most detrimental to system performance, and eliminate them.

- **Flow as a complex adaptive system**—Hardwiring flow requires a deep understanding of systems thinking. If you want to hardwire flow, you must have a clearly articulated and widely understood aim for the system. There must be shared mental models among the team, with a clear sense of the fundamental interconnectedness of the system's parts.

- Just as Maslow's hierarchy of needs applies to individuals, it also applies to healthcare, from basic staffing needs at the bottom to a "Best Practices" learning organization at the top.

- Tools to hardwire flow include demand-capacity modeling tools, value stream mapping, the "5 Whys?", and spaghetti flow diagrams.

CHAPTER 4

LESSONS FROM OTHER INDUSTRIES

by Kirk Jensen, MD, and Thom Mayer, MD

"Don't benchmark. Other mark."

—Ancient Chinese Curse

"Wise men learn from others' mistakes; fools only learn from their own."

—Benjamin Franklin, Poor Richard's Almanac

On January 21, 2009, an Airbus A320 with 155 souls on board departed New York's LaGuardia Airport runway 4 at 3:25 p.m. EST, bound for Charlotte, North Carolina. Two minutes later, at an altitude of 2,800 feet and just past the George Washington Bridge, Flight 1549 suffered a massive bird strike, which immediately extinguished all power to both engines. Within minutes, a sophisticated airliner with state-of-the-art avionics was transformed into…a glider.

First Officer Jeff Skiles, who, ironically, was due to complete his training in the A320 with Flight 1549, was flying the plane, but the captain took control with these two airline-mandated words: "My aircraft." In the remaining 208 seconds of the flight, Captain Chesley "Sully" Sullenberger would put to use every bit of his training and experience from over 20,000 flight hours—including flying United States Air Force tactical fighter-bombers—after making the fateful decision to land the A320 in the frigid waters of the Hudson River. All 155 souls survived with only minor injuries to the crew and passengers.

One week later, in a closed reviewing area of the National Transportation Safety Board, six highly trained accident investigation experts listened to the just-recovered cockpit voice recorder, which captured all sounds emitted in the cockpit of Flight 1549. After the repeated heavy thuds from the bird strikes, which hit not only the engines, but the fuselage and the wind screen of the cockpit (virtually obliterating all sight for a brief time), amid the blaring cacophony of the aircraft's warning system, the calm, measured voice of Captain Sullenberger stood out, including his words to the air traffic controller who had cleared runways at LaGuardia and at the nearer private airport at Teterboro, New Jersey.

He said, "We can't do it. We're gonna be in the Hudson." One of the NTSB members said, in the eerie quiet after the cockpit voice recording finished, "That guy has been training for this his entire life" (Sullenberger, 2012).

In later interviews about the "Miracle on the Hudson," as it came to be known, Sully made clear that the success was not due to his skills alone, but the entire team's skills and training. Despite the fact that he had only just met Jeff Skiles three days prior to the flight, "our training was so thorough that we were interchangeable."

He also confirmed what the NTSB official had said. Captain Sullenberger noted that the successful and unprecedented landing of Flight 1549 occurred because of "engaging in a lifelong commitment to learning, to expanding one's mind and to viewing each day as a cumulative process of preparation." He added, "In seconds, I managed to synthesize a lifetime of experience and training to solve a problem I'd never seen before" (Sullenberger, 2012). And it couldn't have hurt that Sully's hobby—flying gliders—was one that paid dividends when the engines of the A320 went silent.

What can we in healthcare learn from the lessons of Flight 1549, as well as those from other industries? As it turns out, we can learn a lot, as we will discuss in some detail. For the past decade and a half, healthcare has tried to adapt to a rapidly changing environment without its practitioners having had formal training in how to assimilate lessons from other businesses to assist us through the "perpetual whitewater of change" we discussed in Chapter 1.

The pace of change is so fast and the necessity of adapting so acute that one can't help but recall the advice of legendary race driver Mario Andretti: "If things seem under control, you're just not going fast enough!"

The same can be said of the current—and future—environment for healthcare leaders at all levels. Patient safety, patient experience, physician leadership, high reliability, developing evidence-based clinical protocols, and flow are all areas in which the pace of change has been dramatic. Yet the results have been variable, incomplete, or unsustainable in many hospitals and healthcare systems.

When faced with the challenge to improve rapidly, we have three fundamental ways to proceed. First, we can change existing tools and processes to meet these increased challenges. While we certainly need to "fix what's broken." the sheer magnitude of the challenges we face in improving flow cannot help but bring to mind the novelist Rita Mae Brown's wisdom (often incorrectly attributed to others, including Einstein):

One definition of insanity is to keep doing the same things over and over—and expect different results (Brown, 1983).

Thus, while improvement of existing tools and processes is necessary, it is unlikely to be sufficient to produce the results we need. The second option is to *de novo* develop better tools and techniques, starting at "ground zero" and working to craft new solutions to old problems. But that is not a challenge many of us would choose to undertake. It is perhaps an admirable challenge to completely reinvent healthcare processes, but it is, at a minimum, a daunting prospect, particularly given all the other work on our plates.

The third option is the subject of this chapter: learning which solutions have worked well for other industries, finding common ground with healthcare, and adapting those solutions to our work. Innovations and successes from various fields—from restaurants to hotels and gaming to aviation—offer many useful lessons and ideas that, when applied to hospitals and healthcare systems, can greatly improve efficiency and lead to better outcomes.

Many healthcare leaders have written on applicable ideas and models from businesses like major chain restaurants, the hotel industry, and aviation. While other industries offer valuable ideas and strategies, it is important to note that hospitals and care for patients come with many distinct circumstances, and any ideas taken from other businesses must recognize the unique challenges faced by hospitals and healthcare professionals.

The fact that any given idea may be novel, intriguing, and attractive does not necessarily mean that it can be meaningfully and reliably applied in the healthcare setting. That said, it is wise to remember our parents' advice that "You can learn from anyone!"

In other words, don't *just* look at who is performing existing industry processes the best; look outside of healthcare for potential solutions. Whenever you do any of the following activities, you are fundamentally being presented with an opportunity to observe lessons from other industries for healthcare. Each of these things—and more—are what our patients and their loved ones endure when they enter the healthcare system:

- stand in line,
- have to choose a line,
- have service handed off from one person to another,
- have service handed off from one department to another,
- are greeted by someone in a process that is unfamiliar to you,
- wait for important information, and
- approach a situation that is anxiety-inducing.

It would not be an overstatement to say that "common sense could write this chapter", except for the fact that common sense isn't all that common! With these caveats in mind, let us turn to the lessons healthcare can learn from other businesses.

BED TURNS AND THE CHEESECAKE FACTORY

In a well-known article for *The New Yorker*, entitled "Can Hospital Chains Improve the Medical Industry?" Atul Gawande discusses implications of the increasing number of "large conglomerate" hospitals and clinics. He details potential benefits of this phenomenon as viewed through the lens of the success of a major restaurant chain, the Cheesecake Factory. In fact, today, there are roughly 90 "superregional" healthcare systems throughout the United States (Gawande, 2012).

Gawande cites the following factors as key to the Cheesecake Factory's continued success across the country: the size of the chain, the standardization from one restaurant to another, specialized professional development—in which managers are not only taught new recipes but also the proper method for teaching their chefs these new items—and the role of the kitchen manager, who oversees each specialized chef to ensure consistent, high-quality orders.

Gawande contends that many of these factors can be recreated in the hospital to improve service and care. As an example, he cites Dr. John Wright, an orthopedic surgeon at the Brigham and Women's Hospital, and his "decade-long experiment in standardizing joint-replacement surgery" (Gawande, 2012).

Through a review of research and changed practices, the staff at Brigham and Women's Hospital, led by Wright, was able to create a more effective operation for knee replacements, focusing on these issues:

- giving certain pain medications before the patient entered the operating room;
- using spinal anesthesia plus a sural nerve block;
- replacing the use of a continuous passive-motion machine, which was found by large-scale studies to do little good for the patient, with more physical therapy; and
- convincing surgeons to agree to a limited number of prostheses used in the operation. (This represents the greatest cost in the operation, as "the average retail price is around eight thousand dollars, and some cost twice that, with no solid evidence of real differences in results.")

APPLYING THESE LESSONS TO FLOW

To put this example into the context of flow strategy, this is fundamentally an example of *managing variation* to increase value and decrease waste. It minimizes non-value-added variation (using multiple prostheses) and maximizes processes that add value (preoperative pain medications, sural nerve blocks, and early physical therapy).

While these changes are not easy to adopt and surgeons are often reluctant to agree to a restriction of knee prostheses, Wright's role is similar to that of the kitchen manager in the Cheesecake Factory. A kitchen manager is responsible for ensuring optimal performance from those under his or her guidance, praising good performance and, most importantly, reviewing outcomes, informing the chefs when items need to be prepared better, and creating ideas that result in a more efficient environment.

Wright reviewed the knee-replacement procedure and enforced a standardized operation with fewer options in prostheses that led to faster rehabilitation and lower costs. While, as Gawande notes, Wright's position is "not always a pleasant role", it has nonetheless resulted in significant improvements in knee-replacement surgeries, as judged by both costs and outcomes.

The effect on hospital bed turns by this decreased length of stay is an example of *eliminating a bottleneck or constraint* by effectively creating more bed capacity at an earlier time. Ultimately, the standardization implemented by Wright and adopted across the hospital resulted in vastly improved performance and outcomes in regard to knee-replacement surgeries.

Gawande also cites the impact of the rise of the tele-ICU and the efforts of pulmonary and critical care specialist Dr. Armin Ernst. Ernst works primarily with caregivers, rather than patients themselves, in an effort "to get clinicians to agree on precise standards of care, and make sure that they follow through on them" (Gawande, 2012). Ernst operates from an "ICU command center from which his 'tele-ICU' team will have the ability to monitor the care for every patient in every ICU bed in the Steward Health Care System."

Improving the efficiency and operation of ICUs is of the utmost importance. While less than one in four thousand Americans are in intensive care at any given time, they account for four percent of national healthcare costs. Although critical care specialists are in short supply, the tele-ICU covers multiple hospitals, allowing those in the "command center" to monitor patients for multiple issues.

As with Wright's work in orthopedics, there were problems implementing the tele-ICU concept. Some doctors are resistant to the "over-the-shoulder" monitoring created through these centers, with some going so far as to cover up cameras in hospital rooms. In one case, a nurse asked the command center to "not turn on the video system in her patient's room: he was delirious and confused, and the sudden appearance of someone talking to him from the television would freak him out" (Gawande, 2012).

Nevertheless, the remote monitoring allotted through ICU command centers allows fewer individuals to check in on a greater number of hospital rooms and, when necessary, notify nurses and doctors as issues arise. The increasingly widespread use of tele-ICUs is an example of several flow strategies, including *demand-capacity management, real-time monitoring of flow, managing variation, and eliminating bottlenecks and constraints.*

CHECKLISTS AND MANDATORY PROCEDURES

Using Checklists to Improve Safety and Cut Costs

One method businesses use to improve the effectiveness and efficiency of their operations is the checklist. One form of checklist at Starbucks is instantly recognizable, even if you haven't called it by its medical name: *callbacks and call-downs.* Regardless of the seeming complexity of your order, the person at the register records it (on the cup with your name) and calls down the order to the barista (e.g., "Venti triple extra hot, extra caramel skinny macchiato for Kirk").

The barista uses a callback by repeating the order to the cashier—and to you, indirectly—using precisely the same language. This not only helps guarantee customer satisfaction and loyalty, but simultaneously reduces rework and dumping of incorrect orders. Anytime nurses use callbacks and call-downs in the ICU or ED to confirm a verbal order, they are using a technique learned from other industries. (Callbacks and call-downs also owe a debt to naval and aviation safety, as we shall discuss later.)

In *The Checklist Manifesto*, Gawande expands on the importance of checklists and their ability to improve individual performance (Gawande, 2009). He points to the efforts of Dr. Peter Pronovost, a critical care specialist at Johns Hopkins Hospital, and numerous studies, to demonstrate the efficacy of checklists.

Improving performance in ICUs is extremely important given the increasing prevalence of these departments in hospitals throughout the United States. Fifty years ago, relatively few ICUs existed in the country. Now, each day, nearly 90,000 are patients in ICUs and "over a normal lifetime nearly all of us will know the glassed bay of an ICU from the inside" (Gawande, 2009). Increasingly, many healthcare reformers are turning to checklists as a viable means of improving operations within this department, a clear example of *managing variation.*

In 2001, Peter Pronovost implemented checklists at Johns Hopkins Hospital that focused solely on central line infections. Including steps to avoid infections, his checklist detailed that doctors need to "(1) wash their hands with soap, (2) clean the patient's skin with chlorhexidine antiseptic, (3) put sterile drapes over the entire patient, (4) wear a sterile mask, hat, gown, and gloves, and (5) put a sterile dressing over the catheter site once the line is in" (Gawande, 2009). While these steps may seem obvious, they nonetheless resulted in a notable decrease in infection rates.

Specifically, in the year after the hospital instituted this checklist, the ten-day infection rates among its patients dropped from "eleven per cent to zero." Overall, Pronovost and others estimated that at Johns Hopkins Hospital, "the checklist had prevented forty-three infections and eight deaths, and saved two million dollars in costs." Similar programs have been put in place by one of the authors (Thom Mayer) for the National Football League, using simple chlorhexidine cloths to lower the incidence of MRSA.

Following the aforementioned success in Johns Hopkins Hospital, Pronovost started the "Keystone Initiative," which assigned a project manager to implement checklists in each hospital and had each hospital "participate in a twice-monthly conference call with Pronovost for trouble-shooting" (Gawande, 2009). This initiative has produced better outcomes at lower costs, despite initial resistance to mandatory checklists as "cookbook medicine."

Mandatory Procedures to Ensure Consistent Results

A related concept to checklists is that of mandatory procedures. Mandatory procedures assure that all providers at all levels of care are trained in and monitored for compliance with standardized procedures for key aspects of healthcare. These are usually procedures that involve potentially life- or limb-threatening care. And yet some of these lessons come from, of all things, the fast food business. The employees at McDonald's restaurants are not "making it up as they go" when it comes to preparing and serving any of their food, particularly when it comes to signature items like their french fries, Egg McMuffins, or Big Mac Sauce.

Each of these items is prepared the same way, in the same amounts, at the same temperature at *every McDonald's restaurant in the world.* The consistency of the product is a part of branding the product and requires checklists and mandatory procedures to assure that consistency and reliability occur at every location. The same analogy applies at other restaurants, hotel chains, and coffee shops (Starbucks, for example).

An excellent example of mandated procedures in healthcare is the work at Memorial Hermann Healthcare System in Houston, where our great friend Chuck Stokes is the chief operating officer. Since the system mandated the use of ultrasound-guided placement of subclavian vein catheters, they have not had a procedure-related pneumothorax in four years, clearly improving patient safety and provider satisfaction (since no one wants a procedure-related complication).

Other examples of checklists and mandated procedures are the many evidence-based courses for critically ill or injured patients, including the advanced cardiac life support, advanced trauma life support, pediatric advanced life support, and neonatal advanced life support courses. Checklists and mandating certain high-risk procedures all use the key flow strategy of *managing variation* by eliminating non-value-added variation, while assuring that value-added processes are *always* used.

SYSTEMS THINKING, COGNITIVE PSYCHOLOGY, AND PATIENT SAFETY

In an article entitled "Error in Medicine," published in the *Journal of the American Medical Association* in 1994, Lucian L. Leape, MD, a pediatric surgeon and professor at Harvard School of Public Health, discusses causes for error in medicine and presents possible solutions to reducing hospital injuries. He begins with a review of the "medical approach to error prevention" (Leape, 1994).

Under this approach, if healthcare professionals are correctly trained, "then they would make no mistakes." Most importantly, physicians who commit errors are punished "through social opprobrium or peer disapproval." Ultimately, Leape contends that reducing error in medicine centers on altering the way healthcare professionals regard error and the causes of such incidents, as everyone makes mistakes, and "systems that rely on error-free performance are doomed to fail."

He also draws parallels between approaches taken by the aviation industry to reduce mistakes and the application of these principles to hospitals and healthcare professionals. Among the many safety mechanisms implemented in the aviation industry that can be modified and applied to healthcare are: (1) *system design*, which "assume[s] that errors and failures are inevitable and design[s] systems to 'absorb' them, building in multiple buffers, automation, and redundancy," (2) *standardized procedures*, in which "specific protocols must be followed for trip planning, operations, and maintenance," (3) *professional development*, where "the training, examination, and certification process is highly developed and rigidly, as well as frequently, enforced," and, finally, (4) *institutionalization*, where "two independent organizations have government-mandated responsibilities: the Federal Aviation Administration (FAA) regulates all aspects of flying and prescribes safety procedures, and the National Transportation Safety Board investigates every accident" (Leape 1994).

The underlying principles behind these four aspects contributing to aviation safety— system design, standardized procedures, professional development, and institutionalization—can be applied to healthcare to reduce errors in medicine. First, Leape argues for a greater emphasis on the discovery of errors, in which hospital management and medical professionals accept errors as "inevitable, although manageable," resulting in a daily routine that will make "it be possible for hospital personnel to shift from a punitive to a creative frame of mind that seeks out and identifies the underlying system failures" (Leape, 1994). Identifying errors, although this can be expensive, as Leape admits, allows healthcare professionals to identify reoccurring issues and develop solutions to these problems.

Second, in discussion of the prevention of errors, Leape emphasizes two possible solutions: a "reduced reliance on memory" and "improved information access" (Leape, 1994). In regard to the former, Leape points to "checklists, protocols, and computerized decision aids" as methods by which physicians and nurses can minimize the need to rely on short-term memory, since these approaches can provide the information quickly and accurately. In discussion of the latter—greater access to information—Leape argues that statistics and data must be "readily available," and one way of achieving this goal is through computerized medical records.

Finally, another lesson from the aviation industry—institutionalized safety measures—can also be applied to healthcare. Leape does not suggest a national safety board to examine every single accident, as such an organization is "neither practical nor necessary" (Leape, 1994). However, the same principles can be applied at the individual level: expanding the role of "hospital risk management activities."

Leape's key suggestions in this regard consist of expanding managers' responsibilities to "include all potentially injurious errors and deepen[ing them] to seek out underlying system failures." In addition, Leape suggests that the Joint Commission should play a role in "discussions regarding the institutionalization of safety." Overall, while the issues and realities faced by healthcare systems are vastly different than those in aviation, the procedures and methods taken by airlines provide a useful starting point for implementing new methods to reduce error and reexamining existing institutions to improve their role in improving safety in healthcare systems.

More Lessons from Aviation

Advocates of healthcare reform who emphasize the viability of checklists in intensive care units often point to the results of such efforts in the aviation industry when arguing for increasing use of checklists throughout hospitals. A commonly cited example from the aviation industry among healthcare reformers focuses on a 1989 Boeing 747 flight from Honolulu to Auckland, New Zealand.

During the trip, "an electrical short" unsecured a cargo door at an altitude of 22,000 feet, resulting in a "ring-pull" effect. This caused an "explosion [that] blew out the cargo door almost instantly and took with it several upper-deck windows and five rows of business class seats" (Gawande, 2009). The explosion resulted in damage to the engines and loss of cabin pressure.

In the resulting confusion, the pilots consulted the "Door FWD Cargo" checklist (a specific checklist for the damaged cargo door) and "reduced their altitude, got the two damaged engines shut down safely, tested the plane's ability to land despite the wing damage, dumped fuel to lighten their load, and successfully returned to Honolulu." In this incident, the pilots were able to consult a specific checklist for the damaged portion of a plane in order to prevent further catastrophe.

It should be noted that Boeing has released more than 100 checklists a year for specific circumstances and parts of the plane. In Gawande's discussion about the incident with Daniel Boormann, a Boeing flight training technical fellow, Boormann distinguished between good and bad checklists. The latter are lengthy, "vague and imprecise," while the former are succinct, "efficient, to the point, and easy to use even in the most difficult situations" (Gawande, 2009).

Boormann's concept of a "good checklist" appears to reflect many attributes of Pronovost's checklist for avoiding line infections in the ICU. Both Boeing's checklist for "Door FWD Cargo" and Pronovost's list for minimizing infections were to the point and dealt with a specific case. Overall, when considered in light of the success resulting from the implementation of Pronovost's checklist among hospitals in Michigan, the aviation industry's emphasis on this method offers a valuable lesson for instituting such efforts in healthcare systems to minimize risk and improve performance.

For a more recent example of how aviation safety can have an impact on healthcare, we need only return to Flight 1549. As we noted, Captain Sullenberger was a highly experienced pilot who attributed the successful landing of the A320 to both a team effort and a lifelong commitment to learning. Certainly his experience as a glider pilot, in which every landing is a "dead-stick landing" (meaning a landing without power where airspeed controls lift), clearly helped. But what is less well known is that Sully was one of the earliest pilots who committed to a specific type of learning: aircraft safety.

As early as the late 1970s, he was deeply involved in efforts to help pilots understand the precepts of aviation safety. As he said, "We focused not on *who's* right, but *what's* right" (Sullenberger, 2012). This shifted the entire culture from the "blame game" to one where safe and unsafe processes could be distinguished and the essential systems nature of aviation came to the forefront. This is precisely the conversation that is occurring today at the most successful healthcare systems in the country, where it is no longer an "eminence-based" set of rules ("Because I'm the boss, that's why!"), but rather, to an evidence-based, interrelated set of processes, guided by the best science derived from the best experience.

Captain Sullenberger also stresses how early efforts at redefining aviation safety focused on a definition of innovation that meant "changing before you are *forced* to change." Again, all of this is in a culture of teamwork. Contrast Sully's description of Flight 1549 as a total team effort with the image of a doctor arriving at the patient's bedside "in the nick of time to save his life." One cannot help but ask the question in the healthcare setting, "Why didn't you train the *team* to do what was needed instead of keeping those skills to yourself?" If we don't train the team, the doctor remains the *bottleneck or constraint* to life-saving care.

Lessons from Naval Aircraft Carrier and Submarine Operations

Additional lessons from aviation come from nuclear aircraft carrier and submarine operations, which we have been privileged to experience directly, through the generosity of the Department of Defense. There are nine fundamental "Lessons from the Fight Deck" (Mayer 2010) that can help guide flow efforts in healthcare:

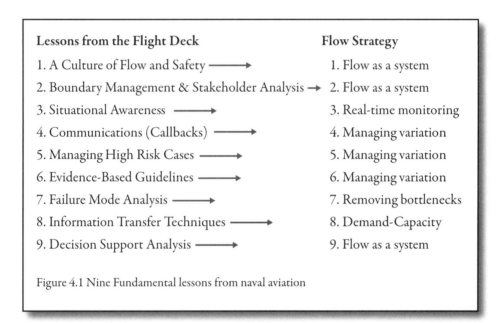

Lessons from the Flight Deck	Flow Strategy
1. A Culture of Flow and Safety ⟶	1. Flow as a system
2. Boundary Management & Stakeholder Analysis ⟶	2. Flow as a system
3. Situational Awareness ⟶	3. Real-time monitoring
4. Communications (Callbacks) ⟶	4. Managing variation
5. Managing High Risk Cases ⟶	5. Managing variation
6. Evidence-Based Guidelines ⟶	6. Managing variation
7. Failure Mode Analysis ⟶	7. Removing bottlenecks
8. Information Transfer Techniques ⟶	8. Demand-Capacity
9. Decision Support Analysis ⟶	9. Flow as a system

Figure 4.1 Nine Fundamental lessons from naval aviation

Both the culture of flow and the combination of boundary management and stakeholder analysis are examples of the strategy of viewing flow as a complex adaptive system, in which transitioning across boundaries is critical. Situational awareness on carrier operations is absolutely essential to assure safe flow of these highly expensive aircraft.

The chatter is very similar to busy healthcare operations, particularly in EDs and ICUs. That chatter is cacophonous and constant and it comes from many sources at once (much like a trauma resuscitation). But what they are monitoring for is deviation from the norm. That is where the danger lies, just as in healthcare, where we are monitoring flow and safety data on a real-time basis.

Communications on both carriers and submarines use redundant callbacks and call-downs, to assure accuracy of vital information to reduce variation. The hand signals used on the flight deck each carry a very specific meaning so there is no question about where and how the aircraft are moving.

Each aircraft is weighed prior to a catapult launch and the information is cross-verified at multiple levels, from the flight deck to the tower (or "Pri-Fly") back to the flight deck and finally to the catapult operator. A nuclear submarine does not change position without an intricate set of communications between the captain of the watch, the officer of the bridge, and the dive master:

Captain: "Make your depth 650 feet, heading 180, 15 degrees right rudder."

Officer of the bridge: "Make my depth 650 feet, heading 180, 15 degrees right rudder, aye, sir."

Dive master: "Making my depth 650 feet, heading 180, 15 degrees right rudder, aye!"

Captain: "Very well."

As we mentioned before, hospitals use similar ways to match demand to capacity and manage variation through redundancy of communication. Managing high-risk situations, such as aircraft launch and recovery or surfacing a submarine (which is essentially "blind" when it comes to the surface), and mandating procedures are additional lessons for carefully controlling variation in healthcare operations.

The use of evidence-based guidelines for high-risk clinical presentations is expanding rapidly and is an additional way to assure that flow and safety are maximized. In our group we developed a program known as "Creating the Risk-Free ED," which is a series of 25 evidence-based protocols for the most high-risk adult and pediatric presentations.

Since mandating that our physicians take this course in orientation and making it available at the bedside, we have seen a sustained 70 percent reduction in loss runs, loss reserves, and malpractice insurance premiums. (The idea came from our experience with carrier operations, as well as from David Letterman, since his "Top 10 List" was evocative of the top high-risk areas from closed-claim experience.)

Failure-mode analysis, including after-action reviews, uses techniques drawn from the military, including not only aviation but infantry branches, with clear application to healthcare in order to remove bottlenecks and constraints and thereby improve the system. Information-transfer techniques and decision-support analysis help manage demand and capacity, manage variation, and assure that the fundamental system nature of healthcare operations, as with aviation, is fully understood and implemented.

LEAN: LESSONS FROM TOYOTA AND OTHERS

Given our definition of flow as adding value and eliminating waste as patients move through the service transitions and queues of healthcare, it comes as no surprise whatsoever that the lessons from the "Lean" approach gleaned from other businesses form a critical part of how we view the ability to adapt Lean to hospitals. Many leaders of healthcare reform point to potential applicable lessons from the auto industry.

Most often, this emphasis focuses on principles developed by the Toyota Motor Company, known as Lean. Unlike other methods discussed in this chapter, Lean is not a tool or policy change, but rather a "cultural transformation that changes how an organization works" with "no finish line" (Toussaint and Berry, 2013).

As defined by Toussaint and Berry, Lean "is an operating system composed of six principles that constitute the essential dynamic of Lean management." According to these authors, the principals of Lean consist of:

- Lean is an attitude of continuous improvement
- Lean is value-creating
- Lean is unity of purpose
- Lean is respect for the people who do the work
- Lean is visual
- Lean is flexible regimentation

Together, these principals are used in the implementation of Lean in hospitals across the country, based on the success Toyota experienced in adopting this philosophy. Many, however, are quick to point out the difficulties in applying a philosophy that was developed from managing a car factory to hospitals.

In this regard, Jan Jennings, the president of American Healthcare Solutions, identified "four rate-limiting factors" to instituting Lean principles in healthcare systems. These consist of "lack of CEO commitment," "[being] starved for resources," "recognition [of] the differences between a Toyota facility and an American hospital," and "failure to recognize and reward success" (Jennings, 2011). Jennings maintains that recognizing and working around these potential mitigating factors can result in improved operations using the Lean philosophy.

IDEO AND DESIGN THINKING

In a 2004 article for *BusinessWeek*, entitled "The Power of Design," Bruce Nussbaum traces the experience and results of a partnership between Kaiser Permanente, a health maintenance organization, and IDEO, a design firm based in Palo Alto, California. Working with IDEO, Kaiser redesigned the patient experience, working on creating a more user-friendly and welcoming environment rather than investing in new infrastructure (Nussbaum, 2004).

As a result, IDEO discovered that many of Kaiser's patients were frustrated before even *seeing* a doctor and that the organization's waiting rooms created unsatisfied patients because "they often had to wait alone for up to 20 minutes half-naked, with nothing to do, surrounded by threatening needles."

In response, IDEO clarified to Kaiser that seeking treatment is "much like shopping—it is a social experience shared with others." Among the many changes resulting from IDEO's recommendations, Kaiser recognized that: it needed to offer more comfortable waiting rooms and a lobby with clear instructions on where to go; larger exam rooms, with space for three or more people and curtains for privacy, to make patients comfortable; and special corridors for medical staffers to meet and increase their efficiency.

In short, Kaiser redesigned much of its restructuring from the user perspective, focusing its redesign on creating a more welcoming and friendly atmosphere for its patients. Kaiser also worked with IDEO to enhance the quality of its medical professionals. One project in particular, which sought to "reengineer nursing-staff shift changes at four Kaiser hospitals," led to vastly improved exchange of information from one nursing shift to another.

A major problem in shift changes centered on the fact that "nurses routinely spent the first 45 minutes of each shift at the nurses' station debriefing the departing shift about the status of patients," but despite this serious time commitment, "nurses often failed to learn some of the things that mattered most to the patients, such as how they had fared during the previous shift" (Brown, 2008). Following prototypes of different shift changes, the hospitals developed a model with "new procedures and some simple software" that gave nurses access to notes from old shift changes and enabled them to add new ones.

The new model allowed nurses to view and alter this information during their shift, rather than at the end. Overall, the new changes cut the time in half between a "nurse's arrival and first interaction with a patient…adding a huge amount of nursing time across the four hospitals."

Ultimately, Kaiser isn't the only healthcare organization to turn to IDEO to improve its services. Indeed, healthcare is IDEO's greatest focus, making up 20 percent of the company's revenues. The firm has offices throughout the United States and abroad, and many organizations have turned to IDEO for its innovative and results-driven approach to improving consumer experience.

IDEO employs a five-step process to create an improved consumer experience (Nassbaum, 2004). These steps include: (1) *observation*, which focuses on "understanding the consumer experience," (2) *brainstorming*, "intense, idea-generating sessions analyzing data gathered by observing people" in which each session "lasts no more than an hour," and (3) *rapid prototyping*, during which mock-ups of working models are created, a phase that "helps everyone visualize possible solutions and speeds up decision-making and innovation."

It also includes: (4) *refining*, where "IDEO narrows down the choices to a few possibilities," and finally, (5) *implementation*, in which the company brings its "strong engineering, design, and social-science capabilities to bear when actually creating a product or service." Each step of the design process involves sub-steps to ensure a standard protocol and an efficient outcome. Overall, IDEO starts by recognizing the problem, identifying potential solutions, developing potential models, evaluating the potential solutions, and, most importantly, executing.

As demonstrated by its work with Kaiser, IDEO's approach to improving the consumer experience has been and can be applied to healthcare to create improved patient satisfaction and work experience of healthcare professionals. Rethinking the hospital from the patient's perspective and developing and experimenting with prototypes can lead to greater outcomes for healthcare providers, as well as improved satisfaction, not only for patients, but also for a hospital's employees. Utilizing IDEO's steps to design thus can prove highly beneficial for healthcare systems in the United States and abroad.

COACHING

Perhaps no other profession has better lessons for leadership to hardwire flow than coaching. As four-time NCAA-championship-winning coach Mike Krzyzewski (Coach K) of Duke Men's basketball said, "I don't look at myself as a basketball coach. I look at myself as a leader who happens to coach basketball" (Krzyzewski, 2014).

Hardwiring Flow™ requires visionary leadership, just as coaching does. We will look at lessons from three legendary coaches: Coach K, Sir Alex Ferguson of Manchester United, and Coach John Wooden of UCLA Men's basketball, winner of 10 national championships. Each of them has extremely important lessons to offer for leading teams in successful endeavors—just as you will have to do to transform your organization to hardwire flow.

Coach K

Here's a way to win a sure bet. Ask a serious college basketball fan this question: What is Coach K's offensive philosophy that has resulted in four national championships and more wins than any other coach in the history of men's college basketball? How about his defensive philosophy? His view on the zone press? These are all trick questions.

As Coach K has noted many times, he assembles the best team possible (more on that in a moment) and then adapts his system to maximize the team's chance of success: "I try to see each new season as a new challenge because I have a new team to work with, new challenges to encounter, and new ideas and theories to try." This requires a primary focus on maximizing the talents of the team first in service to the broader goal of the team's success (Bilas, 2014). And this point raises an important observation, which Coach K phrases this way: "A common mistake among those who lead teams is spending a disproportionate amount of time on 'X's' and 'O's' as compared to time spent learning about people."

These are clear examples of the equivalent of demand-capacity management and managing variation, in that the team must adapt to the changing nature of the situation as it unfolds, as opposed to simply following a prearranged plan, which cannot hope to meet the fluid and changing needs of the situation. Again, Coach K says: "It's not what *I say*, it's what *they do* on the court that matters."

An additional example of managing variation is the need, within any given game situation, to assure that the right team is on the court to meet the needs of the situation. Shutting down the opponent's best three-point shooter when you have a six-point lead with two minutes in the game requires putting your best defender on him. If you are six points down with two minutes to go, that requires different adjustments, both of which relate to managing variation and situational awareness. Let's look more closely at several qualities that make Coach K so effective:

Communication. It's hard to overstate the importance of effective communication to leadership. As Coach K says: "Effective teamwork begins and ends with communication…Communication doesn't always occur naturally, even among a tight-knit group of individuals. Communication must be taught and practiced in order to bring everyone together as one." In fact, communication is a fundamental aspect of both coaching and healthcare leadership. Communication cannot be assumed; it must be pursued in a disciplined, evidence-based fashion.

Trust. Playing a 30-plus-game season against some of the finest competition in the nation and then continuing in the NCAA tournament makes for a long, if satisfying, season. Similarly, attaining and sustaining success in healthcare is a marathon, not a 100-yard dash. Coach K details the implications of this point for leaders: "Every leader needs to remember that a healthy respect for authority takes time to develop. It's like building trust. You don't instantly have trust, it has to be earned."

In leadership, trust is critical. In any organization, trust must be developed among every member of the team if success is going to be achieved" (Krzyzewski, 2012). The nature of healthcare as a complex adaptive system with a high degree of variability speaks to the necessity of building trust among the team, given the challenges it faces to succeed.

Collective Responsibility. Simply assembling a group of talented individuals does not make a team. Those individuals must become a cohesive team with a clear sense of collective responsibility. Or as Coach K puts it: "When you first assemble a group, it's not a team right off the bat. It's only a collection of individuals. Most 'teams' are called by that long before they actually are. The cauldron of competition forges a sense of collective responsibility."

Leaders who hold their teams accountable are important,
but the collective responsibility of a self-motivated team
is even more so.

Hardwiring flow requires developing and nurturing this same sense of collective responsibility and accountability, including clear goals, accessible tools, transparent metrics, and celebrating team success when progress occurs. Leaders who hold their teams accountable are important, but the collective responsibility of a self-motivated team is even more so.

Care. It's an old adage, but a good one: "I don't care how much you know until I know how much you care." What we do in healthcare not only matters, it matters a lot. If we are going to succeed, we have to care not only for the patients and their families, but also for each other. As we continue to find innovative and creative ways to become "high-quality, low-cost" providers of care, the difficult jobs we do will become even more so.

In the context of winning basketball game, Coach K emphasizes the importance of this point: "At the most difficult times of the game, players have to know that their teammates have each other's back. We can make it through anything if we know we are there for each other…People have to be given the freedom to show the heart they possess. It's a leader's responsibility to provide that type of freedom. If a team is a real family, its members want to show their hearts."

Pride. Our work in healthcare makes a difference in the lives of our patients and their families. We truly "leave a legacy" one patient at a time, every day we go to work. "Just enoughers" can never make it in healthcare. It takes passion and pride to do every job that contributes to the success of your hospital or healthcare system.

As Coach K says: "We tell our players they need to play for the name on the *front* of the jersey (Duke), not the name on the *back* of the jersey (your name). You are a part not only of a team, but a great tradition." The same is true of our hospitals, which have a tradition, a reputation, and a brand to protect and maintain. Don't be afraid to motivate your team to the highest possible levels by tapping into their professional and personal pride.

Sir Alex Ferguson, Manchester United

Sir Alex Ferguson is one of the most successful "managers" in the history of the world's most popular sport. Over a period of 30 years, he sustained greatness, despite turnover among players and assistant coaches and owners, which is simply the nature of the sport. Ferguson recently identified these ideas as the foundation for his success (Ferguson, 2013, 2012):

Start with the Foundation

Dare to Rebuild your Team

Set High Standards and Hold Everyone to Them

Never, Ever, Cede Control

Match the Message to the Moment

Prepare to Win

Rely on the Power of Observation

Never Stop Adapting

Figure 4.2 Alex Ferguson's core principles

Like many other leaders and coaches, Ferguson starts with a clear foundation built on a culture of measurable success. He insists that his team members, at every position and every level, have a deep fluency in the system and how it works. Only when this fluency is attained can there be the level of consistency requisite for consistent high performance.

Once this is in place, a deep bond of unity develops, which drives to a culture of success. This is a key insight for flow leaders, who create such fluency on the way to a culture of high performance. As Sir Alex notes, "The job of a manager, like that of a teacher, is to inspire people to be better." This teaching aspect is one that all great coaches share and one that is an essential attribute of healthcare leaders seeking to hardwire flow. As in teaching, there will always be successes or wins, but there will also be setbacks or losses. Not every flow initiative will produce positive results. Again, Sir Alex explains: "Winning a game is only a short-term gain—you can lose the game. Building a club brings stability and consistency."

A culture of hardwiring flow requires building a team dedicated to the long haul and not just focusing on short-term wins. Over time, the flow team will have to rebuild, as members move on or take part in other initiatives. Setting high standards and holding team members accountable to them is essential for the rebuilding efforts. Leadership skills are essential for all team members, but maintaining a clear focus on the vision is an essential trait of the team leader.

As Sir Alex emphasizes, never, ever cede overall control of the team's leadership. Ferguson clearly understands the flow concepts of managing variation and demand-capacity management in his emphasis on "matching the message to the moment," where he notes: "You have to pick your moments. As a manager, you have to play different roles at different times. Sometimes you have to be a doctor, or a teacher, or a father."

The same is true with the always-changing nature of the problems we face as we seek to add value and eliminate waste in healthcare. A broad range of skills—and the wisdom to know which skills are needed at the moment—is an integral part of the skill set of a leader hardwiring flow. The way to prepare to win is by always putting the team in a position to win—a "win" in our case is effectively hardwiring flow.

An additional integral skill set is the power of observation, without which we are "flying blind" in managing variation, identifying and removing constraints, and monitoring flow in real time. Sir Alex considers observation at or near the top of the list of leadership skills: "I don't think many people fully understand the power of observing. I came to see observation as a critical part of my management skills. The ability to see things is key—or, more specifically, the ability to see things you didn't expect to see."

The ability to see things you don't expect to see is particularly important as we develop the requisite situational awareness to lead flow efforts. As we discussed in the naval aircraft operations section of this chapter, this capability extends across virtually all high-reliability efforts.

The power of observing the unexpected leads to the insight that adaptation is the only constant in attaining success. Ferguson notes, "I believe that you control change by accepting it. Most people with my kind of track record don't look to change. But I always felt we couldn't afford not to change." Embracing change requires the ability to look at the broader fabric of healthcare leadership in order to understand the context in which the change occurs. Flow teams must always maintain the power of observation, situational awareness, and the ability to control change by accepting it.

Coach John Wooden

Leadership lessons from John Wooden, coach of UCLA's 10-time NCAA men's basketball champions, not only could fill several books, they *have* filled several books—all of them best sellers (Wooden and Jameison 2005; 2007; 2009). Among the hundreds of lessons he offered over the years, three in particular stand out.

First is the importance of preparation. As Coach Wooden repeatedly said, "Failing to prepare is preparing to fail." The role of preparation in leading efforts to add value and eliminate waste is difficult to overstate. Flow team members almost always come to the table with a deep commitment to do the right thing, but the leader must prepare the effort by assuring that pertinent data, results from previous change efforts, and clear definitions of success are delineated prior to beginning the team's efforts.

The second is a testament to the importance of details. Virtually every player on the Wooden UCLA teams has described how the coach began every season by describing in great detail how to…put on their socks. Put on their socks? Some of the greatest recruits in the NCAA and the coach is teaching them how to put on their socks?

But all of them realized later that the coach was teaching them the importance of a disciplined approach to details, not just to their socks, but also to how they did everything, on and off the basketball court. The lesson for flow teams is to stick to the basics of the fundamental principles of hardwiring flow, including the tools of improving flow.

Finally, Coach Wooden, similarly to both Coach K and Sir Alex Ferguson, understood the importance of adapting his coaching style to the talent available to him. He had already won seven men's basketball NCAA national championships when the nation's highest-rated recruit, Bill Walton, came to UCLA. Moreover, he had just coached one of the greatest players in NCAA history, Lew Alcindor—later known as Kareem Abdul Jabar—with whom he had just won three national championships.

Kareem was one of the most disciplined, coachable players that Coach Wooden had ever had. Bill Walton was, to say the least and by his own admission, one of the most free-spirited student athletes anyone had ever seen, famously lying down on UCLA streets to obstruct traffic in a free-speech demonstration. With Coach Wooden's record, one could have understood if he told Walton that he needed to either change or leave the team.

Instead, Coach Wooden focused on the team, not his ego. He adapted *his* coaching style for the good of the team to meet the exigencies of the situation. Here's how he said it: "It wouldn't have worked with Bill and me if I hadn't found better leadership skills. It would have been a shame if I hadn't been a good enough leader to work effectively with Bill Walton."

A seven-time NCAA championship winning coach adapts his leadership skills to meet the needs of his team, instead of insisting that the team adapt to his coaching style or leadership skills. We submit that is one of the most non-intuitive examples of leadership you may ever see. But that is precisely what leaders who are passionate about hardwiring flow must do. Rather than insisting on "my way or the highway," Coach Wooden adapted his style to meet the team's needs. We will always have diverse and sometimes disparate talent on our teams…and we must adapt to both our patients' needs and to those of our team in order to most effectively improve flow.

CONCLUSION

There are many lessons from other industries that hospitals can profitably turn to in healthcare to improve flow. Studying how such fields as aviation and fast food restaurants handle challenges to flow can inform adaptations of these principles and processes in healthcare to improve not only flow but also patient safety, patient satisfaction, and staff satisfaction, not to mention the bottom line.

Adaptation, however, is a key concept to keep in mind here. Not everything that works in a fast food chain is suitable to implement in a hospital, and some principles or processes that could work well must be modified to fit the specific conditions and challenges in healthcare. Being able to recognize what will work well and how is an important prerequisite for improving flow.

As with any initiative, hospitals need to start small, with limited tests over a short period, and then begin evaluating what works and what doesn't. From there, refine the processes and test again, and repeat the process, continually evaluating and refining. When you set out to improve flow in this manner, using all the tools in the flow toolkit, you're likely to succeed. And your customers—your patients—are going to be the better for it.

HARDWIRING FLOW™ FOCUS: LESSONS FROM OTHER INDUSTRIES

- Lessons from other types of businesses and industries are critical to meaningfully improving the process of hardwiring flow.
- Learning from other industries requires finding their common ground with healthcare and adapting their solutions to our work.
- As Tom Peters said, "Don't *bench*mark. *Othe*r 'mark'."
- Hospital bed-turns and the Cheesesteak Factory's operations have important similarities with regard to anticipating and managing variation, monitoring flow, and eliminating bottlenecks and constraints.
- Checklists, call-backs and call-downs are used in the aviation industry, restaurants, and cafés like Starbucks. Each approach is applicable to specific sectors of healthcare, including surgery (mandatory checklists) and intensive care and ED settings (call-backs and call-downs).
- Mandatory checklists not only assure that your McDonalds' meal tastes the same all over the world, but they can also improve predictability and reliability in healthcare.
- Systems thinking, cognitive psychology, and patient safety all owe important debts to work from aviation, carrier operations, and submarine operations.
- Good checklists are succinct, focused, and easy to use and understand. Bad checklists are vague, imprecise, and open to multiple interpretations.
- As Captain Sully Sullenberger says, "Focus not on *who's right,* but *what's right.*"

- Innovation means changing before you are forced to change.
- If physicians don't train the entire team on requisite skills, the physician will become the bottleneck and the sole source of error.
- Lessons from the world's great athletic coaches can be very helpful, including: Coach K: "It's not what *I* say, it's what *they do* on the court that matters;" Sir Alex Ferguson: "I came to see observation as a critical part of my management skills. The ability to see things is key—or, more specifically, the ability to see things you didn't expect to see;" and Coach Wooden: "It would have been a shame if I hadn't been a good enough leader to work effectively with Bill Walton."

CHAPTER 5

EMERGENCY DEPARTMENT SOLUTIONS TO FLOW: FUNDAMENTAL PRINCIPLES

by Thom Mayer, MD, and Kirk Jensen, MD

"There is a tide in the affairs of men,
Which, taken at the flood, leads on to fortune:
Omitted, all the voyage of their life
Is bound in shallows and miseries.
On such a full sea are we now afloat,
And we must take the current when it serves
Or lose our ventures."

—*William Shakespeare,* Julius Caesar, Act IV, Scene III, 218-224

"Diseases, desperate grown
By desperate appliance are relieved,
Or not at all."

—*William Shakespeare,* Hamlet, Act IV, Scene III, 9-11

Because some of the earliest work in Hardwiring Flow™ came from the emergency department (ED), we have dedicated two chapters to this work. The first discusses the fundamental principles and the following chapter dives into more detail on highly sophisticated, but attainable ways to "frontload flow."

There are numerous reasons that, in many institutions, the journey toward flow started in the ED. First, the emergency department is inarguably the "front door of the hospital." Regardless of the size, location or acuity of the hospital or its ED, far more patients come to the ED than are admitted to the hospital. National figures indicate that only 15-35 percent of patients who present to the ED are admitted to the hospital, meaning that the remaining 65-85 percent of patients will be treated and discharged from the ED (Emergency Department Benchmarking Alliance, 2013).

Thus, the vast majority of ED patients are discharged, meaning that all they know about the hospital is what they see in the ED. For many patients, it is their first contact with the hospital and the staff. As we noted earlier, many of them walk in on their own and can choose to go elsewhere if they're not happy or if they wait too long. If they "vote with their feet" and go elsewhere for ED care, they are likely to go elsewhere for future healthcare needs as well.

Second, comparing ED volumes to other areas of the hospital offers ample evidence that EDs form a major impact on the communities they serve. For example, the average ED utilization per 1,000 population members appear so have risen from 368 to over 400 (Emergency Department Benchmarking Alliance, 2013). Thus, over one-third of any given population base will be seen in any given year in the local ED. Third, the current US family size is 3.6 per household, though, of course, there is variation depending upon the geographic area and urban-suburban-rural mix.

Clearly, an ED visit is, at an absolute minimum, a "family-affair," affecting the perceptions of an additional 3.6 people (on average). Given the community-based nature of our society, those who visit an ED will, to understandably variable degrees, be a "community event", in that the ED visit, whether positive or negative, will be shared with others who know those who have actually gone to the ED.

Third, the ED is by nature a "process-rich environment," in which there are nearly constant service transitions and queues built into the system, which creates multiple opportunities to improve flow by adding value and eliminating waste. These transitions occur across multiple areas that are traditionally "siloed,"—from nursing and registration to physicians and essential services personnel (e.g., laboratory, imaging, bed-board)—which also creates opportunities to improve those hand-offs.

Fourth, while the majority of ED patients are discharged, those who are admitted typically constitute over 50 percent of total hospital admissions, thereby serving as the life-blood for the hospital in terms of sustaining its revenue stream. However, the process of admitting patients to the hospital means that the inpatient side is the "back door" of the ED, often creating a constraining bottleneck, which we will discuss in more detail in the input-through-put-output" section of this chapter and in Chapter 6.

In most hospitals, the impact that obtaining and assigning inpatient beds has on ED operations has been vastly underappreciated, creating more opportunities for flow improvement. And finally, in addition to the revenues generated from admissions, the ED is a major source of the work that goes on in a hospital. In many hospitals, three-fourths of the plain radiographs are done on ED patients, as well as half the CT scans and ultrasounds (Mayer, 2014a; Emergency Department Benchmarking Alliance, 2013).

> In most hospitals, the impact that obtaining and
> assigning inpatient beds has on ED operations has
> been vastly underappreciated

It has also been our experience that, while change is difficult for everyone, emergency departments by their very nature tend to draw people who are more amenable to change and who understand, at least intuitively, the concepts that form the 7 strategies of hardwiring flow we have recommended: demand-capacity management, forecasting demand, real-time monitoring of flow, queuing theory, managing variation, theory of constraints, and flow as a complex adaptive system. This is probably because emergency department operations by their very nature are nearly textbook examples of the ways in which application of these principles can predictably result in dramatic improvements (Mayer and Jensen et al., 2014).

For all of these reasons, much of the early work on flow led to an ED leadership philosophy to develop and implement systems to "front-load flow" in the ED, particularly during times when patient demand predictably exceeds available capacity. These demand-capacity mismatches have become widespread and predictable, particularly in large volume emergency departments. The stressors and pressures on emergency department personnel, including caring for a high volume of high-acuity patients in an increasingly capacity-constrained environment with dramatic demand-capacity mismatches surely qualifies, in Shakespeare's phrase as "diseases, desperate grown."

But understanding the inexorable reality of those stressors and pressures can give rise to creative and innovative processes designed to benefit the patient, as well as those who care for those patients. In the face of adversity in a busy ED, these creative solutions constitute a way in which the "tide…which, taken at the flood, leads on to fortune."

THE BEGINNING, THE MIDDLE, AND THE END

Input, throughput, and output are concepts used in systems thinking. In an ED context, "input" refers to the patients coming into the department, whether through the front door at triage, by ambulance, or even by helicopter. "Throughput" consists of the patients in the department during their stay there, being diagnosed, treated or waiting at various stages. "Output" refers to patients who leave the department, those who are discharged home, and those admitted to the hospital (or transferred to another facility):

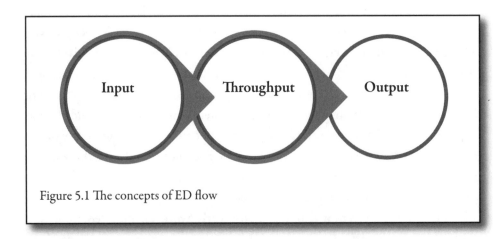

Figure 5.1 The concepts of ED flow

When asked where they should concentrate to reduce crowding, many healthcare professionals would likely respond by focusing on throughput. Obviously, that's important. In fact, from practical experience working in hundreds of EDs, enhancing flow occurs more effectively by concentrating on input and output first, and then focusing the lens on throughput (Asplin et al., 2003; Mayer and Jensen, 2009; Jensen, Mayer et al., 2014).

Enhancing flow occurs more effectively by concentrating on input and output first, and then focusing the lens on throughput.

INPUT: THE FRONT-END

Input is susceptible to flow improvements because the ED controls where and when patients go once they enter. Streamlining processes here tends to have a cascading effect. The chief principle to keep in mind is forward motion. As we showed previously but reproduce here, Figure 5.2 illustrates this principle as it applies to movement through an ED with a layout of the flow process from an actual ED entrance and a proposed reconfiguration of that process to smooth flow through the department.

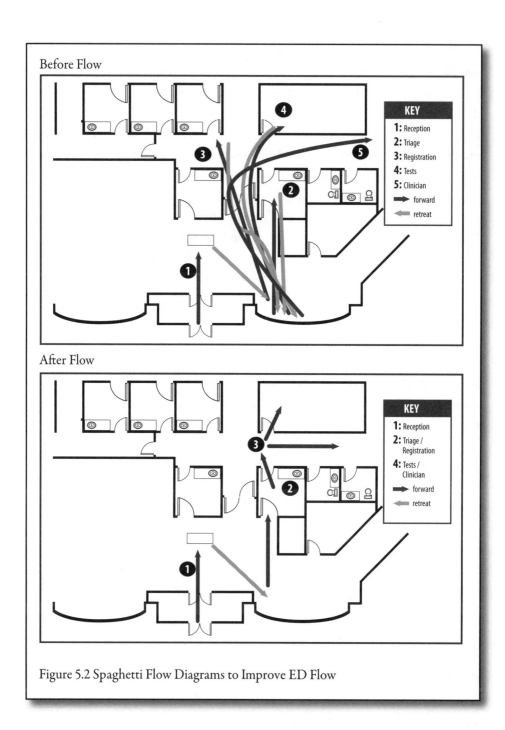

Figure 5.2 Spaghetti Flow Diagrams to Improve ED Flow

In other words, do not send a patient from reception to a waiting area, then to triage, then back to the waiting area, then to registration, then back to the waiting area, and so on. Handle triage and registration in the same place and same step, and do the same with meeting the physician, and conducting tests. Keep the patient moving forward throughout the process. Triage is a critical point in the process. Before that, however, is an opportunity to enhance front-end flow: realize who the patients are or are going to be.

Using demand-capacity management, forecasting, and variation. Emergency departments may think they do not know who is going to be entering them, but in fact they do—or they can. By measuring current demand on an ongoing basis, ED staff can gain an accurate picture of the state of their department, throughout the year, which will enable them to predict how many patients will come, what services they will need, and what resources they will require.

Thus, effective measurement means tracking the number of patients hour by hour to indicate what times of day, which days of the week, and which months in the year are going to be busier; types and frequency of complaints; types and amounts of ancillary services needed; and how many beds will be required throughout the day. The more data a department can gather, and the more it can analyze the data by category, the better it can predict ED volume in the future and how to handle it effectively.

A related concept, which EDs must consider as well in making these projections, is variation, which we discussed in detail in Chapters 2 and 3. Not every patient with a particular condition will have the same severity, and not all will respond the same way to treatment. On some days, more patients with complex conditions will show up than on others. This kind of variation is natural; it occurs in all systems. EDs need to manage it by tracking and forecasting, as discussed above.

Other variation is not "natural," it is "artificial"—the time of discharge, for example, when a physician has completed a patient's treatment and the patient is simply waiting to be released. The more an ED can reduce artificial variation by refining processes so that such variation becomes predictable—and therefore adds value—the smoother flow in the department will be. In addition, increasing variation in order to increase value can be a highly effective strategy to improve flow, if it is used to reflect matching variation in patient arrivals and acuity with processes to match capacity through such variation. We discuss this in more detail in the section on "the flow cascade."

Once an ED knows what to expect, it can plan accordingly to match staffing requirements to anticipated volume. Armed with detailed data gathered over a long period, an ED can forecast down to the hour what needs are likely to be, with a high degree of accuracy. Forecasting for this purpose gives an ED a great opportunity to improve flow with some simple changes.

Administrators may think they need more staff when that may not be true if they schedule more realistically, based on what their tracking and forecasting tells them. Figure 5.3 illustrates what can happen when the scheduling is not realistic. However, it is equally important not just to forecast ED arrivals and acuity, but also to use real-time dashboards to alert us when patient flow is different than forecasted. This is important because these data can help us to change processes to meet the demands of the "new reality" represented by the actual situation in the ED, as opposed to the forecast.

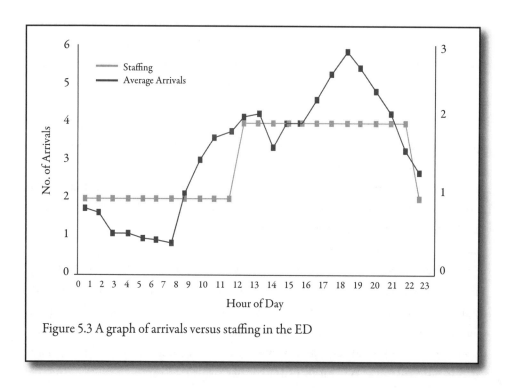

Figure 5.3 A graph of arrivals versus staffing in the ED

In the example above, the department's scheduled staffing does not match the pattern of patient arrivals. The ED can predict this pattern by careful, detailed tracking and forecasting as described above. If administrators in this case had done so, and paid attention to the results, the cause of the problem—inevitable crowding when staff could not handle volume—would have been obvious. Here is a good illustration of our point earlier that processes may not work as they should and may cause problems rather than solve them. Through its scheduling practices, this ED is creating a mismatch between staff and patients.

Improving flow does not necessarily require adding
staff or space. It starts with creating better processes
and using staff more effectively.

This example and its implications reinforce an important principle to keep in mind about improving flow: Improving flow does not necessarily require adding staff or space. It starts with creating better processes and using staff more effectively.

When an ED knows what to expect in patient volume, patient complaints, and resources required, it can move on to improving front-end flow. The next step is optimizing the effectiveness of triage. The specific ways in which triage can be improved are addressed below.

OUTPUT: THE BACK-END

Output includes both patients discharged home and those admitted to the hospital (or transferred to specialty centers or hospitals participating in managed care plans). Unlike in the front end, the ED does not control where and when patients go in the back-end (ED discharge to hospital admission), at least not to the same degree. The ED may have little say on when and where patients are admitted to the hospital. Still, this phase does present opportunities for enhancing flow in ways that, like front-end improvements, have a cascading effect…this time in a backwards fashion. Taking full advantage of those opportunities means involving other units in the hospital, so it needs to be part of an overall plan to improve flow in the hospital.

A useful concept in envisioning flow through an ED is "pulling" rather than "pushing"; in other words, think about what needs are going to be in the future rather than reacting to needs that are already there, and pressing. A bed coordinator should be focusing continually on where the next patient who will need a bed is going to go (even when that patient has not yet entered the ED). If coordinated effectively throughout the facility, this approach can reduce delays significantly in moving patients from the ED into other units. Just as with front-end flow management, this approach becomes effective when the ED uses patient flow tracking and predictive modeling to learn how many patients are going to need to go where and when they will need to go.

In the same way that the ED should use demand-capacity management, dashboards, and managing variation, the hospital should track types of admissions and number by day of the week, even by shift. Track which units' patients go where. From the results, project admissions for a day, for a week, and give the projection to the hospital staff members who place patients.

Keep track in real-time by making sure current information on patients is available to ED staff, ideally using an electronic monitoring system. Once a physician has decided to admit an ED patient to the hospital, contact the placement coordinator—quickly. The ED process in place should deal with moving patients into the appropriate inpatient unit within 30 minutes of admission communication. Figure 5.4 summarizes important points about admissions and flow in the ED.

- Current information on the status of patients in the ED should be on an electronic monitoring system
- When a physician decides to admit a patient, the patient flow coordinator should notify patient placement promptly
- The ED should have regular bed rounds and huddles
- From those rounds and huddles, the flow coordinator should predict admissions for the next 4 hours
- The coordinator should transmit those predictions to patient placement

Figure 5.4 Expected admissions and potential admissions

Another approach that requires coordination across units is to instill in other units' staff the mindset that they will communicate with the ED about whether any patients might need their services and will cooperate in moving them from the ED to the appropriate unit. This is commonly known as "decision to admit to bed time." Not only does this process help improve flow in the ED, it smooths flow in the receiving units as well. Achieving this level of cooperation across units may seem daunting, but it can be done.

One very effective principle to keep in mind is demonstrating to people how an activity is in their own interest. When staff in other units view moving patients as in their own best interest, they will be more motivated to do so. The best way to do that is to align strategic and financial interests so that the hospitalists and emergency physicians both understand their respective target metrics and mutually benefit when they are attained. Additionally, some facilities have implemented programs that financially reward hospitalists for earlier discharges, thus aligning the self-interest of the hospitalists with the overall interest of the hospital.

It is impossible to overstate the importance of aligning strategic incentives across service transitions, including across services. Integration of services, from emergency medicine to hospital medicine and intensive care is one of the key attributes of highly reliable and successful healthcare organizations. The key is assuring that an integrated approach is taken at every step in managing these patients.

This requires that emergency physicians, specialists in hospital medicine, consultants, and physicians in essential services all share a common goal of moving patients in a value-added fashion. As Figure 5.5 illustrates, it is important that emergency physicians not only know what the target metrics for hospitalists are, but are incentivized to help them meet these goals, and vice versa, of course. For example, the hospitalist should care about how backed up the ED waiting room is and how ED service scores are trending, just as the ED team should care about core measures and inpatient HCAHPS scores (Studer et al., 2010).

Do Your ... If Not, Why Not?

Hospitalists care about...
-ED boarders, LOS, patient satisfaction?

Emergency physicians care about ...
-Hospital bed turns, LOS, core measure compliance, finances, readmissions?

Radiologists care about ...
-Oral contrast in abdominal CTs, plain film TAT?

Figure 5.5 Efficient flow depends upon shared goals.

This requires leadership at the highest levels, including the CEO, COO, CMO, CNO, CFO and the chairs and section chiefs of the main medical staff departments, to not only instill a culture of integrated value, but also to support this by with goal metrics that cross all service lines.

If the ED tracks in detail and is able to project demand effectively, then other units will soon learn that their own flow improves if they can count on the estimated number of patients they can expect on a given day and schedule them. Once they learn this, cooperating with the ED is in their own interest.

Finally, a brief word on one major obstacle to flow in the department: boarding. Chapter 6 addresses this topic in detail, but we point out here that if an ED consistently experiences significant boarding of patients awaiting admission, then it faces serious problems in flow, and tactics for improving flow will be of limited value. If boarding just occasionally causes problems, then the techniques outlined in Chapter 6 can be highly effective.

Output also includes the large number of patients who are not admitted to the hospital, but are instead discharged home. EDs should have a formal process for discharging patients that encompasses a clear understanding of discharge instructions, follow-up with physicians, instructions to return if certain signs or symptoms develop, and elements of patient safety.

Many EDs have created a "discharge window" at the point of exit from the ED, where patients stop to verify instructions, re-check demographic and insurance information, and, in some cases, collect co-pays and monetary payment. Patients in which follow-up is critical (but resources are limited or unclear) deserve particular emphasis, including uninsured patients and those with behavioral health problems.

THROUGHPUT: THE BIG MIDDLE

Triage marks a boundary in the ED: When patients reach triage, they cross into the middle phase of their ED experience. Improving flow in the front end and the back-end, as noted earlier, presents the greatest opportunities, but flow in the middle is significant. Throughput in the ED thus refers to the myriad, interconnected processes and sub-processes that occur in "mainstream" ED operations (Mace and Mayer, 2008).

As we've noted previously, patient segmentation into clinical pathways and geographic treatment areas matching patient demand to our capacity to meet those demands is essential to hardwiring flow. Regardless of the size or acuity of the ED, there is, in fact, not a single ED for our patients, but rather "many EDs," depending upon individual patient demand. Even if a patient with a relatively minor illness or injury is being taken care of by the same nurse and physician as a patient with an acute illness or injury, they will use different processes and pathways to care for each of those patients.

This is accentuated even more when patients are seen in different areas or pods of the ED by different team members. Thus, each patient will experience a "different ED," depending on his or her needs. Throughput is thus a complex system unto itself within broader emergency department operations, so we will devote a large part of this chapter to throughput and how it can be improved.

CRITICAL ED PATIENT FLOW CONCEPTS

We were fortunate to have done a great deal of our original work on hardwiring flow in emergency departments. We have a combined experience of over 50 years in this endeavor. These concepts have been developed and implemented in literally hundreds of hospital EDs, either because our physician group manages them or because we have consulted or advised them.

This has led to 13 critical patient flow concepts that drive our improvement efforts to add value and decrease waste. Figure 5.6 summarizes these concepts:

- Front-Load Flow-The front door and your front end processes drive flow
- Triage is a process, not a place
- Get the patient and the doctor together as quickly and efficiently as possible
- Get the (right) patient to the (right) doctor/team as quickly and efficiently as possible
- The more horizontal you are, the more you are a patient; the more vertical, the more you are a customer
- Keep your vertical patients vertical and in motion
- For horizontal patients, real estate matters; for vertical patients, speed matters
- Patients who do not require many resources should not wait behind patients who do, no matter how high the volume of patients in the ED
- Fast Track is a verb, not a noun
- The "MVP of the ED" is...the Bed!
- Be fast at fast things and slow at slow things
- The #1 sign of the health of the ED is the relationship between the doctors and nurses
- Making people unhappy, making them wait without explanation, and then sending them a bill is a bad business model!

Figure 5.6 13 Critical ED patient flow concepts

We will address specifically how these critical concepts can be implemented in some detail below, but let us first turn to an understanding of how to think about ED operations from a "not from a philosophical viewpoint, but a practical lens" (Mayer, 2014b). One of the most important of the flow concepts noted here is "The Flow Cascade." (See Figure 5.7.)

The Flow Cascade recognizes that the bottlenecks of patient flow move and change during the course of a single day, depending upon time of day, patient arrivals, patient acuity, and a multitude of other factors. Thus, the processes employed to meet these needs must adjust and adapt to meet the changing needs of the patients and providers over the course of time. A solution that works very effectively at one time of the day with a certain group of patients may be completely ineffectual, or even harmful, if it is applied at the wrong time with the wrong patients. This is why we have stressed repeatedly that variation that adds value enhances flow. This is precisely what the solutions of the flow cascade are intended to address.

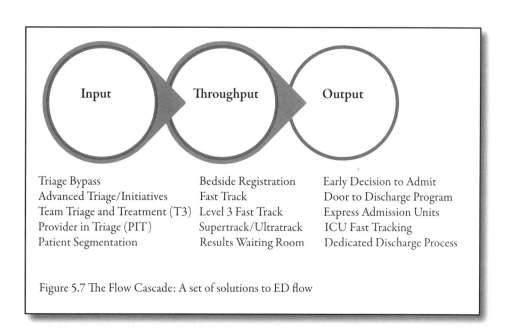

Input	Throughput	Output
Triage Bypass	Bedside Registration	Early Decision to Admit
Advanced Triage/Initiatives	Fast Track	Door to Discharge Program
Team Triage and Treatment (T3)	Level 3 Fast Track	Express Admission Units
Provider in Triage (PIT)	Supertrack/Ultratrack	ICU Fast Tracking
Patient Segmentation	Results Waiting Room	Dedicated Discharge Process

Figure 5.7 The Flow Cascade: A set of solutions to ED flow

Triage Solutions. Remember: Front-load flow. The front door and front-end processes drive flow. As we mentioned, the majority of patients arrive at the ED through triage, with national averages ranging from 72-90 percent, depending on the acuity of patients. As all of our parents taught us, "You never get a second chance to make a first impression." The first impression for the majority of ED patients will therefore be how they are greeted, processed, and moved through the system at triage.

"Triage" is universally used, but is actually poorly understood, in our experience. We think we know what it means, but far fewer would be able to supply a concise definition of what it is. The key to optimizing triage is understanding this concept:

"Triage is a process, not a place."

In most EDs, triage is considered a static function occurring at a fixed location. Even our language is evidence of this when we say a patient or a staff member is "at triage," meaning the physical area "out front" where we perform the function. But triage is—or should be—an active process seeking to match demand with capacity. It is not a place, an assigned location where this process occurs. Most EDs use triage to solve this equation: Triage = Who can wait and who can't.

Think about it: Doesn't your ED largely have a clear, if unwritten, decision tree where triage is fundamentally "sorting" people into lines of who can wait the longest to who can't wait at all? The derivation of "triage" comes from the ancient French "trier," which meant "to sort bad fruit from good fruit" (Mayer, 2009). This mind-set is a prescription for delay. Indeed, it is an absolutely logical consequence that a "who can wait" definition of triage will create delays. That's what it's for! Instead, triage should solve this equation: Triage = expediting flow by segmenting patients into demand-capacity pathways.

If triage means, "who can wait," then that is largely, but not exclusively, an activity done on behalf of the ED staff to figure out who can wait the longest. That is fundamentally different from acting on behalf of the patient by segmenting them into the right value stream. As we have previously emphasized, "always do the right thing for the patient." If we are going to do that, we need to rethink our definitions, our processes, and even our culture at triage.

The new culture is front-loading flow by defining triage as a process where patients are expedited to the right pathway, not a place where delays are created and fomented. A new way of thinking about triage is: "Triage is value acceleration!" It is the place where patients should be accelerated into the pathway most likely to result in the best outcomes in the most efficient way possible. That is a culture change worth making! If that patient were you, or a member of your family, isn't that how you would want the staff caring for you to view triage?

Triage Bypass/Direct Bedding. If patients arrive via triage at hours of the day when beds are available in the ED, why even triage them at all? Does it add value to do so? The answer, of course, is no. All you need is "name, basic demographics, and chief complaint" and they can be sent to the ED bed, which is the first solution to hardwire flow—**triage bypass.** (Triage bypass is also known by other names, including "direct-to-room," "direct bedding," and "pull until you are full.")

Triage bypass was first initiated in the late 1980s at several institutions, including Inova Fairfax Hospital in Virginia, Nash General in North Carolina, and Christiana Medical Center in Delaware. Each of these large volume, high-acuity EDs recognized that there were predictable hours in the morning, typically from about 7am and lasting for a few hours, when there were actually ED beds in which patients could be placed without triaging them. Triage, in effect, was a wasted step, since delaying patients at the triage area was of no added value and simply delayed them getting to the nurses and doctors who were waiting to care for them.

Dr. Robert Cates, the chairman of the Department of Emergency Medicine at Inova Fairfax Hospital, describes the genesis of the concept: "I was scheduled to give a lecture at a large medical center back in the days when you had to go to the airline ticket counter to get your ticket and boarding pass. I was running late when I got to the airport and was distressed to see the 'cattle gates' up, in which the ropes force you to go through the 'maze' before getting to the ticket agent. Fortunately, no one was in line, so I cut around the ropes and went straight to the agent at the counter.

She looked at me and said, 'Sir, we have a policy here at this airline that states that I cannot take care of you unless you have gone through the line.' I looked back and there was no line, but having been happily married for a number of years, I take direction from women well. I quickly hustled back around the ropes, entered the maze, and making some left turns and right turns I was quickly back at the same agent, who then smiled and said, 'Next!' It suddenly hit me, 'That's what we do every morning at triage! We make people go through a maze when there is no need to'" (Mayer and Cates, 2014).

Triage bypass effectively recognizes that in addition to not adding value, waste is created when patients are put through a "maze," going from triage to the waiting room to registration back to the waiting room, only to then be called by the primary care nurse to be taken back to precisely the same open room that they could have been placed in directly from triage. It requires the ability to do bedside registration, but was found at Inova, Nash, and Christiana to improve patient turnaround and patient satisfaction while showing no erosion of patient safety.

Triage bypass has been shown to:
- decrease waiting times,
- reduce length of stay,
- decrease left prior to medical screening exam or without treatment (LPMSE or LWOTs), and
- increase patient satisfaction.

In fact, triage bypass is a seemingly simple and eminently logical way to ensure that the system is able to front load flow by getting the patient and the patient care team together quickly, which is precisely what the patient wants. However, there are always "pockets of resistance" to any meaningful change, no matter how logical and well-intended the change may be. The primary resistance to change in triage bypass is typically not the triage nurse, registration, or the treating emergency physician, but rather the primary care nurse, who perceives a loss of control of the rooms to which he/she is assigned, which are now being filled directly from triage by the triage nurse. The traditional system empowers the primary care nurse or the charge nurse to determine when and "when not" to bring patients back to fill the rooms, inherently creating patient delays. It is a classic remnant of the "triage = who can wait" mentality.

Get the patient and the doctor together as
quickly and efficiently as possible.

Triage bypass is a sea change of control for the primary care or zone nurse and many institutions have found it hard to sustain this change. Nonetheless, it is a highly effective strategy to front-load flow by adding value (getting the patient in a room and seen by the ED team faster) and decreasing waste (avoiding triage and registration), at least during the hours when there are beds readily available. It derives from a simple concept, which nonetheless requires substantial leadership to effectively implement: Get the patient and the doctor together as quickly and efficiently as possible.

Bedside Registration. A related strategy to triage bypass is bedside registration. While bedside registration is often thought of as having been used since the late 1980s, in fact, EDs have always used it for a subset of critically ill or injured patients, usually arriving by ambulance. Bedside or in-room registration for patients arriving at triage who have been direct-bedded typically involves an initial rapid registration (often called quick registration or "Quick-Reg"), comprising patient name, date of birth, social security number, presenting complaint, and vital signs.

The patient is then placed into a patient care room, where, when the patient is not being attended to by medical and nursing staff, registration personnel can complete the more detailed process of full registration. In-room registration is typically accomplished using a "computer on wheels" if terminals are not available in each room. This immediate bedding process allows the staff to immediately begin patient treatment, including ordering lab tests, imaging studies, and medications either while the ED physician and nurse meet with the patient or shortly afterward.

Fundamentally, this concept allows parallel processing of the patient with multiple activities occurring simultaneously, as opposed to the more traditional sequential processing. The majority of large volume, high acuity EDs use bedside registration for their patients. When first introduced, it was common for ED staff to resist this "new" change until it was pointed out that just such a process has always been used in EDs to register trauma codes, chest pain patients, and the majority of acute patients arriving by EMS.

The vast majority of EDs currently use some form of bedside registration. Triage bypass and bedside registration are an important part of the ED solution to hardwiring flow, but are largely limited to times in which there are beds available for the patient. Once all beds are full, different processes are needed to improve flow. The most important of these are advanced triage/advanced initiatives (AT/AIs) and patient segmentation into flow streams.

Advanced triage/advanced initiatives. Triage bypass uses ED beds at those times when they are immediately and readily available and relies on the use of bedside registration. But once all ED beds are filled, how can flow be front-loaded when there are no appropriate treatment beds? Advanced triage/advanced initiatives (AT/AI) were developed specifically to address those patients, in which the likely diagnostic and/or treatment regimens were known, but in which there were no spaces in the treatment area to begin the evaluation or care (Kokiko and Mayer, 1997).

While AT/AIs are also known by many names, they share a fundamental strategy. Using standardized evaluation and treatment protocols (usually supported by standing physician order sets), AT/AIs allow the nurses at triage to initiate diagnostic, therapeutic or management regimens for specified patients based on presenting complaints and vital signs. Now widely used, AT/AI shortens patient turn-around time and, when combined with appropriate scripts, can be an important contributor to patient satisfaction.

At one point, The Joint Commission briefly criticized this strategy on the basis that each and every physician order required prior physician contact with the patient and approval of the order. However, once the self-apparent folly of this approach was pointed out (e.g., if a physician is busy with a trauma code and another patient has a cardiac arrest, should the nurse withhold CPR until the physician can evaluate the patient?), EDs quickly turned back to AT/AI as a highly effective strategy. Data from multiple reports are clear that AT/AI:

- decreases LOS,
- decreases time to pain relief,
- increases patient comfort,
- decreases time to antibiotic therapy in community-acquired pneumonia, and
- decreases time to open artery in chest-pain patients presenting to triage.

These then are the concepts fundamental to driving efficient flow in the emergency department. Think in terms of opportunities in input, throughput, and output as you begin to more deeply consider the flow cascade in your own ED and work to apply the solutions identified here.

HARDWIRING FLOW™ FOCUS: EMERGENCY DEPARTMENT FUNDAMENTAL

- Because the emergency department is the "front door of the hospital," some of the earliest work in hardwiring flow arose from here.

- By nature, the ED is a "process-rich environment," involving multiple service queues and transitions. This makes it a perfect place to add value and reduce waste.

- While admissions constitute only 15 to 35 percent of total ED patients, the hand-off from the ED to the hospital is a critical one.

- In general, even those close to ED operations probably don't fully comprehend the actual processes in action, largely because of their complexity and variability. So the first step to improving flow is taking a deep dive to understand it.

- ED flow can be viewed as three fundamental processes: input, throughput, and output.

- Input is susceptible to flow improvements; the front door and front-end processes drive flow.

- Improving flow does not necessarily require adding staff or space; it starts with creating better, simpler processes, and using staff more effectively.

- Reliability and predictability require real-time monitoring of flow data, since the number, type, and acuity of ED patients changes over the course of the day and by day of the week.

- Aligning strategic incentives across service lines is a critical concept.

- Output for discharged patients is discrete from admitted patients but equally important.

- Critical ED patient flow concepts include: (1) Triage is a process, not a place; (2) "Triage" should mean to expedite flow by segmenting patients into value-added demand-capacity streams, not deciding who can wait and who can't; (3) Get the patient and the doctor together as quickly as possible; (4) "Fast Track" is a verb, not a noun.

CHAPTER 6

ADVANCED EMERGENCY DEPARTMENT SOLUTIONS TO FLOW

by Thom Mayer, MD, and Kirk Jensen, MD

---

*"Before we can consider the ultimate things,
we must first consider the penultimate."*

—*H Richard Niebuhr,* The Responsible Self

Having considered the basics of Hardwiring Flow™ in the emergency department, we now turn to more advanced concepts, which can be put in place once the basic culture of adding value and eliminating waste has been addressed and progress has been made toward adopting and leveraging change.

SEGMENT PATIENTS INTO APPROPRIATE FLOW STREAMS

Patient segmentation certainly begins at the triage area as we seek to expedite flow, but it is on ongoing process as well. As we learn more about the patient through clinical observation, the course of their care, and the lab and imaging studies we perform, we continue to evaluate how best to segment their needs into the value stream. For now, let's focus on patient segmentation at the front-end of their care. Important concepts which drive this work are:

"Get the (right) patient to the (right) doctor/team as quickly and efficiently as possible" and:

"The more horizontal you are, the more you are a patient. The more vertical you are, the more you are a customer."

Once all the treatment areas are full, we need to ensure the patients get to the "right" bed and team of people who will be caring for them. Certainly patient acuity is the key driver of this equation, particularly for EDs who operate "Fast Tracks" (areas of the ED with dedicated space and staff to care for these more minor problems).

We will discuss Fast Tracks in more detail below, but it is important to understand that sending a more severely ill or injured patient to Fast Track is an example of a demand-capacity mismatch, since the demands for that patient almost certainly exceed the capacity to care for that individual in the Fast Track area. Another useful perspective in regard to patient flow is to see patients as "vertical" or "horizontal." The essential distinction between them is that vertical patients either do not need a bed (or need one for a highly circumscribed time and purpose) while horizontal ones do.

Vertical

- Ambulatory
- Arrival at Triage
- Well
- Younger
- Perceived Urgency
- Convenience Factor
- Value (Starbucks, Fast Food)
   Speed
   Convenience
   Non-medical factors

Horizontal

- Stretcher
- Ambulance Arrival
- Sick
- Older
- Perceived life-threatening
- Acuity and Anxiety Factors
- Value
   Speed
   Safety
   Technical Ability

Figure 6.1 Keep vertical patients vertical...and moving!

Vertical patients walk into the ED. Often, there is no reason a vertical patient needs a bed for other than a brief period of time for evaluation and treatment. Horizontal patients usually arrive by ambulance and need more critical care. The typical perspective in the past has been that attention should be focused on the horizontal patient, and as a result, vertical patients have often waited awhile to be seen…and then waited some more.

There's no denying the need for immediate attention and urgent care for horizontal patients. But if an ED is to exploit triage as a way to expedite patients' care rather than delay it, it needs to change this perspective. Two ideas can help accomplish this. First: "Keep your vertical patients vertical and moving." Not all patients need beds. Those who do need beds need them only so long as the bed adds value. The second principle that an ED working to enhance flow needs to embrace is: **"Patients who do not require many resources should not wait behind patients who do, no matter how high the volume of patients is in the ED."**

"Keep your vertical patients vertical and moving."

Horizontal patients require attention and resources, and they should receive them. But in giving them those resources, departments should not simply park patients with less urgent needs. This principle may seem to lead inexorably to a dilemma: If you're going to devote attention and resources to critically ill patients, how do you attend at the same time to patients who aren't very ill at all? There is a solution: segment patients at triage into streams, and have processes and staff in place to handle the different streams.

Each stream is a form of demand-capacity management, in that the streams should match patient needs with the timely ability to meet or exceed those needs. The underlying principle is the one we gave earlier for enhancing front-end flow: to get patients and doctors (or physician assistants or nurse-practitioners) together as quickly as possible. Vertical patients, after all, may need only simple care quickly administered, and the sooner they receive it, the sooner they can be discharged, making their experience in the ED more pleasant and increasing the flow of patients through the department.

Segmentation systems are tools that can help you implement this principle. There are various systems, notably the Emergency Severity Index (ESI) and the Canadian Triage and Acuity System (CTAS). These systems help triage personnel divide patients into different streams; both ESI and CTAS use five levels to classify patients, based on how severe the patient's condition is and the amount of resources that patient will likely need. These levels range from patients who need immediate care to save their lives (level 1) to those who likely will require very few resources (level 5).

The initial assessment in triage should not take much time and should classify the patient into one of the streams. The ED should have different pathways established for patients falling into the different categories. A nurse in triage directs the patient into one of those pathways, as Figure 6.2 demonstrates. Patients enter them directly from triage, and do not return to a waiting area.

Those patients who do not need beds should not be placed in beds. The goal is to keep vertical patients vertical and moving through the system. Again, forward movement is the idea. Horizontal patients will go into beds, in the traditional ED pathway. Obviously, they need to be seen quickly. But so do vertical patients. Because the pathway for many of them will be a fast track, the ED should have dedicated staff here.

FAST TRACK SERVICES

As with triage, it helps to think of fast track as a process rather than a place. Having such a process in the ED enables a department to quickly treat patients with minor needs, and move them on. A useful phrase to emphasize this notion of fast track as process is: **"Fast Track is a verb, not a noun."** Fast track is a place in one regard: it should be near the triage area, so patients with few needs can get there quickly for treatment. (A side note: This small detail of physical layout is the sort of obstacle to flow that you may observe by considering current processes and analyzing their effectiveness. Do you see patients required to walk a good distance from triage to fast track?)

The segmentation concept raises an important question: Who gets a bed? If an ED routinely puts a large percentage of its patients in beds before treatment, then beds can easily become a constraint (as we discuss below), leading to backups. In the assessment for segmenting, staff should carefully consider whether a particular patient needs a bed at all, or if so, for how long? A patient who needs to be in a bed for ten minutes of treatment, who can then get vertical again, will keep moving forward, and will improve overall flow.

A particular opportunity to enhance flow appears when patients wait for the results of tests. If the ED has a designated area where patients who have no need to be horizontal can wait comfortably for the results, then it frees beds for those patients who truly need them. As with the fast track, location matters. This waiting area should be near triage and fast track. If vertical patients can move relatively swiftly from reception to triage to fast track to waiting area, they are likely to both increase flow and be more satisfied.

Combining the concept of segmented streams with that of fast tracking enables an ED to resolve the dilemma mentioned earlier. Patients directed into the Level 4 and 5 streams can generally be fast tracked. So can a significant percentage of those in the Level 3 stream (which represent up to a third of patients in many EDs operating this kind of segmentation system today).

Since a sizable majority of emergency patients are typically Level 3 patients, fast tracking that many patients in this stream contributes substantially to improving flow. For all five streams, EDs operating with effective flow can treat as many as 40 percent of patients through fast tracking, often including use of a "super track," and team triage. A super track is designed to handle patients in the Level 4 and 5 streams, in a designated area with two or three beds, and sometimes two treatment rooms, staffed by a physician or mid-level provider (MLP), and a technician.

Because the fast track can contribute so powerfully to flow, ensure that you use tracking and forecasting of patient volume, particularly in relation to the fast track and super track. Aligning staffing and ensuring supplies are on hand to match expected patient volume for the fast track is as necessary as having a fast track in the first place. Having a central triage where patients are quickly assessed, then directed into multiple streams, takes advantage of queuing theory, which has found that a single sequential line processes people faster than multiple lines to multiple stations (just like cash registers in a store, for instance).

The reason is not hard to grasp: When there is one line, if one register takes longer than normal with a customer, other registers continue to process the next person in line; whereas if each register has a line, the chances of someone delaying multiple lines is greater. Figure 6.2 illustrates the concepts discussed here for expediting flow, particularly for less ill patients.

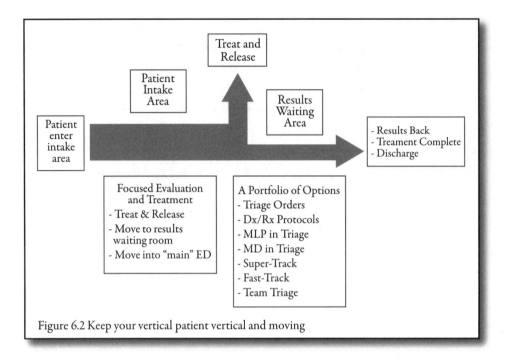

Figure 6.2 Keep your vertical patient vertical and moving

One other concept an ED staff needs to understand is constraints. If, for example, the services of a lab technician on a particular shift in the ED are called on to a higher degree than is usual, that person becomes a constraint; A constraint, in essence, is any resource that becomes scarce. It doesn't have to be a person; it could be a bed. When constraints develop, they often lead to bottlenecks, which start to back up the system in queues. As we have discussed earlier, a bottleneck results when demand for a resource passes its capacity.

Systems like EDs are networks, and have two kinds of bottlenecks: critical bottlenecks and non-critical ones. Knowing the difference is essential for improving flow. Responding to conditions that create a critical bottleneck in ways that will alleviate the bottleneck leads to better flow through the system as a whole. But reacting similarly to a non-critical bottleneck—though it may clear that bottleneck—will not help flow in the system as a whole.

Another aspect of bottlenecks is that they depend on conditions at the time. What is a bottleneck one day or on one shift may not be on another, but a different bottleneck may easily develop. Clearly, this aspect often makes them difficult to detect and respond to. The way to handle constraints and bottlenecks is to, once again, track processes and events in detail over time, and study the results carefully to identify which factors create bottlenecks at particular times.

An ED staff needs to examine the department's processes, too, and analyze them for potential constraints. Once an ED identifies possible bottlenecks, it should develop a potential solution and then test it on a small scale to see what kind of difference it makes. If it does in fact address a critical bottleneck, it will increase flow in the system. If it does not do so, then it is probably not responding to a critical bottleneck.

For some extremely high volume emergency departments, there are highly predictable times when their resources are so taxed and outrun that they can reliably and predictably use forecasting to project that there will be hours at a time when all beds are not only full, but likely to remain full for extended periods of time. This is often, but not always due to hospital boarders occupying ED beds, a subject dealt with in depth in Chapter 6. Solutions for emergency departments in these circumstances include team triage and treatment as well as several alternatives.

TEAM TRIAGE AND TREATMENT

In the first several years of the 21st Century, United States safety net hospitals were nearly constantly faced with the problems of ED crowding. National averages for ED crowding in 2001 were at 21 percent, whereas safety net hospitals were overcrowded up to 80 percent of the time. To address this situation, the Robert Woods Johnson Foundation created the Urgent Matters grant program, which sought innovative and creative solutions to the problem of ED crowding in large volume, high acuity EDs serving as safety net hospitals to their communities (Mayer, 2004).

One of the 10 national $250,000 grants was awarded to Inova Fairfax Hospital, which at the time was a 72,000 visit ED and a level I trauma center with a dedicated pediatric emergency department. The ED faced crowding 79 percent of the time on a consistent basis. The grant was for the nation's first development and implementation of a concept called "Team Triage and Treatment" or "T3."

Using statistical process control methods, the peak hours of ED crowding and boarding were determined to be a predictable 10-hour period from 10 am to 8 pm. Team triage and treatment deployed these resources in a front-loaded fashion at the triage area for this 10-hour period: emergency physician, emergency nurse, ED technician, scribe, and registrar.

This team used two to five designated treatment beds (depending upon patient flow) in or immediately adjacent to the triage area to begin, and in many cases to complete, the ED evaluation at the initial point of contact for the patient. Several points deserve emphasis regarding team triage:

Components of Team Triage and Treatment. First, it is essential that this program utilize a "team" approach, not simply placing an emergency physician or mid-level provider at triage. The physician, nurse and other members of the team must work closely together in a designated space and according to clearly delineated protocols. Without an additional emergency nurse dedicated to team triage, blood drawing, IV lines and medication administration would fall either to the triage nurse or to already over-stressed and overworked ED nurses, who would have had to leave their duties in those areas and care for these patients. In this initial formulation, the triage nurses continued to perform their duties and assisted the T3 nurse when patients were waiting to be triaged.

Second, after a "Quick-Reg" occurs at traditional triage, lab and imaging can occur so that patients never wait to have full registration completed. Third, the ED technician is also a critical part of the team, since T3 functions occur within a discrete area with dedicated staff. The technician can perform designated procedures, freeing up the physician and nurse to perform their responsibilities.

Fourth, scribes are essential to the team, as this allows the emergency physician to maintain flow in the T3 area. A key attribute of team triage is ensuring that the emergency physician is available to provide bedside patient care, and, to the maximum extent possible, freed from charting and electronic medical record (EMR) responsibilities.

Successful implementation of team triage and treatment. The results of team triage and treatment have been dramatic at Inova Fairfax Medical Center (Mayer, 2004; 2009; Mayer et al., 2014). While patient velocity (patients seen per hour of physician coverage) in the ED generally was 1.9 during the study period, the T3 physicians averaged 3.7 patients per hour. Patient satisfaction improvements were also substantial, increasing from the 60th percentile to the 97th percentile, with a 100 percent patient loyalty rating (likelihood to return or recommend).

While the 212 minute reduction in length of stay (LOS) for T3 patients is perhaps not surprising (330 minutes to 118 minutes), even more notable was the 46 minute mean decline in LOS for patients not seen at T3 (a 15 percent reduction, from 330 minutes to 284 minutes). This supports the long-held but never previously documented concept that, if ED crowding can be avoided, it has an impact on flow in the entire ED.

Of specific interest is that 34 percent of patients had their entire ED evaluation and treatment completed while in the triage area. An additional 18 percent of patients had their ED work-up completed and were admitted directly to an inpatient bed from team triage. Patient safety incidents also declined by 80 percent, demonstrating the important improvement in risk reduction from front-loading flow.

Because of ED staffing shortages, more recent iterations of team triage have used an emergency physician and scribe dedicated to team triage, with ED nurses and technicians "pulled" into the area as needed to support the diagnostic and therapeutic orders from the emergency physician. This version of team triage has also been successful and is currently in use at Inova Fairfax Hospital. It has resulted in length of stay reductions of 17.5 percent, decreased door to doctor times, reduction in boarder hours, an increase in patient satisfaction, and creation of additional patient care capacity (Mayer et al., 2014). It was also noted that team triage and a physician incentive compensation plan improved outcomes.

Obstacles to Team Triage. While improvements are usually dramatic, there are predictable obstacles to overcome when implementing and sustaining such a program. The first of these is expense; the costs of deploying a five-member team account for a substantial investment on the part of the physician group and the hospital. In particular, the cost of having a dedicated emergency physician in team triage for six to 12 hours per day (depending upon demand-capacity curves and their prediction of times when ED beds will not be available for sustained times) may be prohibitive for some physician groups.

Alternatives include using mid-level providers in team triage or variants of providers at triage. Nonetheless, the return on investment (ROI) for team triage exceeded 200 percent in a high acuity level I trauma center, taking into account the reduction in LWOT patients (i.e., seeing more patients), increased admissions, decreased risk, and increased functional capacity. The reduction in LWOTs is an important part of this equation, as is the increase in hospital admissions. Generally speaking, if ED crowding results in persistent delays of three or more patients per hour for more than five to six hours, team triage is a highly effective strategy to decompress the ED and improve its standing in the community.

High visibility. This program is highly visible, since the waiting room and the triage/team triage areas are typically in direct line-of-sight. While triage nurses are accustomed to this, emergency physicians may have to adjust to this "on-stage" concept, as Disney refers to it.

Resistance among physicians. While a third of patients may have their evaluation and treatment completed at team triage, the remaining patients are eventually moved to ED rooms in the main ED. There is typically some resistance from the emergency physicians "in the back" to the transfer of care of patients who are partially through their care. (Nurses are typically less resistant, probably because of the fact that it is more common for them to transfer care.)

However, this resistance can be overcome by simply pointing out that transfer of care from one emergency physician to another routinely occurs at change of shift. In addition, team triage greatly reduces risk, as the data clearly shows. While there are many refinements and alternative options to team triage, it remains an attractive option for large volume, space and capacity-constrained EDs. They routinely face situations where demand exceeds capacity for several hours of the day. It should be noted that members of the T3 teams have also reported increased job satisfaction.

VARIATIONS OF TEAM TRIAGE

Since the initial report of the team triage and treatment concept in 2003, the concept has not only become much more widespread, but has also been parent to many effective variations. These include: ESI level 3 fast tracks, "ultra tracking" ESI level 4s and 5s, and using providers at triage.

Team triage, both at its inception and in subsequent iterations, is not weighted towards care of ESI 1 to 2 patients (i.e., those with more severe acuity, who are typically recognized quickly and sent to the acute care area of the ED) or level 5 (minor) patients. For example, team triage at Inova Fairfax Medical Center is comprised of nearly 90 percent ESI level 3 and 4 patients. Alternate ways of dealing with these patients are presented below.

Anne Arundel Team Triage. Anne Arundel Medical Center in Annapolis, MD is a busy community ED, with an annual volume exceeding 50,000 patients. Because of recognized capacity constraints at peak-level flow times of the day, the ED staff implemented a variant of team triage. During peak flow times, an emergency physician, nurse, and ED technician are deployed at the triage area to evaluate and begin treatment of patients at times when rooms are not immediately available to place patients.

The emergency physician does a complete evaluation and order sets are implemented according to previously established treatment protocols. Once the evaluation is completed, the patient is placed into the next available treatment area and is accepted for follow-up care by a mid-level provider (MLP). The MLP then completes the work-up, considers the results of the lab and imaging studies ordered, as well as the patient's clinical course, and, in most cases, makes a disposition of the patient. In cases where the patient's clinical course changes or the results of the work-up require further emergency physician involvement, an ED physician re-evaluates the patient.

This system has been in place for over seven years and has worked very effectively (Gummerson, 2012). Dr. Ken Gummerson, the medical director at Anne Arundel, also uses a "middle-linebacker shift," which is a dedicated emergency physician shift that is not assigned to a specific area, but "plugs the holes" wherever they may be at the time. This is an example of real-time demand-capacity management utilizing the emergency physician.

PROVIDER AT TRIAGE

As described, "team triage" is usually intended to indicate that a physician and a team of providers are available at the triage area during certain hours of the day or certain days of the week. "Provider at triage" is somewhat less descriptive and may include an MLP at triage, with or without a nurse, tech, scribe or registrar as parts of the team.

The following chapter describes this concept in more detail, but the basics of these programs are briefly described here. There are many ways to identify these programs, including "provider at triage," "immediate care physician," "immediate care provider" (MCP), "rapid care assessment," and "rapid medical evaluation (RME)."

All of these approaches share the basic goal to bring patients and providers together as rapidly and safely as possible upon patient arrival to the emergency department. In addition, all programs share a "parallel processing approach" to these patients, in which either physicians or MLPs work closely with their nursing and support colleagues to front-load the care of the patient.

A data-intensive approach that allows all ED providers to visualize and monitor the progress in patient flow is essential to success. Whether the "provider at triage" is an emergency physician or MLP will depend on volume, acuity, risk factors, financial issues, and local circumstances. However, use of both emergency physicians and MLPs has been successful, depending upon local circumstances.

ESI Level 3 Fast Tracks. For EDs that choose not to deploy a team of providers at triage, other "front-loaded" flow options have been developed to address the issues of flow. All are fundamentally based on the concept we noted earlier that: "Fast Track is not a noun—it is a verb!"

Current approaches consider "fast tracking" to be a way in which patients with certain identifiable clinical entities are processed in a highly evidence-based fashion (a verb). Thus, patients with numerous high acuity illnesses or injuries are now "fast-tracked" in EDs, based upon their presenting symptoms. The concept is critical to understanding a number of ways in which flow is front-loaded. For example, some EDs do not deploy personnel to the triage area to evaluate and treat patients, but instead create a "split flow" or segmented flow process. In this way, they create processes by which patients with ESI level 3 acuity can be "split" and moved through the system in an expedited fashion.

Results waiting areas. Typically, what is the most rate-limiting constraint or bottleneck in your ED? In other words, who is the "MVP" of the ED? Is it the physician? The nurse? A simple answer might be "the team." However, the true rate-limiting step or bottleneck for most EDs is "the bed." Do all ED patients need a bed? The answer is "no," since some low acuity patients may be seen in chairs, whether in a room or a hallway, depending on availability.

Perhaps more important, for those patients who do need a bed, do they need it for their entire length of stay in the ED? Patients with critical illnesses or injuries, those with protracted vomiting, and those who require monitoring usually do require a bed for their entire stay. But for many patients, the bed "adds value" only for the period during which the nurse and physician evaluate and initially treat the patient.

Our staff need to be able to "make the diagnosis" of how the bed adds value to the patient through the course of their care and not simply use this most valuable resource for convenience. Recognizing this temporary need and the capacity constraints that the bed (or other horizontal surfaces in the ED) represent, many EDs have developed "results waiting rooms," in which patients wait until their diagnostic studies are completed.

Properly set up, these rooms have comfortable chairs and are readily visible either to nurses or to other qualified ED personnel in case patients develop problems. The results waiting rooms are often physically next to the triage area in the front of the ED. These patients must also be tracked in the patient tracking system, so that there is a clear understanding of where they are located.

Here is a simple way of thinking about who needs a bed, for what purpose, and for how long:

Bed needed? (i.e., for exam, laboratory, imaging, consultants). If no, evaluate where they are to be evaluated and assure a process is in place to do so.

Predictability of discharge: If no, keep the patient in the bed. If yes, move the patient to the results waiting area. If discharge is likely in less than 30 minutes, keep the patient in the bed. If discharge is likely after more than 30 minutes, move the patient to the results waiting room.

Super Track or Ultra Track: "Super Track" or "Ultra Track" is a concept first implemented at Mary Washington Hospital in Fredericksburg, VA. Super Track "is thus a Fast Track that is located at or near triage for the purpose of promptly treating patients who require very low resource utilization." Typically it utilizes two to three beds or chairs, has an adjacent results waiting area, and is staffed with a physician or MLP, a nurse, and may or may not have an ED technician, depending on the number and flow of patients.

This concept is an example of segmenting patient flow and creating a separate process and area for those patients who have very low acuity problems. Patient flow data should guide both whether such a concept is needed and the hours of the day that it is needed. For obvious reasons, such programs are usually utilized in large volume EDs (greater than 50,000 annual visits), since these EDs have enough high acuity patients to fill the beds in the main treatment areas, while simultaneously having a "critical mass" of lower acuity patients to necessitate a separate and dedicated flow pattern and process. This concept again illustrates that variations in process can add value for this specific group of patients by reducing waiting times, decreasing length of stay, and improving patient satisfaction.

ED FLOW: TEAMWORK

Because EDs by their nature are complex adaptive systems delivering care by many people from different backgrounds across multiple processes, improving flow requires a dedication to teamwork of unprecedented levels. Solutions should not be doctor, nurse, ED tech or essential services-based, but team-based, with active input sought throughout flow improvement efforts. It also requires transparency and communication of results. In this way, change can be sustained and even accelerated.

Hardwiring Flow™ Focus: Advanced ED Solutions to Flow

- **Demand-capacity management**—Patient arrivals are highly predictable with the right data and IT. Also, the times they arrive can be plotted by hour of the day. Use acuity data, ESI levels, and E/M codes to predict what they will need. Ask: "Do we have the correct staffing patterns and essential services to meet these needs?" and "What will we do if we don't?" Plan to correct demand-capacity mismatches when they occur, using clinical huddles and bed rounds.
- **Forecasting demand**—Once demand-capacity data is known and widely shared, use that data to forecast changes from typical flow patterns.

Similar data on hospital admissions should be used to assure that the hospital anticipates when, how many and what type of admissions will predictably come from the ED. Use this data to assure the bed board has a "Be-A-Bed-Ahead" program, which anticipates admissions and pre-assigns beds when available.

- **Real-time monitoring of flow**—Use the EMR and IT systems to monitor flow to predict when demand is about to exceed capacity. When more than the expected number or type of patients arrive at triage, these data should be used to alert the "staff in the back" to the downstream effect this will have as those patients move through the system. When patients are boarded in the ED, the rest of the ED and the EMS system need to use these real time data to change processes to meet the needs of the patient.

- **Queuing theory**—Anticipating and addressing the needs of patient flow before they occur and have their maximum negative impact reduces the effects of queuing. When delays do occur, small changes at the ascending limb of flow problems can have a dramatic impact on queuing and flow. Since ED rooms or beds can create unnecessary queues, programs like level 3 fast tracks, super-tracks, and results waiting rooms can reduce or eliminate them.

- **Managing variation**—Remember that the "paradox of variation" is that some variation adds value, while some causes waste and delays. Accentuate the former and eliminate the latter. Use flow data to predict where and when different processes are needed to meet the needs of the patients. Hours and criteria for Fast Track may be flexed to meet variable patient flow needs. Flex staffing on certain days or hours may be needed to meet variation. Triage bypass or "pull until full" are used when beds are available, but add no value when the ED is full.

- **Eliminating bottlenecks**—Assure that triage expedites flow by segmenting patients into value-added streams to decrease wait times. Triage bypass, AT/AI, provider in triage, "Be-A-Bed-Ahead", evidence-based clinical protocols, and Team Triage are all ways to reduce or eliminate bottlenecks by recognizing that those bottlenecks move and change during the course of the day.

- **Flow as a complex adaptive system**—Assuring that the entire hospital has aligned strategic understanding and incentives connects flow across boundaries and stakeholders. Hospitalists need to care about ED delays and patient satisfaction, just as the ED needs to understand core measures, hospital LOS and case-mix index. Leading up or managing up is critical across these dimensions, particularly for admitted patients, since ED satisfaction drives HCAPHS scores. Express admission units, ICU fast-tracking, door-to-discharge and early decision to admit are all recognition of the system nature of hospital operation.

- **Critical ED patient flow concepts**—(1) The more horizontal you are, the more you are a patient. The more vertical you are, the more you are a customer; (2) Keep your vertical patients vertical and in motion; (3) Horizontal patients value real estate (the bed) while vertical patients value speed; (4) Be fast at fast things and slow at slow things. (This requires different processes for each); (5) The number one sign of the health of an ED is the relationship between the doctors and the nurse; and (6) Making people unhappy, making them wait, and then sending them a bill is not a healthy business model.

CHAPTER 7

HOSPITAL SYSTEMS TO IMPROVE FLOW

by Kirk Jensen, MD, and Thom Mayer, MD

"One definition of insanity is doing the same thing, over and over again, but expecting different results."

—*Rita Mae Brown,* Sudden Death, *1983*

"Everything must be made as simple as possible. But no simpler."

—*Albert Einstein*

The ED may be the hospital's front door, but the various parts of the hospital form an interrelated system where occurrences in one affect the other. This has far reaching implications. To improve overall flow, efforts must be coordinated across units. Flow and functional siloing are incompatible. As a leader, you *must* assure your team sees the hospital as a complex adaptive system. Hire, train, promote and reward for that.

The most visible such relationship is between the ED and inpatient units. Emergency departments can implement strategies to improve flow, but the process is not a one way street. This chapter examines coordination across units. As background, let's first highlight an important factor affecting ED flow and its relationship to general hospital flow: boarding.

BOARDING: A SYSTEM-WIDE SOLUTION

A major determinant of ED flow is the number of patients who have been admitted, but are being held in the ED awaiting beds, i.e., boarders. As previously noted, these patients should be called "hospital boarders," not "ED boarders," because while they may be housed in the ED, the problem is on the hospital bed demand-capacity side of the ledger (Druckenbrod, 2004). Boarders occupy beds and consume resources that are best invested for new ED patients. Extensive literature documents the negative effects of boarding (Asplin et al. 2008, Bernstein et al. 2009), which is the major contributor to increased ED length of stay and correlates most strongly with decreased throughput in the overall healthcare system.

For an ED faced with frequent boarding, the biggest challenge is dealing with hospital wide patient flow. Other hospital units also have a stake in meeting this challenge, however. Remember, for example, that the ED is the hospital's front door to the community.

The exact percentage of boarders that is cause for grave concern or even danger is unknown. Two patients boarding in a 20-bed department is an unfortunate situation, a patient safety problem, and a worrisome circumstance for the staff. But it's an operational nuisance—not an operational nightmare—since 90 percent of functional patient care capacity remains.

We often see that when boarders exceed
10 to 15 percent of capacity, then the ED
has a significant flow problem.

Ten patients boarding in a 20-bed department eats up 50 percent of care capacity. This is now an operational disaster. Boarding is always a problem from patient safety and satisfaction perspectives, but operationally, whether it is a significant patient flow problem depends on the percentage of productive capacity boarding patients occupy. This "tipping point" percentage will vary by hospital. Based on our experience with queuing theory and variation, we often see that when boarders exceed 10 to 15 percent of capacity, then the ED has a significant flow problem.

When boarding approaches 20 percent, the department loses the flexibility required to cope with demand and variation in patient presentations and throughput. If boarding is a constant problem, recruitment and retention of highly motivated staff will be a problem

Fortunately, a number of strategies will help decrease ED boarding and accelerate movement into the hospital. We'll look at several in the sections that follow.

START STRONG

Get in early. After an initial patient assessment, experienced emergency physicians and nurses know—90 percent of the time—whether a patient needs to be admitted. This is a major opportunity to accelerate flow on the back end. Why wait four to six hours before formally requesting admission? Most commonly, we wait because of typical human caution: doctors (either the ED or the attending) want every lab result and diagnostic study returned and charted. Though understandable, this tendency is often a source of waste. Making an early decision to admit, followed by early engagement of the admitting team (to be discussed later in this chapter) can be a potent tactic for improving flow.

Early to bed—and the right bed. A closely related tactic to making an early decision to admit is an early request for the inpatient bed. As soon as the emergency physician realizes what type of bed is necessary, he or she should order an inpatient bed. Fifty to seventy percent of total hospital admissions arrive from the ED, so early bed requests can have a major impact on hospital wide patient flow.

If a hospital provides bed assignments rapidly following a request, the early request tactic may be unnecessary. However, if obtaining a bed often takes longer than 60 minutes, it can become an important tool. The early bed request is an example of parallel processing—occurring at the same time as diagnostic evaluation rather than following it—and can be a powerful tactic to enhance flow.

Timely notification of the admitting team. When an ED physician determines the patient needs to be admitted and submits a request for a bed, notifying the admitting team early in the process can help insure cooperation between the inpatient team, ED, and nursing units. ED physicians should be prepared to answer four questions:

1. Does the patient need admission?
2. Which service in the hospital should admit the patient (particularly determining surgical or medical and hospitalist versus specialty physician)?
3. Does the patient need to go to an intensive care unit?
4. Does the patient require emergent consultation, intervention, or procedures?

There can be legitimate differences of opinion as to which type of bed and location will best serve the needs of the patient. Admitting physicians may think a patient needs a bed on a different floor from that requested by the emergency doctor. Nursing units may have restrictions on the use of interventions or monitoring, such as continuous pulse oximetry or neurological checks every two hours. The inpatient team may feel that the admission decision is premature or disrupts their workflow and process.

Since early admission or early engagement may be resisted for a number of cultural and operational reasons, full use of these tactics may require changing the culture in the hospital. Written agreements on bed selection negotiated in advance and based upon mutual respect and caregiver consensus make the process much smoother. (See Figure 7.1 for an illustration of such a tool.)

All of these elements are examples of making prospective, evidence-based decisions regarding bed placement, and thus illuminate the importance of demand capacity management, managing variation, and eliminating bottlenecks or constraints. It is impossible to overstate that evidence based leadership requires senior leaders to have the courage of their convictions. They must insist that such prospective discussions on what data points will drive bed placement and admitting physicians simply *must* occur.

Admitting Service: _____Diagnosis:_____

Level of Care:
___Admit as Inpatient   ___Place in Observation Status

Special Needs:
___Confused/Falls/Wander Risk   ___Suicide Precautions
___ Isolation ___ Negative Pressure Room (patient infectious)
               ___ Positive Pressure Room (Neutropenic)
               ___ Contact
___Titrating Drips   ___ ETOH/Drug withdrawal protocol
___Pulse Oximetry   ___Continuous   ___Q4h   ___ Q8h
___Serial Cardiac Enzymes

Special Unit Designation: Preferred Unit: _____
___Intensive Care   ___CHF
___Progressive/Step Down   ___Dialysis Patient
___Stroke or TIA   ___Oncology 7
___Transplant Patient   Type of transplant: _____
___Telemetry   Cardiac _____   Medical _____
Medical/Surgical Floor _____
___Observation Unit   ___Pneumonia

SIGNATURE _____ DATE_____
TIME _____

Figure 7.1 Bed Selection Agreement

USE CONSULTING AGREEMENTS
TO SET EXPECTATIONS

Consulting agreements can help minimize potential conflicts associated
with the timing of a consult. It is rational for an admitting physician to want
chest X ray results for suspected pneumonia, but it is not necessary to wait

for a complete blood count, unless the patient is post chemotherapy and neutropenia is suspected. For the majority of chest pain patients, an EKG and bedside troponin level may be sufficient to make bed placement decisions. By spelling out expectations and protocols in advance, consulting agreements help make this process smoother (see Figure 7.2).

Consulting agreement with the hospitalist group. The emergency medicine physician will see most patients who will be admitted to the hospitalist group in the ED and perform a history and physical examination. If the patient requires admission, the emergency medicine physician will order all indicated studies (including labs) that are central to the evaluation before calling the hospitalist.

Timing of consult and diagnostic testing. The hospitalist should be called as soon as it becomes clear that the patient requires admission. If the need for admission is clinically apparent, the study results do not have to be completed prior to calling the hospitalist. However, if chest X ray, ECG, or dip urinalysis are central to the evaluation, these studies should be completed prior to calling the admitting physician. If it is likely that ED point of care (POC) laboratory tests including bedside troponin will significantly accelerate the patient evaluation, these tests should be ordered before calling the hospitalist physician.

Bed order. When the emergency medicine physician calls the hospitalist, they should discuss the type of bed needed so the ED unit secretary can place an order for the desired bed. The hospitalist should see the patient in the ED within 30 minutes. In the case of stable patients, he or she may elect to give phone orders and see the patient on the floor.

Admitting orders. Hospitalist standing orders will be kept in the ED to aid in the admission process. Any order designated as "STAT" or "NOW" will be carried out in the ED before the patient goes to the floor.

Transfer to floor. If the hospitalist agrees, stable patients may go to their rooms when the bed is available, where they will be seen by the hospitalist on the floor. This does not apply to patients who are going to an intensive care setting.

Patients transferred from a physician's office or outside hospital. Clinically stable patients who are accepted in transfer from a clinic, private office or outside hospital should be admitted directly to a floor bed without being seen in the ED.

Consulting Agreement with the Hospitalist Group

The emergency medicine physician will see most patients who will be admitted to the Hospitalist Group in the ED and perform a history and physical examination. If the patient requires admission, the emergency medicine physician will order all indicated studies (including labs) that are central to the evaluation before calling the hospitalist.

Timing of Consult and Diagnostic Testing

The Hospitalist should be called as soon as it becomes clear that the patient requires admission. If the need for admission is clinically apparent, the study results do not have to be completed prior to calling the Hospitalist. However, if chest X-ray, ECG, or dip urinalysis are central to the evaluation, these studies should be completed prior to calling the admitting physician. If it is likely that ED point of care (POC) laboratory tests including bedside troponin will significantly accelerate the patient evaluation, these tests should be ordered before calling the CHG physician.

Bed Order

When the emergency medicine physician calls the Hospitalist they should discuss the type of bed needed, and the ED unit secretary will place an order for the desired bed. The Hospitalist should see the patient in the ED within 30 minutes. In the case of stable patients, they may elect to give phone orders and see the patient on the floor.

Admitting Orders

Hospitalist Standing Orders will be kept in the ED to aid in the admission process (Attachment A). Any order designated as "STAT" or "NOW" will be carried out in the ED before the patient goes to the floor.

Transfer to Floor

If the Hospitalist agrees, stable patients may go to their rooms when the bed is available where they will be seen by the Hospitalist on the floor. This does not apply to patients who are going to an intensive care setting.

Patients Transferred from a Physician's Office or Outside Hospital

Clinically stable patients who are accepted in transfer from a clinic, private office or outside hospital should be admitted directly to a floor bed without being seen in the Emergency Department.

Figure 7.2. Example of a consulting agreement

Convincing the consultant. Sometimes the emergency physician must guide the consultant into doing the right thing. In a humorous article on this subject, Dr. Grant Innes, a Canadian emergency physician, proposes a number of strategies for convincing admission staff to admit patients who probably require hospitalization, but don't have a typical admissible presentation (Innes, 2000).

This article, in addition to being potentially helpful, is entertaining: Some of the suggestions are made with tongue firmly in cheek. "Select an appropriate diagnosis," the author advises. "The ideal diagnosis is exotic, difficult to disprove, and mandates hospitalization." Some of his favorites include Tumarken's otolithic crisis (weak and dizzy) and familial periodic paralysis without hypokalemia (patient won't move).

"Order a large number of tests," he continues in this vein. "Admitting physicians are more impressed by abnormal values than by sick patients. It is therefore helpful to order a huge battery of nonspecific tests on anyone who may require admission. A skilled ED physician should be able to generate two to three intriguing false positives on any patient." He recommends C reactive protein, antimitochondrial antibodies, thick smears for malaria, and India ink stains.

We don't recommend you go that far, but Dr. Innes does make the point that effectively communicating a patient's likely need for admission is often the right thing for that patient. This type of conversation should begin: "Bill, this is Thom Mayer in the ED. I need you to admit this patient. Here's why…" Stating precisely what you need the admitting physician to do at the outset of the conversation is essential. They can always ask about the "blood rubber or serum porcelain" if they choose.

Our friend and colleague Dr. Dighton Packard tells the story of seeing a 90 year old man who came to the emergency department having never seen a doctor in his entire life up to that point. All of his work up was negative, but Dr. Packard called the hospitalist to admit him and, when questioned why he wanted to admit him said, "I am the first doctor he has ever seen. I'd like to make sure I'm not the last!" The hospitalist cheerfully admitted him.

PERFORMING ACCELERATED TESTING

An important aid to flow is quickly and efficiently conducting tests early in the ED process. ED clinicians typically form a well-educated hypothesis as to whether patients will need admission and where they will need to go; clinicians also generally know which tests are likely necessary. Also, accelerated testing can break through an important barrier to flow in some hospitals: lab test turnaround time. In fact, point of care lab studies can decrease lab turn-around time by as much as one to two hours, a time savings that equates to earlier, accurate decision making (Murray et al., 1999; Hsiao et al., 2007).

Admitting teams can request or even demand results of lab testing, although the key decision makers in this process need to determine whether this information is "need to have" or "nice to have." That said, using evidence from clinical pathways and flow studies can help guide which lab studies need to be done by point of care testing. (Those that are constraints or bottlenecks—versus those that can be done in the lab—need to be identified.)

As mentioned above, an electrocardiogram and a single troponin or creatine kinase (CK) will indicate clearly where many chest pain patients should go. If diabetic ketoacidosis is suspected, point of care electrolytes, venous arterial blood gas, and dip urine for ketones can provide all lab tests that are necessary within minutes of the patient's arrival. A portable chest x-ray, electrocardiograph, urine dipstick, and point of care electrolytes will suffice for many medical admissions, all of which should be readily available in the ED.

HOW TO HANDLE HIGH FLOW HOURS OF THE DAY

Ensure use of an efficient admitting officer. Having an efficient medical admitting officer stationed in the ED can be a valuable tactic to expedite flow. This approach is more common in larger hospitals, often in tandem with a residency program or a hospitalist service. To be effective, an admitting officer must understand that the goal of the healthcare system is to admit sick patients and keep patients who aren't sick out of the hospital.

Understanding the goal is key. Diagnostic and treatment sensitivity and specificity are critical: Sensitivity speaks to: *"Who is sick and who isn't?"* Specificity speaks to: *"What is the actual need for admission and what is the quickest way to accomplish this?"* The admitting officer must focus on the need for admission and make frequent use of standardized, streamlined admission orders, along with any required emergency medications.

In a sense, this process is a type of refined fast track triage approach. The admitting officer must also avoid temptations to perform an exhaustive evaluation in the ED, order extensive testing, or work up comprehensive admission orders. Such testing and preparation of comprehensive orders can wait until the patient enters the inpatient unit. Fundamentally, this process—properly used—adds value and eliminates waste because it is an example of parallel versus sequential processing. It assures that "the baton is passed" at the earliest appropriate time in the patient's journey.

Use an admitting agreement. There are a number of reasons and situations that may impede the rendezvous of an admitting physician or an admitting team with the patient. These sources of delays in the admitting process can benefit from a coordinated, system wide approach. One component of such an approach is the admitting agreement.

Under an admitting agreement, the ED can send stable patients to the appropriate inpatient floors for evaluation by the admitting team. When there are consult delays, these agreements provide that workups happen in the inpatient unit and not in the ED. They also specify which patients are eligible to move to inpatient units under the agreement. Figure 7.3 shows how a typical such agreement might look:

ED Direct Admission Process

Overview
The most stable ED patients who require admission to the hospital will be evaluated by the admitting team on the inpatient nursing unit rather than the ED. For such patients, the emergency physician will write brief holding orders after discussion with the upper level resident or the admitting physician. The admitting team will complete the history and physical examination on the floor and submit more comprehensive orders at that time.

Eligible Patients
Clinically stable adult patients going to a floor or monitored bed who are being admitted from the ED.

Diagnostic Exclusion Criteria
• Active or recent chest pain, unless EKG and initial enzymes completed,
• Undiagnosed abdominal pain, unless abdominal imaging completed (CT or US),
• Any undiagnosed neurological condition (e.g., focal weakness, confusion, paresthesias), unless neuroimaging completed (CT or MRI),
• Patients who require intensive or progressive care, or
• Patients who require emergent operation or procedure.

Figure 7.3 Example of an admitting agreement

Bridging or transition orders. Bridging orders (also known as transition or holding orders) offer another way to move patients out of the ED, a way that decreases time to admission and which many hospitals have used regularly in their emergency departments. Bridging or transition orders are not admission orders. They are *time limited* orders that permit stable patients to be moved safely from the ED to an inpatient or holding unit.

In its revised policy on "Writing Admission and Transition Orders" of April 2010, the American College of Emergency Physicians asserted that "in the interest of patient care and safety, an emergency physician may be compelled to write transition orders…[which] may include essential treatment and assessment parameters required before preparation of suitable admission orders."

We would emphasize the point that in decreasing the number of boarders and the time to admission, holding orders when carried out properly aid patient safety. In fact, the American Academy of Emergency Medicine has issued a statement to the effect that writing orders that "define any necessary treatment and assessment parameters required in the interval until completion of admission orders" is acceptable (see http://www.aaem.org/positionstatements/admissions.php).

Conventional healthcare thinking once held that emergency physicians should not write bridging orders because doing so could open them up to medico legal liability in inpatient areas. Experts now believe there is little legal risk for the emergency physician who writes holding orders as long as they are executed within certain limits. Indeed, some experts believe that hospitals and doctors face far more legal risk in boarding patients in an overcrowded ED than in using holding orders.

Well written bridging orders make clear that the inpatient team is responsible for all further orders. They also stipulate that the *admitting team* (and not the emergency physician) must be notified of any change in the patient's condition. Figure 7.4 shows an example of a bridging order for moving a patient into an inpatient unit while awaiting admission.

<u>Initiate: ED Patient Admitted to Hospital – Holding Orders</u>

Verify Allergies

Diagnosis: _____

Admit to Patient Type: _____ Inpatient _____ Observation

Admit to Service:

Admit to bed type: ___Medical Floor ___Cardiac Tele ___Medical Tele __

___Neuro ___Orthopedics ___Trauma Other _____

Isolation Precautions: ___None ___Contact ___Airborne ___HR-MDRO

Old Chart to the Floor

Consult _____ for: _____

Treatment Parameters

If the admitting physician has not evaluated the patient within 1 hour or arrival to the nursing unit, page and notify the senior resident on call in the case of a staff service, or the on-call physician in the case of the hospitalist group.

Call Dr. _____ on beeper # _____ immediately when the patient arrives to the unit to request admission orders. Notify the admitting team of any significant changes in vital signs, or any changes in the patient's condition.

Pharmacy

Patient Weight: _____ kg. ___Estimated ___Measured

___ IV PRN Adaptor

IV Fluids _____ @ _____ml/hour Max Volume: _____ ml

Figure 7.4 Transition order for ED patient admitted to hospital

Refusing to play telephone games. We've discussed how emergency physicians may have to maneuver around barriers created by admitting teams. Similarly, emergency nurses can face obstacles in giving reports to floor nurses who often say they're too busy to take a phone ED report an hour before or after a shift change, because they're short staffed, just had a code, and so on.

A simple way around this obstacle is to standardize reports and streamline the process. One way to accomplish this is to fax the ED nurse report to the inpatient unit secretary. (See Figure 7.5 for an example.) Email and voicemail work too. The key take home point here is to establish a method for a "no delay" nursing report.

The ED nurse does place one call: to the unit secretary on the floor to alert the secretary that a fax or e-mail is on the way. A floor nurse who has any questions can call the ED for clarification. If there is no call and no reason to delay, the ED sends the patient to the floor 15 to 30 minutes after the report is faxed, in a process agreed on in advance by all parties.

Emergency Deportment   Patient Sticker

Admitting Diagnosis: Admitting Physician:

Date:_____ Pt. Room number:_____ Time faxed:_____
Report by:_____ at phone number:_____
Estimated transport time:_____ Transported by:☐RN ☐EDT
Equipment needed: ☐monitor ☐pulse ox   ☐oxygen   ☐IV pump ☐other_____
Precautions:☐suicide ☐ respiratory isolation   ☐ contact   ☐immunocomprised
              ☐droplet ☐ other_____

Allergies:_____
Past medical history:_____
Past surgical history:_____
Home medications:_____

Oxygen source:_____ L/min   ☐ NA   O2 sat_____%
VS: T_____P_____R_____BP_____cardiac rhythm_____
IV: #1 site___size_____solution_____rate_____DC credit_____
IV: #2 site___size_____solution_____rate_____DC credit_____
Other: ☐ foley catheter ☐NG tube   ☐ other_____

Lab results:
Other abnormal labs:_____
Radiology:☐chest ☐KUB ☐pelvis   ☐obstruction series   ☐c-spines   ☐ head CT ☐abd CT
          ☐helical CT ☐other
Abnormal radiology results:_____

Medications given: Name_____dose_____route_____effect_____
                   Name_____dose_____route_____effect_____
                   Name_____dose_____route_____effect_____
Interventions still needed: meds_____xrays_____IV_____
other _____

Comments_____
_____

Figure 7.5 Example of a faxed nursing report

Express admission and holding units. When EDs start to get busy, moving patients through efficiently before boarders begin to fill the hallway is important. Express admission units (EAUs) and holding areas for ED patients are other tactics to increase patient flow. Stable ED patients requiring admission are moved to one of these staging areas using holding orders to start admission diagnostic and treatment plans.

These units are typically nearby, although geographically separate from the ED. Their size varies according to the number of ED admissions per day. (We have observed that the best express admission units are often physically located outside the ED.) In some hospitals, the EAU and the ED holding areas differ in that express admission patients are the responsibility of the admitting team while holding area patients remain the responsibility of the ED team until the arrival of the admitting physician.

Here again, EAUs or holding units can improve or impede flow, depending on how they are operated. When not well implemented, they become easy substitutes for decision making, or way stations for selected ED patients. The unit's mission must be clear cut, with time measured in minutes and hours.

EAU and ED holding area nurses must be relentless in their pursuit of admitting orders from the inpatient team. Incentives must also be aligned across the hospital, with the goal of getting patients in and out. Leaders need to be clear on their goals and how they will be reached, and they need to be vigilant in maintaining accountability.

AN IMPORTANT FLOW RELATIONSHIP: ED AND THE ICU

A specific and significant stream of patients coming to the ED involves those who will need treatment in the intensive care unit (ICU). ICU management is one of the two most powerful drivers of hospital-wide patient flow (the other is surgical management). ICU patients in the ED require significant amounts of nursing and physician resources, and they divert monitoring and care from other patients in the department.

In addition, how long an ICU patient remains in the ED correlates with subsequent mortality, especially for ED stays longer than six hours (Chalfin et al., 2007). The more quickly patients can be moved to the ICU to receive the appropriate care, the better off they will be and the smoother flow will be. So developing an "ICU Lean" program improves flow, the quality of care, patient safety, and patient satisfaction.

Hospitals have developed various programs to achieve these goals. At Northwest Community Hospital, a "Swoop Team" has operated for several years. When patients arrive in the ED who meet certain criteria, spelled out in a written policy, the Swoop Team springs into action.

A nurse practitioner or senior nurse comes to the ED and then takes the patient to the ICU, where the patient receives a speedy, full evaluation. A policy for activating this kind of program might include the following criteria:

- Sepsis or sepsis syndrome;
- acute respiratory failure requiring mechanical ventilation;
- resuscitation post-arrest;
- unstable hemodynamics requiring vasopressor intervention; or
- intracranial hemorrhage with evolving neurological deficits or airway compromise.

Intermountain Medical Center in Salt Lake City developed a similar program it calls "Priority One" (Welch, 2009). Under Priority One, a critical care team comes to the ED for patients who meet the written criteria and transports them to the ICU. An intensivist writes the ICU order after a patient arrives in the unit. After Intermountain established the program, the ED length of stay for Priority One patients dropped from 300 minutes to less than 60 minutes.

The most effective process involves the ED physician making a single call to the intensivist instead of separate calls to multiple physicians. Also, medical staff agreements for automatic ICU consults can allow bypassing the admitting physician for this initial call; the intensivist then consults the admitting physician from the ICU.

In some ICU Lean programs, the patient goes directly to the ICU after the ED physician has a phone consult with the intensivist and carries out appropriate ED stabilization, without the intensivist coming to the ED. If the intensivist or the patient's physician needs to come to the ED, the ICU Lean policy should ideally spell out that the physician should arrive in the department within 30 minutes. In addition, the policy should require the ICU to respond within 30 minutes of notification with a bed assignment and a team to transport the patient. The patient's ED nurse should accompany the patient with the transfer team to give a bedside report.

Whatever form an expedited ICU admission program takes, it should aim to decrease the time from initial activation to the patient's arrival in the ICU, preferably to less than 60 minutes. Figure 7.6 outlines the typical process for an ICU Lean program:

ED–ICU Patient: An Expedited Admission Process

1. Request ICU bed.
2. If ICU bed available, determine consult based on code critical (intensivist) or non-code critical (general admission).
3. If code critical: Page intensivist and discuss patient status.
   Notify ED secretary to text or page admission team with patient identifiers.
4. If not code critical: Page appropriate admitting physician.
   Select the consult icon in status board to start the 60-minute timer.
5. Notify the secretary to page the care team for patient transfer to the ICU.

Figure 7.6 The ICU expedited admission process

LEARNING THE PROCESS FIRST-HAND

Regarding hospital-wide coordination in connection with hospital wide flow, we recommend that ED and inpatient personnel spend two to four hours observing the inner workings of the hospital admitting team (people and process) and learning intimately how the admission system works. Witnessing this process will drive home the impact of admissions on flow. Understanding the complexity of admissions also provides valuable insights that can be applied to improving overall flow across the hospital.

BEDS AND BOARDING: SPECIFIC STRATEGIES

There are other specific tactics available to decrease the incidence of boarding and smooth flow; we've seen these work in our own experience. At Inova Fairfax Hospital, we participated in a project to improve flow in the hospital by improving coordination between the ED and the inpatient units. If the ED is the front door of the hospital, we reasoned, the transition for patients between the department and other units is the back door, and the presence of large numbers of boarders functioned to lock the back door.

We realized that we would not likely succeed in improving flow if it remained locked. If we could unlock that door though, we could improve flow. And so we created the Boarder Patrol Team. It included leaders from the ED and from inpatient units, and it focused on eliminating or at least dramatically reducing boarding. To achieve that goal, the team developed a couple of innovative programs. Together, they worked to significantly improve flow, with some gratifying corollary results.

The Adoption Agency. One innovative project that the Boarder Patrol created was the Adopt a Boarder program. (A similar program was developed independently at Stonybrook and Inova.) It grew from an observation about the quality of boarding, as well as the quantity. Specifically, patients who are boarding often spend hours in the ED hallway waiting for an inpatient bed; sometimes, patients wait 12 hours or more in that hallway.

This observation led us to wonder, if 10 patients are waiting in the ED hallway for inpatient beds and, instead, if each of those patients were placed on a hallway in a different inpatient unit, would those patients get better care? Would they be safer? Would they be more satisfied? Intuitively, we would answer yes. And a number of studies have shown that patient satisfaction is much higher when they move to inpatient hallways. Patients believe they are getting more personal attention and better care, and they are happy to be closer to their inpatient beds.

Many of the largest hospitals in the United States have implemented the Adopt-a-Boarder program, including Duke, William Beaumont, and UCLA. We should acknowledge up front that it is a work-around to the problem of boarding and not a true solution. (A solution would be expedient admission of all patients to the appropriate inpatient units.)

Nonetheless, it greatly improves patient satisfaction and, if implemented well, improves teamwork among ED and inpatient staff. And hospitals across the United States found something interesting when they implemented the program: It often accelerates bed turnover so that patients who are designated to move to a bed in an inpatient hallway instead go directly to a room.

Perhaps the reason is because staff on inpatient floors don't want their hallways crowded with beds, or perhaps coordination and teamwork just improve in general. In any case, beds get cleaned in a much shorter time than usual. This was the experience at Inova Fairfax. After we implemented the program, we rarely had to use it. Usually, the inpatient unit found a bed in a room before the patient arrived.

At Inova Fairfax, the program dramatically reduced the time it took to place admitted patients in beds. It had an automatic trigger: When more than four ED boarders waited more than four hours for inpatient beds, it went into effect. The nursing supervisor and administrator on call put it into effect when conditions reached that trigger point.

Giving those persons the responsibility to do so meant that adequate authority was behind the move to make the program succeed. Such authority is necessary; in the typical hospital, nurses in inpatient units resist accepting boarding patients. So leadership accountability is essential if the program is to succeed.

One important caveat about the Adopt-a-Boarder program in this regard is that inpatient leaders need to develop and implement the program. When an ED tries to do so, it faces resistance from inpatient staff with little incentive (or so they perceive) to make it succeed. It is, in fact, extraordinarily rare for an ED to succeed in its implementation.

Someone with authority in inpatient units has to drive the program. When that happens, it often leads to a change in mind-set and behavior in inpatient units' staff as well as better teamwork and communication. A similar program at Stonybrook is called "Full Capacity Protocol." Dr. Peter Viccellio, who led development of the program, makes many useful resources on it available at www.hospitalovercrowding.com.

Huddle before the play. One of the central principles of effective flow management is this: *Be proactive.* Implementing this principle is particularly important in bed management in a hospital. Establishing and maintaining an effective bed coordination process combines some theoretical components of flow with basic, old fashioned information gathering. The bed huddle is a good illustration.

A daily bed huddle involves a group of people: the hospital's bed coordinator, floor nurses, and housekeeping staff, who meet to review the status of beds on particular floors, particularly to anticipate discharges that will free beds. This group also predicts likely admissions from the ED, surgical unit, ICU, and any other relevant sources, basing predictions on information from demand capacity management. The group then projects a net surplus or deficit of beds for specific units. This projection should trigger specific responses from individual units to facilitate availability of needed beds, through such measures as early discharges.

The bed huddle makes use of real-time monitoring to fit capacity to demand and predict staffing requirements. During times of high volume, holding two (or even more) huddles will improve flow more than just one. Having one person designated "bed czar" is an important part of the bed huddle strategy.

Finding out for yourself. The commander of the U.S. Army's 82nd Airborne Division during World War II, General James M. Gavin, recounted an anecdote from his combat experiences in his memoir, *On to Berlin*. He received orders to send his troops across a forested canyon, where another U.S. division had suffered a terrible defeat with heavy casualties months before, to seize a German town.

Gavin himself led a reconnaissance of the canyon. The trails were impassable for tanks; wrecked tanks still littered the terrain, and Jeeps sank into the mud. Well camouflaged German pillboxes on ridges to both sides of the trail had been able to concentrate murderous fire. In examining the terrain, the general realized that an alternate route following a paved road across land favorable for tanks would have required much simpler maneuvering.

When he asked in corps headquarters why the canyon route had been chosen, a staff officer dismissed the question. Gavin noticed the corps commander and another general bent over a map, drawing lines representing battalions. He was struck by "how remote they were from the realities" (Gavin, 1978). He also wondered if the earlier disaster "had some relationship to the lack of understanding in higher headquarters of what the actual situation on the ground was." He found out subsequently that indeed it did.

The central lesson here—find out for yourself—applies not just to military engagements but to business and organizational leadership, including healthcare. Leaders who take the time to explore what's going on at ground level in their organizations are better able to make informed decisions. For hospital flow, leadership rounding is one of the main forms this awareness takes.

Leaders who routinely carry out rounds among admitted patients are engaging in the most basic form of real-time monitoring. We can call this approach "management by walking around," as Tom Peters popularized it in the book *In Search of Excellence*, having observed it at Hewlett Packard (Peters and Waterman 1982).

Studer Group® and others have taken this concept to the next level with "Leadership Rounding." Leaders round on direct reports as well as on patients to verify and validate care for continuous improvement. It's not a haphazard method; it's a purposeful one comprising deliberate efforts to be aware of conditions, above all from the patients' perspective. Its principal components are to look, listen, ask, coach, problem solve, communicate, and plan.

The leaders of individual units should round in their own units, but to optimize flow management, they should also follow patients from their units when they're moved to other units and round on those units with their leaders. This type of joint rounding helps avoid the erection of silos by improving teamwork and creates a more unified sense of hospital wide flow.

Staying ahead of the game. As we began our work as the Boarder Patrol, one of the first questions that occurred to us was this: *Why can't we be a bed ahead in the process rather than a bed (or often more) behind?* Asking this question led us to wonder whether we could develop a process in which the bed board proactively identifies which bed (or beds) will be the next one assigned to patients, not just from the ED but also from operating rooms and transfers.

The answer was yes: we created the Be A Bed Ahead program, whereby a bed team worked to identify beds that would likely be needed, based on patients' conditions in the ED or operating rooms, and have those beds ready to assign (see Figure 7.7 for an outline of the process). It quickly became clear that to succeed, the program would need not just ED monitoring and forecasting but cooperation from inpatient units and input from them.

To achieve this cooperation and effectiveness, we started bed rounds two times a day. Those involved in the rounds included the ED charge nurse, the charge nurse in each inpatient unit, the nursing supervisor, and the administrator on call. When beds were scarce, forecasting discharges became a priority. Real-time monitoring of conditions was critical for achieving effective demand-capacity management. The process worked.

One of the gratifying side results was the genuine spirit of teamwork that developed as a result of this joint approach. Charge nurses in inpatient units commonly volunteered to the ED charge nurse to take specific patients and acted to expedite admission of those patients. This attitude and the better communication that the process entailed led to better team spirit. This better spirit, in turn, sparked more progress in improving flow, which led to better team spirit, and so on. The process became a positive feedback loop of innovation.

Traditional Bed Assignment Process	Be-A-Bed-Ahead Process
- ED calls for an inpatient bed	- Beds are identified as available only when they are clean, unoccupied, and staffed
- Bed board begins to "search" for a bed	
- Board makes multiple calls to multiple floors	- Bed board prospectively identifies 33 beds by types (e.g., surgery, ICU, telemetry)
- Floors engage in "bed hiding"	
- Board locates bed	
- Environmental services cleans the bed	- Bed board informs unit of its "next-up" status
- Bed is in service	- Charge nurse informs nurse of "next-up" status
- Bed is available	
	- Bed is assigned when requested

Figure adapted from Chapter 38, "Disposition Decision to Departure: Finishing Strong," Emergency Department Management, McGraw-Hill, in press, Jody Crane, Robert W. Strauss, Suzanne Stone-Griffith, Thom Mayer

Figure 7.7 The elements of a bed-ahead program compared with the traditional process

COORDINATING HOSPITAL WIDE FLOW

The importance of patient flow in healthcare has become increasingly recognized in the past decade or so. Hospitals are taking steps to improve flow, healthcare professionals are seeking out training in flow improvement, and national organizations are acting to emphasize the need to improve flow. In the first years of this century, The Joint Commission established an accreditation standard requiring hospital leaders to "develop and implement plans to identify and mitigate impediments to efficient patient flow throughout the hospital" (Joint Commission Resources Leadership Standard LD.3.10.10, effective January 1, 2005).

The Joint Commission recently put into effect new performance standards whereby the chief executive officer, medical staff, and other senior managers in a hospital must set specific goals to improve patient flow, including ensuring availability of patient beds and maintaining proper throughput in labs, operating rooms, inpatient units, telemetry, radiology, and post anesthesia care units. These new requirements became effective January 1, 2013 (Schneider 2013).

The Joint Commission has said recently that "boarding in the ED requires a hospital wide solution" (Schneider, 2013). Lynne Bergero of The Joint Commission added, "We want to make sure that organizations are looking at patient flow hospital wide, even if the manifestation of a flow problem seems to be in the emergency room."

To reach this goal, The Joint Commission has mandated that hospitals form hospital wide flow committees to examine processes, analyze data, and implement ongoing improvements. This kind of committee can be key in coordinating flow improvement efforts. To succeed, it must include senior leaders—for example, the chief executive officer, chief operating officer, chief medical officer, and chief of emergency medicine—as well as appropriate representatives from various units.

Since few healthcare professionals understand flow and systems management better than ED practitioners, for whom minutes and hours are critical concerns, ED clinicians are essential participants on—or chairs of—these committees. In fact, few understand the timely management of people and resources better. As in any effort of this kind, the commitment and persistence of the leaders will determine how well the hospital improves flow. But when a hospital-wide committee with clout is serious and determined, it can achieve impressive results.

FINISHING STRONG: ORCHESTRATING THE DISCHARGE

An important point about hospital flow should be clear from this chapter: The process of patient transition is one in which simple changes can have significant effects on flow throughout a hospital. Admission is one part of that process. Another part contains some of the greatest potential for improving flow: the discharge process. If a hospital can improve it, the effects cascade: the bed assignment process becomes easier to manage, and patients flow out of the ED and surgery into inpatient units.

> The process of patient transition is one in which simple changes can have significant effects on flow throughout a hospital.

Perhaps no other activity within the hospital is such a likely candidate for hospital-wide coordination, and often that coordination is lacking. Many hospitals, for example, typically discharge patients in the morning. The discharge process, however, takes time and often requires participation of several units, such as pharmacy and dietary departments, so many patients are not actually discharged until late afternoon. A hospital that sets a regular time for discharging all patients is setting itself up for bottlenecks. When a number of patients are going through that same process at the same time, a number of departments begin to be tied up. So when patients are not discharged efficiently, space needed for other patients becomes unavailable. Delays begin to spread throughout the hospital. The bottlenecks get worse when departments don't communicate with each other.

Improving the flow of discharge requires a focus on process and the coordination of activities among departments and units; a hospital wide flow committee should focus on these aspects early in its work. It should create a process for scheduling all discharges and it should ensure that the work of all staff members involved in the process is orchestrated.

As with any flow initiative, it should use real-time tracking, data compilation and analysis, and forecasting to predict discharges—then use those predictions accordingly. The criteria for discharge must be clearly understood in each unit, and tracking of patients should occur in light of those criteria, with results monitored. Some specific methods to coordinate discharge and smooth flow are these:

- pull patients through the hospital by incorporating discharge in the admission process and scheduling discharge;
- stagger discharges through scheduling—they should not all be set at the same time;
- orchestrate discharges between the particular departments involved in each case, including housekeeping;
- make earlier discharge rounds, with a specific discharge team;
- coordinate any necessary follow-up services before discharge; and
- develop relationships with long-term care facilities and outpatient clinics to coordinate transfers.

How scheduling works. The final decision concerning a patient's readiness to leave the hospital rests with the physician who writes the discharge order, but others can identify who is a likely candidate. These include: a case manager, a multidisciplinary team, and a nurse or nurses.

The best approach is to use a team. When teams carry out bed rounds, and then discuss possible discharges, they often make safer and better decisions than individuals do. A team could be as simple as a physician and nurse who make rounds and then agree on which patients can leave the next day.

Or it could involve an ICU team with doctor, nurse, social worker, and respiratory therapist. Hospitals that use this approach, spending five minutes per patient on average, find it highly effective and a great time saver. Such teams can predict with about 80 percent reliability which patients will be ready to leave the next day (Roger Resar, via personal conversation, 2012) and can predict with 60 to 70 percent reliability which patients will be ready to leave in two days.

Scheduled discharges can be set for several designated times throughout the day: 10:00, 2:00, and 5:00, for example. They can also be set for every hour, with a patient scheduled for each hour throughout the day, for example.

Discharge schedules can also be arranged by asking patients what time they would like to be discharged.

The most effective approach is establishing a set of appointment times based on historical demand. (These numbers are available in the records.) Study data for the unit for a week, a month, and a year to determine the times that patients were discharged on average. Those average times become the discharge slots. The average numbers of patient discharged on particular days are in the records, too. Number and time can be mapped.

Giving patients a choice of available slots involves them in the process and helps them and their family plan for the transition. Offering the patient such a choice, rather than asking the patient to name a time, works well: "You are going home tomorrow, and we have discharge appointments at 9:00, noon, and 3:00. Which time would you prefer?"

How orchestration works. For discharge to work smoothly, many departments that need to perform tasks—pharmacy, nursing, respiratory therapy, dietary departments, for instance—must know when specific patients will leave. Communication of their scheduled discharge times can occur by use of fax, white boards, or phone calls. White boards are usually the most effective. A small one in the patient's room is particularly effective, though they can also be placed at the nurses' station. The white board contains two pieces of information: the estimated day of discharge and the scheduled time.

Use of such a white board achieves three results. First, it involves the patient in his or her care, giving the patient a sense of control and increasing satisfaction. Second, it enables the patient's family to schedule for the patient's homecoming (or a follow up facility to plan accordingly). Third, it holds the system accountable. Once the hospital has promised patients they can go home in four days at a designated time, the departments involved are more likely to work toward that clearly defined goal.

To orchestrate the discharge, the flow manager, whether case manager or nurse or someone else, can give each department involved a specific time to complete its role in the discharge—pharmacy at 8:00, respiratory therapy at 9:00, and so on, for example—or can provide each with the discharge time and leave them all to complete the necessary work. Generally, using the second option works better for flow, allowing the people involved to figure out for themselves how to get the work done in time and giving them the ability to complete it earlier, thus smoothing the work load.

Learning from the process. Once a hospital implements the process for scheduling discharges and orchestrates the work that needs to happen for that process to work smoothly, it should study the resulting procedures and results. What it learns will help it fine-tune the process to smooth flow. If it becomes clear that the hospital needs many more beds in the morning than the afternoon, for instance, then it can focus on scheduling discharges for the mornings and can coordinate activities aimed at meeting the schedule.

At first, the goal should be simply to establish discharge slots and fill them. After that process is in effect, factors that inhibit smooth flow will become apparent. Generally, only a few reasons cause delays:

- waiting for tests,
- waiting for somewhere to go,
- waiting for a doctor to write the discharge order, or
- waiting for nurses to complete their work.

Whatever delays the process, the hospital can find solutions. For example, suppose one reason for delays is arranging transportation for patients home. Several possible solutions are available: vouchers for taxi rides, volunteers in the community, or even ambulance services (if predictable hours can be arranged). If discharges during the day reach too high a volume, evening slots can be assigned. Examining the causes and thinking creatively about solutions should help smooth out wrinkles in the process.

Tracking these reasons can be as simple as a daily huddle with members of the discharge team, to consider why a patient did not go home when scheduled. The team can plot the reasons on a quality control chart, which includes the patient's name, scheduled time of discharge, actual time, and reason for the delay. Common factors will show up in this kind of tracking.

Remember the goal. Whether the patient's discharge order is predicted and scheduled two days ahead or written the previous day or four hours before the discharge, the method involved in successful on time discharge is always the same: the order or predicted order should set in motion an orderly, predictable set of coordinated activities that are designed to join the patient, the patient's family, and the staff in reaching the same goal: discharging the patient at the predetermined time.

For patients who don't have a predicted discharge, the process can often still be implemented once the physician writes the discharge order. If the physician receives the order at 9:00 am, for example, an afternoon discharge slot might be available. Discharge activities take an average of four hours to complete, so if the patient is scheduled for four hours later, the process is still smoothly orchestrated. The goal is still the same for those patients whose discharge has not been predicted: scheduling the slot when possible and organizing the process necessary to have the patient ready to go then.

A hospital that coordinates discharge effectively will find that flow improves noticeably throughout the system. More beds are available for inpatients. Staff workloads become more easily predicted and managed. Admissions and transitions between units become smoother and backlogs diminish. The ED is less stressed as the incidence of boarding goes down. And not least, patients are more satisfied when their waiting times for services and transitions are less. The effects of smoother discharge enable other flow initiatives in other processes within the hospital to succeed more easily. Benefits accumulate, and smoother flow is good for everyone.

HARDWIRING FLOW™ FOCUS: HOSPITAL SYSTEMS TO IMPROVE FLOW

- The various parts of the hospital form a system, whether we recognize it as such or not, where changes in one part have important effects on others.
- Patients boarding in the ED hallways are not "ED boarders", but rather "hospital boarders," since it is a failure of inpatient services that causes this bottleneck or constraint.
- The value added, waste reduction calculus needs to be applied to the boarding issue to come up with effective solutions.
- A fundamental question to answer: "If those boarders were members of your own family, would you tolerate laying in the ED hallway?"
- If boarding is a constant and recurring problem, recruitment and retention of highly talented and motivated staff will be a problem.
- Failure to deal with the board challenge is a fundamental test of your leadership legitimacy.

Strategies to Hardwire Flow:

- **Demand-capacity management**—Get the right bed early. (The majority of acute chest pain patients can have accurate bed placement decisions made with a history, physical exam, EKG, and bedside troponin and/or creatine kinase.)

- **Forecasting demand**—Understand normal and abnormal patterns. (Assure all parties know how many admissions occur each day, what number and types of beds will be needed and how the team will respond when delays and backups occur.)

- **Real-time monitoring of flow**—Constantly monitor flow and watch backups closely. Use clinical huddles and bed rounds to get ahead of the flow curve.

- **Queuing theory**—Use service-written, negotiated service agreements between key physician groups. (Start with hospital medicine-emergency medicine, since this is a key rate-limiting step.) Use parallel processing instead of sequential processing whenever possible.

- **Managing Variation**—As utilization increases above 80-85%, expect more waits, delays and rejections (boarding). Anticipate this and make necessary changes in process. Use Express Admission and Transition Units when beds are unavailable. Use ICU Fast Tracking when ICU beds are tight

- **Reducing constraints and bottlenecks**—Assure there are evidence-based, mutually agreed upon physician order sets and clinical guidelines between key services. Use point-of-care testing to reduce bottlenecks. Eliminate "telephone games."

- **Flow as a complex, adaptive system**—Link the pieces of the system together with common purpose, metrics, motivation, and aligning strategic incentives. Start with the units that most frequently interact in service transitions and queues. Celebrate even small successes publically across the system.

CHAPTER 8

HOSPITAL MEDICINE AND FLOW

by Kirk Jensen, MD, Thom Mayer, MD, Mark Hamm,
and Nathan Goldfein, MD

"The best preparation for tomorrow is to do today's work superbly well."

—*William Osler*

"Cure sometimes, treat often, comfort always."

—*Hippocrates*

The emergence of the hospital medicine specialty in the 1990s marked the evolution of the responsibility for inpatient care from primary care physicians to dedicated hospital medicine physicians, whose practice is restricted solely to managing inpatients through the course of their hospital stay (Hamm et. al, 2014).

But that evolution can become a revolution if hospital medicine is married to the principles of Hardwiring Flow™. We have often said that there should be a distinction between a "hospitalist,"— a physician whose clinical practice occurs totally within the hospital—and "specialist in hospital medicine."

The latter not only cares exclusively for inpatients, but does so with a focus on flow as the patient moves through the inpatient process:

Hospitalist	Specialist in Hospital Medicine
On-call	"Hospitalist PLUS..."
Focuses on inpatient management	All of the hospitalist functions and...
Rounds at least daily on patients	Applies flow strategies and tools to inpatient care
Works on discharge planning	Keeps PCP informed through the course of care
	Focused on EBM protocols, LOS, core measures, HCAHPS scores

Figure 8.1 Specialists in hospital medicine must hardwire flow

However, for the sake of brevity and convenience, we will refer to "hospitalists," here, with the understanding that there is nothing about having physicians on-call for admissions *per* se that results in smoother flow. While improving flow was not the only reason this specialty developed, it has a central place in any effort to make flow smoother.

Hospitalists and the related subspecialties (see Figure 8.2) should be highly effective allies in improving flow throughout the hospital. However, it is not simply having these physicians available but having them committed to flow that is critical to success. Our view is that hospital medicine is not only an essential, but also a central component to hardwiring hospital-wide flow. Physicians must not only be at the table, but must be fully committed to a culture of flow and managing to results based on flow metrics.

Hospitalist Type	Care Provided
Hospitalist	Adult inpatients
Pediatric hospitalist	Pediatric inpatients
Surgicalists	Surgical patients
Intensivists	ICU patients
Nocturnists	Night care for inpatients
Laborists	Inpatient obstetrical care

Figure 8.2 Hospital medicine subspecialties

There are barriers, though, that can impede this effectiveness, and you need to be aware of those. In this chapter, we'll look at what hospitalists do and how you can incorporate those activities into your flow toolkit. The benefits of programs that are successful at marrying hospital medicine with flow are abundant. (See Figure 8.3.) In fact, utilizing hospitalists who know how to hardwire flow provides hospitals a distinct competitive advantage as they seek to establish their position as the "high-quality, low-cost" provider of care in their market.

Length of stay reductions

Increased bed turns and capacity

Decreased cost per case

Fewer lab and imaging studies

Higher patient/family satisfaction

Higher HCAHPS scores

Improved quality measures

Core measure compliance

Improved Medical Staff satisfaction

Figure 8.3 Advantages of hospital medicine programs

AN OVERVIEW OF HOSPITALISTS

Simply put, hospitalists are physicians who work exclusively in an inpatient setting and focus on hospital medicine. The Society of Hospital Medicine describes this focus as "general medical care of hospitalized patients" and the primary patients served as "frail, elderly, and medically complex, with chronic diseases" (Society of Hospital Medicine, 2008).

However, in the ensuing years since the genesis of the specialty, hospitalists care for patients of every age and complexity with both acute and chronic diseases. Hospitalists increasingly care in consultation, or as the admitting physician, for general surgical or orthopedic patients, for example. When they are effective, hospitalists work with hospital staff to improve the general operations of the institution and to better the patient experience.

Benefits include greater patient safety, higher patient satisfaction, and lower levels of ED crowding. An essential point about hospitalists, and the most relevant to flow, is that they direct all aspects of care for patients admitted to the hospital. How effectively and efficiently they actually perform across the service transitions of patient care determines how well they hardwire flow.

The role of hospitalist developed in the 1990s as part of hospitals' efforts to increase efficiency and cost-effectiveness in response to changing conditions in the field. Rather than depend on the intermittent rounding of primary care physicians on their hospitalized patients, hospitals began to make use of physicians who worked only in the hospital full-time, and thus increased both efficiency and the quality of care.

A bonus of the growth of these programs is the opportunity to relieve primary care physicians of the task of rounding on patients in the hospital, allowing them to increase the efficiency and quality of care in their practices as well. In the mid-1990s, about 1,000 hospitalists worked in the field. By 2004, that number had risen to an estimated 13,000 physicians serving about 5.4 million patients (Society of Hospital Medicine 2008), and by 2010, the number of physicians had grown to more than 27,000 (Harbuck et al., 2012). Though hospitalists have varied and specialized medical backgrounds, about three-fourths come from general internal medicine training (Society of Hospital Medicine 2008). In addition to providing patient care, many teach and conduct research as well.

HOSPITALISTS AND THE ED

Hospitalists' most significant relationship in the facility is with the emergency department. Since a large percentage (typically 50% or more) of hospitals' patients enter from the ED—where bottlenecks often manifest most seriously—that relationship needs to be a good one for patient flow to be optimal. We might expect relations to be excellent, because the two types of physicians practice in a similar context and interact in their work to a high degree. They both work exclusively in a hospital setting and deliver a broad range of care rather than practice in an organ, system-based or skill-based specialty. An ED physician turns a patient over to the hospitalist, and theoretically they collaborate on their care.

The reality is often different. In part, the discrepancy between theory and practice results from the different focuses of the two types of physician. Emergency physicians concentrate on the immediate evaluation and treatment of patients with both common and severe illnesses, while hospitalists are more concerned with managing a continuum of care from admission to discharge.

Ideally, hospitalists create more efficient flow by effectively managing admissions and discharges, adding value for both hospital and patients. Poor patient flow can occur if hospitalists do not fully understand their role as part of the care continuum. The resulting lack of cooperation and collaboration between hospitalists and ED physicians can lead to bottlenecks in the ED and increase the number of walkaways (Patients who leave the ED to visit another hospital with a shorter wait).

DIFFERING PERSPECTIVES

Hospitalists and emergency physicians frequently fail to cooperate fully because they operate from different perspectives. Though many of their concerns coincide and they serve many of the same patients, they also operate differently, driven by different priorities and attitudes. ED physicians focus on operating swiftly, moving patients through the department quickly and into the hospital or on to discharge, and then moving on to the next patient.

They must make critical decisions quickly, both in the interest of operational efficiency and for effective treatment of many patients they encounter.

Focused as they are on the whole stay of a patient, hospitalists operate at a more deliberate pace and are prone to be more analytical. Treatment of many of their patients is a considered decision that is not quickly made. When physicians operate from these different perspectives, misalignment often occurs, resulting in prejudiced views of the other.

Emergency Medicine	Hospital Medicine
- Goals not aligned with hospitalist group	- Goals not aligned with E.D. goals
- Compensation based on volume and productivity	- Compensation is fixed and providers have average daily census limits
- ED physicians want to increase visits, fast track admissions	- Believe ED physicians are dumping patients on them
- Believe hospitalists refuse patients	- Hospitalist-centered admission process
Progress = Minutes	**Progress = Days!**

Figure 8.4 Difference between the mental models of emergency medicine and hospital medicine

Here's a typical experience: the ED doctor pages the hospitalist to admit a patient and expects the hospitalist to respond within 30 minutes, but the latter is caring for patients and doesn't arrive until later, then wants more tests, adding more time. Once those tests are completed, the ED doctor contacts the hospitalist again, who takes a while, again, to arrive, then reviews the test results and evaluates the patient to confirm the diagnosis. More time passes. In many cases, the theoretical 30 minutes from decision in the ED to admit to actual admission of the patient to the inpatient unit can take three hours or more, with a national average of nearly three and a half hours.

Such experiences and the differences in perspective can lead ED physicians to believe that hospitalists procrastinate in seeing emergency patients, generally want more data and more tests than necessary, and do not realize that the ED is short on beds and that bottlenecks are likely. For their part, hospitalists often believe that ED doctors request admission for patients who don't need it, don't conduct full evaluations, and don't supply all the information necessary for admission. Different perspectives are not the only source of misalignment. Two other factors can contribute to poor relationships:

Differing Incentives and Metrics. In many hospitals, the two types of physicians work for different groups, which use different incentives and measures of productivity. The differing incentives and metrics for the two groups often lead to conflicting motivations. ED doctors' performance is measured by efficiency—number and acuity of patients—and incentives are structured accordingly.

ED groups, as well, use number of patients who have left without treatment, boarding time, and patient satisfaction to measure performance. ED physicians must diagnose patients' conditions and determine where the patient should go next as quickly as possible to keep ED beds free for incoming patients.

Hospitalists, on the other hand, often have performance metrics and incentives based on the quality of their interactions with patients, and not on productivity or length of stay (LOS). Satisfaction matters, but the number of walkaways in the ED, for instance, or the number of patients moving through the system often doesn't affect the hospitalists. They thus have little explicit incentive to drop everything else and hurry to the ED.

Frequently, the result of these factors is silos; physicians in the two groups work independently, sometimes at cross-purposes, and relations between them can characterized by poor communication, minimal collaboration, mistrust, and even an adversarial atmosphere. Silos and the conditions that cause them lead to poor flow.

The admission process is inefficient, and boarding occurs in the ED as patients who should have already gone to inpatient units are still in the ED. The backups cascade throughout the hospital. What should be a tool for improving flow becomes instead an impediment to flow.

And yet data from Studer Group® clearly indicates that patient satisfaction in the ED is extremely closely tied to patient perception of the inpatient hospital experience, as measured by inpatient HCAHPS scores:

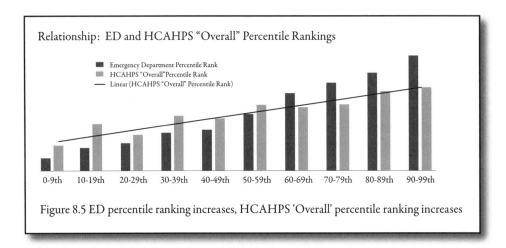

Figure 8.5 ED percentile ranking increases, HCAHPS 'Overall' percentile ranking increases

We simply must assure that we improve flow across these transitions or we will have no hope of hitting targeted patient satisfaction scores. So let's consider ways to reverse this outcome next. To begin, consider the overall role of the hospitalist in caring for hospitalized patients.

The hospitalist's role. A helpful analogy is to think of the hospitalist as the quarterback of inpatient care as the patient's journey unfolds. He or she is in the best position to expedite the patient's journey through the hospital:

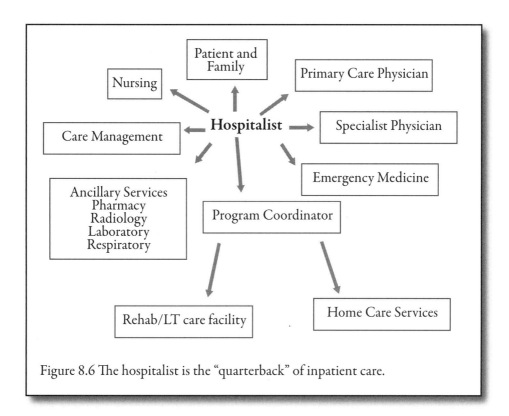

Figure 8.6 The hospitalist is the "quarterback" of inpatient care.

This hospital "quarterback" can often provide better care than would be the case in an uncoordinated process, since he or she has a view of the whole journey of the patient, can focus on what needs to be done, and can monitor that appropriate treatment occurs in a timely way.

To continue the quarterback analogy, the hospitalist coordinates efforts among many different "players," from patients and their families to ED physicians, primary care physicians, specialists, nurses, case managers, lab and radiology personnel, program coordinators, home care providers, long-term care providers, and rehabilitation personnel.

Once an ED doctor or primary care physician has determined that a patient needs admission, the hospitalist begins work, seeking to provide the appropriate care. Once the patient is admitted, the hospitalist monitors progress, supervises care each day of the patient's stay, coordinates planning for discharge and follow-up, and discharges the patient.

An effective hospitalist program has great potential for both improving the quality and timeliness of the patient's care and increasing the hospital's operational efficiency. These improvements lead to higher patient satisfaction and lower hospital costs. Some of the reasons why hospitalists can be highly effective are listed are:

- conducts patient rounding throughout the day,
- is available both immediately and constantly,
- operates under longer schedules (for better observation and understanding of patient's needs),
- coordinates necessary services across service transitions, and
- creates a more positive and unified environment for patients and families.

As with any other flow tool, when hospitals predict the demand for hospitalists' services and manage staffing to fit that demand, they are likely to improve flow significantly. With many full-service hospitals shifting to providing laboratory services, radiology, and other essential services 24 hours per day, effective 24-hour hospitalist programs, with staffing matched to predicted demand, will result in visibly better flow.

One other aspect of the hospitalist's role is highly important for both flow and relationship with the ED. The hospitalist plans, prepares for, and executes timely discharges of patients. For an effective hospitalist, this goal is in sight as soon as a patient is admitted into the hospital, and the hospitalist focuses on how to expedite care so that the patient is ready for discharge as soon as is appropriate. Well-planned, timely discharges help to reduce the length of inpatient stay as well as ensure appropriate care after discharge. They can also reduce the number of unnecessary readmissions.

Hospitalists are perhaps better positioned to realize this goal more than anyone else. They are also well positioned to monitor and make sure the process moves smoothly towards that goal. Hardwiring flow requires that metrics are in place to measure, in reality, how effective the hospitalists are at achieving these goals. In addition, a clear vision of success, the tools required to achieve the metrics, and accountability are necessary.

HANDING OFF THE BATON: TEAMS AND TEAMWORK

Probably nothing encapsulates the whole issue of smooth versus sluggish flow better than the relationship between the ED and hospitalists. Links between the ED and hospitalists are numerous, so increasing the impact of hospitalists on flow depends on strengthening those links.

The intersection between ED and hospitalists is one of the most critical for flow. Flow largely depends on the strength of their relationship. Many hospitals, though, struggle to integrate and align the work of hospitalists and emergency physicians. How these two groups work together has an enormous effect on patient care metrics, underscoring the importance of ensuring efficient teamwork between them.

There is probably no flow tool better than a good hospitalist program… if incentives of ED doctors and hospitalists are aligned; if hospitalists' pay is based on patient volume and length of stay; if adequate staffing is provided at peak hours and for peak loads; and if the two groups work cooperatively as a team.

But if these two groups aren't aligned, then nine times out of ten, flow will decrease. And if they are misaligned, what may seem to affect only one of the groups will ultimately affect both.

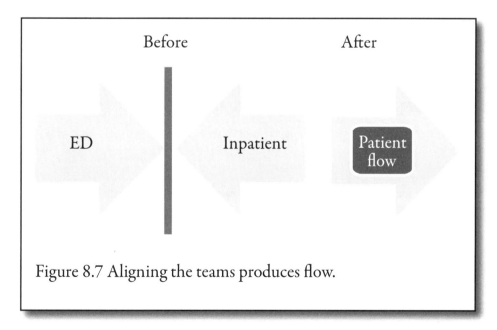

Figure 8.7 Aligning the teams produces flow.

The ideal is for seamless patient care from the ED to inpatient treatment and ultimately, to discharge. Some hospitals achieve this ideal. Doing so requires the two groups—ED staff and hospitalists—to work together to improve admission processes, communicate openly, share goals, and cultivate better relationships.

In an ideal, smoothly flowing process, the patient enters the ED and is evaluated; the ED physician and hospitalist collaborate in the admission process (using established, agreed-upon admission orders, criteria, and timelines); the patient enters an inpatient unit as quickly as possible under the hospitalist's care; and the hospitalist determines the further course of treatment. Figure 8.8 illustrates how this process should flow. This model is what hospitals should use as a guide and should aspire to put into practice.

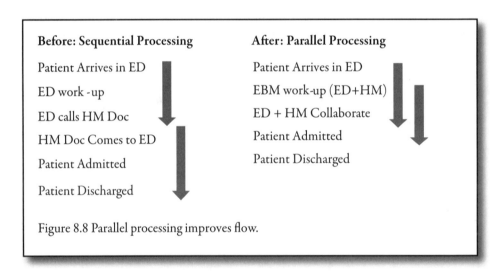

Figure 8.8 Parallel processing improves flow.

If your current atmosphere is less than ideal, here are some steps to take, ideally with both groups working together. First, observe the bed control process and revise it if necessary (see Chapter 6). Second, follow the progress of one or several patients from entry to the ED through to admission into inpatient units all the way to discharge. This step provides both groups with a visceral understanding of the processes and the patient's journey.

Third, ED staff should spend time with the hospitalist staff to observe and understand their work flows and habits. Fourth, obtain relevant data about processes, problems, and progress toward goals. With this foundation of experience and knowledge, the ED manager should discuss the hospitalist program separately with the appropriate hospital manager and the lead hospitalist. The aim of these conversations is to determine where the gap lies between current conditions and the desired working relationship between the two groups. These discussions should include examination of people, processes, and performance; incentives; and what is aligned or misaligned. Finally, the two groups should develop a plan to move forward together.

Two highly effective communication skills that help assure that patients and families understand the close and collegial working relationship between the ED and hospital medicine teams are "managing up" (Studer, 2008) and "rounding on next", (Mayer and Cates, 2014). "Managing up" assures that we are communicating that our transition of care is to colleagues and teammates who share our vision of excellence in clinical and service aspects. For example, the emergency physician may say to the patient:
"You will need to be admitted to the hospital. Fortunately, one of my colleagues, Dr. Martinez, is on today. She is one of our best and she will take great care of you and communicate with your primary care physician about your care."

Similarly, when the patient arrives on the inpatient unit, the hospitalist can also "manage up" the ED: "Hello, Mrs. Jones, I am Dr. Rodriquez and I have been fully briefed about you and am looking forward to taking care of you. I see you saw Dr. Mahaney in the ED. He's great, isn't he?"

"Rounding on next" is a disciplined and evidence-based program developed at BestPractices and EmCare where emergency physicians routinely visit patients they have admitted to the hospital medicine service. These are not clinical rounds, but rather a chance to reconnect with patients to see how they are doing.

"Rounding on next" is the single most powerful and underused strategy at our disposal. To use it, keep a log of admitted patients. The rounding goal is typically five patients per week (usually one at a time). You will often need ten names to get the five interviews. (Leave a card.) Use the key words, "I don't know if you remember, but I just wanted to check and see how you are doing."

Almost without exception, patients and their families are extremely pleased that emergency physicians (and nurses) have taken the time to come up to visit them. By far the most common response we hear on our "rounding on next" visits is, "Thanks for checking in on me. I was so sick in the emergency department that I didn't have the chance to thank you properly."

Managing up and "rounding on next" are two excellent ways of hardwiring hospital-wide flow that result in improved service transitions and higher HCAHPS scores. An additional program we have developed in EmCare's hospital medicine program is designed to assure that our patients are clearly and consistently informed regarding their care.

In our "information excellence" program, we provide notepads and pens at the patients' bedside, so they can write down their questions and concerns when they arise. These are typically centered around diagnosis, treatment, tests, medications, and progress (Figure 8.9).

Information Excellence

Diagnosis	What is my diagnosis?
Treatment	What is being done?
Tests	What tests and why?
Medications	What new medications?
Progress	When will I go home?

Figure 8.9 Notepads can be used so that hospital inpatients can write their questions down for the hospital medicine team

---

This allows the patient and family to record their questions real-time, so they are not dependent on raising the questions only when the nurse or doctor is in the room. They can be used as an adjunct to white-boards in that the patient can write their own questions down at the bedside. We have found it to be an effective tool to assure that patients have the information they need when they need it.

SMOOTHER FLOW UNDER
EFFECTIVE COLLABORATION

When hospitalists and ED doctors collaborate effectively, they produce constructive teamwork, an improved admission process, and greater communication. The easiest way to achieve this collaboration is to ensure a unified approach and defined governance structure for both emergency physicians and hospitalists. When the goals, reporting pathways, and incentives of both sets coincide, the two groups work together as one team more easily and their motivations are more likely to align.

If they are aligned, they will integrate their care from an overall perspective of the patient's journey through the hospital, focusing on how to optimally achieve the goal of discharging the patient. As a result, conflict diminishes and commitment to the team increases. Both sets of physicians aim at the goal of increasing value for the team and the hospital they serve.

One can go even further, integrating these two groups clinically, operationally, technically, and financially. The hospital benefits from improved patient flow and better care. Patients are more satisfied. Additional signs of improvement include faster bed turnover in the ED, decreased numbers of walkaways, and more efficient handling of a greater volume of patients. Value increases, and so does the hospital's profitability.

One management group can often more easily motivate physicians in both groups with incentives aimed at bringing them to work together for their common interest. As we saw earlier, hospitalists are likely not to concern themselves with such metrics as number of walkaways and number of patients moving through the system.

However, a unified management can use incentives for hospitalists that include measures of hospitalist productivity in number of daily encounters, for example. This could incorporate patient volume as a factor, as well as ED throughput time, reduced boarding, and decreased numbers of walkaways, thus aligning incentives and motivations of ED doctors and hospitalists.

While integrated management may be the most effective way to align the goals and work of the two groups of doctors, operating both types of service is a challenge for one company, and hospitals may not be able to implement such an arrangement. If they can't, they do not lose the opportunity to induce the two groups to work together. There are other ways, as we'll see next.

A UNIFIED, OVERALL APPROACH

Hospital administrators, along with ED and hospitalist program managers, can implement a program to smooth working relationships between the two groups so that they function as a team, which increases the effectiveness of both. Even without joint financial incentives, hospitalists and ED doctors can be motivated to work well together.

When they realize that a more coordinated approach based on seeing the overall journey of the patient through the hospital makes life easier and more pleasant for them, they are more inclined to take part willingly. And such an approach, effectively monitored and managed, does indeed make their lives easier and more pleasant.

One such initiative is the "Door-to-Discharge Program™" developed by EmCare. It coordinates the work of hospitalists and emergency physicians and has resulted in improved patient throughput (EmCare, 2011).

One of its key components is a "rapid admission process…designed to increase capacity by quickly moving patients from entry to treatment." Under this process, when a patient comes to the emergency department with "certain common medical conditions…and subsequently meets predefined criteria for those conditions, he or she is rapidly admitted to the hospital." The Door-to-Discharge Program thus builds coordination between hospitalists and emergency physicians, using established criteria and procedures to improve patient throughput.

Programs such as this one have drastically improved the movement of patients through the hospital. The Door-to-Discharge Program has notably improved conditions for patients, physicians, and the hospital. By 2010, it increased ED volume by 10 percent, decreased length of stay for adult patients from 6.5 days to under three days, increased physicians' daily patient encounters from 12 to 40, and increased ED throughput by 30 percent. It also "increased hospital capacity, decreased cost per case, and improved [the] case-mix index" (EmCare, 2011).

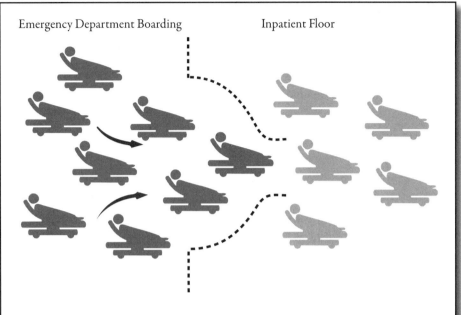

Figure 8.10 Before implementing a door-to-discharge system, there is a major bottleneck in getting patients out of the ED. Afterwards, this bottleneck is dramatically improved with smooth patient flow.

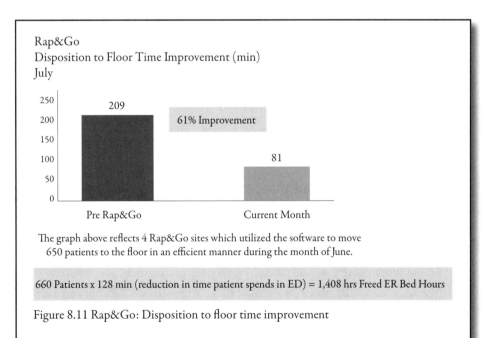

Rap&Go
Disposition to Floor Time Improvement (min)
July

The graph above reflects 4 Rap&Go sites which utilized the software to move 650 patients to the floor in an efficient manner during the month of June.

660 Patients x 128 min (reduction in time patient spends in ED) = 1,408 hrs Freed ER Bed Hours

Figure 8.11 Rap&Go: Disposition to floor time improvement

THE BEGINNING AND THE END

To most effectively improve collaboration and improve flow, any program must focus especially on two points. The first is admission from the ED to the inpatient units. As we've made clear (see Chapters 5 and 6), when ED staff and hospitalists cooperate, with predetermined triggering criteria and admission protocols, then patients flow more smoothly and quickly through the ED and into the inpatient units. So the processes involved in admission are critical for achieving collaboration between the two groups and efficient flow.

The second is discharges. As we noted earlier, a good hospitalist is ever mindful of the patient clinical course, expected timeline, and potential for discharge. That goal should guide the hospitalist's efforts. A hospitalist who is focused on getting the patient to the point of discharge is naturally going to focus on the best and most effective way to do so, and thus the best and most appropriate care.

And when patients flow smoothly through the hospital to their discharge, other patients can flow smoothly from the ED into the inpatient units. In focusing clearly on the patient's discharge and working appropriately toward that goal, the hospitalist is working in conjunction with the ED's best interests.

CULTURE AND LEADERSHIP

To achieve better patient flow, hospitals often will have to change the prevailing culture. Processes often need to change, and personnel need to adjust to new conditions. Such culture change requires excellent, committed leadership. Great leaders will motivate people in the system to willingly help implement the necessary changes in order to reduce or remove bottlenecks, increase teamwork and commitment, and provide excellent care to patients.

Hospital leaders must focus both the hospitalist and ED groups on how changes are in the best interest of each group, their patients, and the hospital as a whole, particularly when those doctors report to different management groups. They must facilitate understanding about how collaboration expedites the admission process, moves patients quickly and efficiently, and concentrates everyone's attention on what best serves those patients. Help them understand how their cooperation will have a major impact on flow and the quality of the care that the hospital provides.

BENEFITS OF SUCCESSFUL HOSPITALIST PROGRAMS

When hospitalists are effective, they are working smoothly and cooperatively with the ED and other departments, providing patients with high quality care, and moving those patients toward discharge. The improvements are notable for the hospital. These include reduced boarding in the ED, better relationships between staff members, and improved bed turns.

Not surprisingly, one recent study identified a link between hospitalist programs and improved patient flow in the emergency department. Simitha R. Chadaga and others compared 1,901 patients boarded at the Denver Health Emergency Department before inception of the institution's hospitalist program with 1,828 patients after the program was implemented and found notable improvements in boarding time.

Specifically, the hospitalist program resulted in "boarded patients being seen by a hospitalist an average of two hours and nine minutes earlier than they previously would have been seen by a physician" and diversion resulting from a full ED "decreased by 27 percent" (Chadaga et al., 2012). The Denver program also resulted in many financial benefits, including reduced loss of revenue from overcrowding.

In considering benefits of good hospitalist programs, we should not overlook the most basic. Improving flow is not an end goal in itself. We want to create smoother flow in order to provide better care to patients. That's the ultimate goal and the primary reason we look for ways to increase operational efficiency. One demonstrated aspect of hospitalist programs is their potential to improve patient safety and the quality of care.

A study by the Mayo Clinic, for example, found notable improvements in patient safety in cases co-managed with hospitalists. Specifically, "61 percent of patients co-managed by hospitalists and orthopedic surgeons were discharged with no complications, compared to 51.2 percent managed by orthopedic surgical teams alone. Approximately 30.2 percent of patients co-managed by hospitalists experienced minor complications, compared to 44.3 percent of patients managed by orthopedic surgical teams" (Society of Hospital

Medicine 2008). Reducing the number of complications improves overall patient safety in the hospital.

We may tend to see hospitalists as generalists, but in fact, they are specialists: in care within the hospital. That is all they focus on. Because hospitalists are in place for longer periods and are more easily accessible to patients than primary care providers or specialists, they provide more attentive and flexible care, leading to higher patient satisfaction. They are able to round at various times throughout the day, and can modify their rounding to better fit the needs of patients and their families.

THE HOSPITALIST'S CRITICAL ROLE

Since their beginning in the 1990s, hospitalist programs have grown rapidly. Hospital medicine is "considered by many to be the fastest-growing medical specialty in the United States" (Hamm et. al, 2014). That growth is no surprise. The many benefits a good hospitalist program provides patients and hospitals are clear. An effective hospitalist helps create better flow, particularly through coordinating admissions with the ED and planning and managing discharges. A good hospitalist also provides high quality patient care. Both aspects of effective hospital medicine contribute significantly to better flow of patients through a hospital and a more satisfying journey for those patients.

Through their role as directors of overall care for hospitalized patients, hospitalists have great potential for expediting that care and making it more effective, more efficient, and faster. And because hospitalists are "trained to treat all aspects of the patient experience, the 'whole patient,' including the environmental and social aspects" (Hamm et al., 2014) and are in place for many hours during the day and many days during the patient's stay, they are finely tuned toward the patient's needs and well placed to tend to them. They therefore have great potential for dramatically improving overall quality of care for hospitalized patients.

HARDWIRING FLOW™ FOCUS:
HOSPITAL MEDICINE AND FLOW

- The development of the specialty of hospital medicine has been a disruptive innovation in shifting the responsibility for inpatient care to a group whose practice is solely focused on inpatient care.
- The evolution from "hospitalists" to "specialists in hospital medicine" is that the latter are fluent in and committed to the principles of hardwiring hospital-wide flow.
- This evolution is critical for hospitals seeking to become the "high quality, low cost provider of care" in the marketplace, which gives them distinct competitive advantage.
- The most important source of service transitions and queues for hospital medicine physicians is the emergency department. The "baton must be passed" effectively and efficiently during the course of these transitions.
- For a number of reasons, the mental models and perspectives of hospital medicine and emergency medicine physicians are fundamentally different. Aligning strategic incentives between them is essential.
- ED satisfaction and inpatient HCAHPS scores are tightly correlated, illustrating the importance of this transition.
- The hospital medicine physician is the "quarterback" of inpatient care, and can be a bottleneck if not trained and incentivized properly.
- Seamless patient care from the ED to the inpatient units and throughout the inpatient stay requires using parallel processing, not sequential processing.
- Two of the most effective communication skills in this regard are "Managing Up" and "Rounding on Next."
- Once the patient is admitted, there must be a clear and effective way for patients to communicate their questions, using white boards or notepads.
- Evidence-based clinical protocols between the ED and hospital medicine groups are a critical way to assure that value is added, waste is reduced, and reliability is improved throughout the process.
- In our experience, these programs reduce decision to admit to bed placement times from 3.5 hours to 78 minutes, on average, which creates substantial capacity for the hospital.

- This requires a fundamental cultural change to assure that the imprimatur of the hospital's leadership is on hardwiring flow into the hospital medicine service.

CHAPTER 9

USING REAL-TIME DEMAND AND CAPACITY MANAGEMENT

by Kirk Jensen, MD and Thom Mayer, MD

Let's begin with a sample scenario: Facing increasing crowding, a hospital embarks on a project to improve flow throughout all of its units. It forms a flow committee and introduces flow concepts to the various units. The committee makes use of the flow tools we've described in earlier chapters, tracking historical data and making predictions about demand.

On a particular day, the critical care unit, using these predictions, prepares to receive eight patients it anticipates will arrive. Instead, 12 patients need beds in the unit, a number that historical data showed as unlikely for this day of the week in this season. As a result, the unit doesn't have beds for all of them. Some patients have to board in the ED, and delays begin to build throughout the system. What went wrong?

Actually, nothing…all the flow tools are useful and valuable. This hospital's approach, though, lacks a component we address in this chapter: real-time demand-capacity management (RTDC)). You've heard the old saying "the devil is in the details." That principle applies here as well. RTDC is an essential part of improving flow in the daily operations of the hospital.

Throughout earlier chapters, we've emphasized coordination throughout the hospital and breaking down silos, not focusing solely within a unit, but thinking more broadly of the whole system. That advice applies in regard to RTDC, too, but in this case, work must begin by focusing in detail on the unit level and then working out from there. (It's important to recognize that the work initially begins at the unit level but must be coordinated hospital-wide). While we've emphasized turning to the past to uncover patterns in the data, here, we will be more focused on the present…on what's going on *now*.

To understand the importance of keeping track of current conditions, recall our discussion of constraints and bottlenecks. What is a constraint one day may not be a constraint the next, and on the other hand, what was not one yesterday may be one causing a bottleneck to form today. Bottlenecks can shift in complex branching systems, so monitoring what is occurring in individual units, as well as the hospital as a whole, every day is critical to achieving smooth flow.

THE PROCESS: A FOUR-STEP SEQUENCE AND REFINEMENT

The RTDC process can be best described through its four sequential steps, shown here:

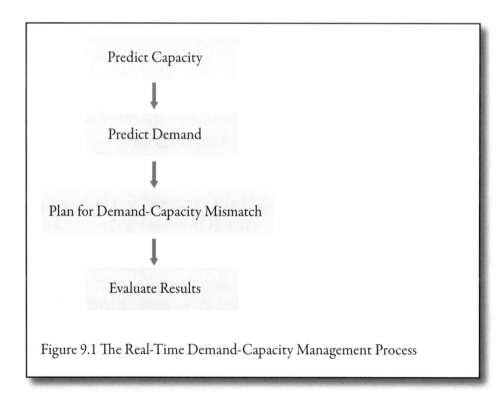

Figure 9.1 The Real-Time Demand-Capacity Management Process

The steps are straightforward and easy to grasp; but again, the details within each step are what really matter, and there are a number of details to take into account. Simply put, to match demand and capacity in real time, a unit predicts capacity (step one) then predicts demand (step two).

If those two match or if predicted capacity exceeds predicted demand, assuming your predicted discharges match, your unit is ahead of the game. But if the predicted demand is greater than the predicted capacity, then you need a plan to deal with the anticipated mismatch (step three). Regardless of expectations and actual results, the fourth and final step is evaluating the previous ones.

Evaluation leads to refinements, and the process repeats. Repeated refinements will lead to increasing effectiveness in the daily management of matching capacity with demand. So while the basic process may be simple in its structure, the continual refinement adds complexity; a key word is *adaptation*. You predict, plan, then see what worked and ask why. You see what didn't work and ask why not; then you adapt to what you've discovered, and so on.

Real-time demand-capacity management itself is an outgrowth of initial interest in improving flow—and what hospitals learned from early efforts to do so. In 2004, The Joint Commission developed standards for managing patient flow, which called for hospital leaders to come up with plans to more effectively manage flow and reduce impediments to it. Many hospitals did respond by forming flow committees and initiating projects to improve flow.

However, in many cases, flow did not significantly improve. We've identified three reasons based on our experience for the underlying the lack of progress:

1. Improvement projects often were not connected to true bottlenecks holding up flow at the time.
2. Changes improved conditions in one or more units but did not optimize flow throughout the hospital.
3. Hospitals tried to implement more projects than they had the resources to devote to them.

In many cases, a hospital would come up with a plan to improve flow, by adding a discharge lounge or a discharge nurse, for example. But because such projects addressed only *one* aspect of flow, and often one that wasn't a critical bottleneck or *today's* bottleneck, they did not improve flow throughout the hospital.

As a result of the lack of progress in many hospitals, the Institute for Healthcare Improvement in 2006 introduced the Real Time Demand Capacity Management approach to improving flow and tested the method in its Improving Hospital-wide Patient Flow Community. This community consisted of a group of hospitals involved in working to improve flow.

One of the hospitals in the community that took the lead in testing the RTDC approach was the University of Pittsburgh Medical Center (UPMC) at Shadyside (Resar et al., 2011). As a preliminary step before introducing changes, the flow team at Shadyside assessed the daily hospital-wide bed meeting and noticed two important characteristics of the meeting:

- It usually did not produce a specific plan to meet patient demand that day.
- A "discharge" or "available bed" in one unit did not necessarily mean the same thing in another unit.

Effective unit-based huddles and hospital-wide bed meetings are an essential part of successful RTDC. The regular hospital-wide meeting at Shadyside took place at 8:30 am. As the flow team began its work on RTDC, it held a new, additional meeting following the regular one, which continued to function as it had previously; this new meeting consisted of managers of a couple of units involved in testing the pilot project and the bed coordinator as well as the "RTDC Project " team leader.

The meeting was limited to reports from the unit managers on how many available beds and discharges they expected by 2 pm., as well as the number of admissions expected by 2 pm. They also then reviewed predictions from the previous day. As the team began testing the RTDC, the pilot units each started holding a unit-based huddle early in the morning prior to the regular hospital-wide meeting. These meetings included the unit manager, case manager, unit secretary, and specific nurses whose patients were being considered. The meetings last about 10 minutes. Each potential discharge was discussed along with the action needed to ensure the discharge happened when expected.

As hospitals have gained experience with this method, a unit-based huddle in a typical unit might also include a social worker, physical therapist, and home health coordinator. The purpose of the unit bed huddle is to finalize a unit's prediction of discharges before 2 pm that day. The time 2 pm. was selected through experience. (If capacity and demand are matched by that time, then demand-capacity mismatches that arise after 2 pm in a hospital can often be avoided.)

Once multiple units have engaged in real-time management, the hospital-wide bed meeting can be at its most useful. It typically includes the nursing supervisor and other nursing leaders from units, case manager, and representatives from the post-anesthesia care unit (PACU), ED, radiology, cardiology, catheterization lab, infection control, housekeeping, and transportation.

No new format for meetings, though, will be effective in the long run if various units do not agree on the meaning of the terms used and if they do not understand and communicate effectively with each other. This process of real-time management must establish clarity and shared understanding by defining the terms from the outset.

Here are the definitions the Shadyside team introduced:

- *Available bed*—a bed that has been cleaned, for which staff is present, and which is ready for a patient to occupy.
- *Discharge*—a patient who has left a bed and will not return to it.
- *Capacity*—number of discharges plus available beds.
- *Admission*—a patient who has been physically placed in a bed.

With this clarity and the format of the bed meetings in place, a hospital is ready to undertake the four steps to RTDC.

PREDICTING CAPACITY

The first step, predicting capacity, is the primary purpose of the bed huddle. Projecting expected capacity begins with those in the unit bed huddle listing potential discharges. In its simplest form, this list is a piece of paper with handwritten names. At Shadyside, the case manager in the pilot units would compile a list of potential discharges for the next day, posted at the nurses' station. Evening nurses updated the list after physicians had completed rounds and also upon noting changes in patients' conditions.

An accurate discharge list, ideally, was ready by 7 am the next day. The form such reporting takes can also be more sophisticated. At Northwest

Community Hospital near Chicago, the flow team developed a spreadsheet on bed status, which units update with their own reports. The overall spreadsheet is visible electronically at the hospital-wide bed meeting each morning, giving a projection of bed status that day (Weintraub et al., 2010). The spreadsheet is on a shared drive in the hospital's computer system, so different departments are aware of capacity in real time.

Some important points in predicting capacity are to base these projections on what is realistically likely to happen, not on what ideally should happen, and to predict one concrete number, not a range of numbers. The goal is to predict available beds by 2 pm; accurate predictions and sufficient capacity for that time period will alleviate typical overcrowding later in the day.

And the predictions should be *specific*, with individual patients' names tied to concrete actions that are necessary to achieve discharge, and linked to specific individuals to act by a designated time. The morning bed huddles should address these questions:

- Which patients will be discharged today?
- What needs to be done for those discharges to occur?
- Who will perform the necessary actions?
- When do they need to complete those actions by?
- Can the patient be discharged by 2 pm?

Figure 9.2 presents a sample discharge worksheet. The final column—whether discharge occurred by 2 pm—can be filled in later and used for evaluating the accuracy of predictions. This column should be completed during the huddle discussion on the unit. It allows the unit to know the number of discharges by 2 pm. If there is a need to search for additional discharges through escalation of discharge criteria, review the patients originally identified as "no's" on this list.

Patient Name	Room Number	Need for Discharge	Person Responsible	Time	2 p.m. Discharge (Y/N)

Figure 9.2 Discharge Prediction Worksheet

Evaluation of prediction accuracy is a key step for refining predictions so that they become increasingly on target. The Shadyside redesigned hospital-wide bed meeting in conjunction with the pilot project evaluated accuracy by recording whether the specific patients projected for discharge by 2 pm were in fact discharged by that time. The goal was to continuously improve the accuracy of the discharge prediction to reach 80 percent. Figure 9.3 shows what happened: the accuracy rate climbed quickly; within two years, the goal was adjusted to 85 percent, and units mostly met that higher target.

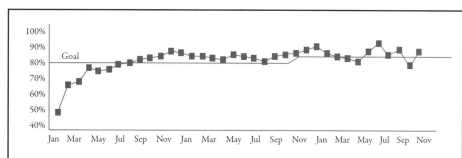

Figure 9.3 The accuracy of discharge predictions by month, 2007–2009, University of Pittsburgh Medical Center, Shadyside

Combining a report on bed status, as in the Northwest Community practice, with a projection of discharged patients gives the expected capacity. If the status report shows that two beds are available this morning and the bed huddle predicts four discharges by 2 pm, then the expected capacity by 2 pm is six. Northwest "refined and re-refined to improve the prediction formula through repeated testing and learning from inaccurate predictions" (Weintraub et al., 2010).

At first, facing some reluctance to predict discharges for patients who lacked written discharge orders, the Northwest flow team emphasized to staff that the forecasts were predictions and incorrect ones did not cause problems. (As we note, inaccurate predictions help flow teams learn to make more accurate ones.) Experienced nurses realized when patients were ready to go home.

PREDICTING DEMAND

Knowing how many patients and what types will be coming to particular units requires coordinating with other units. Historical data/trending is valuable for ED and direct admissions. (Elective procedure demand—e.g., catheterizations/ORs—is best obtained from schedules.) The OR, with scheduled surgeries, and PACU are other likely sources of admissions.

Historical data on admissions are helpful, though Winetraub and colleagues noted that in the Northwest Community experience, "collecting months of historical data on admissions is usually not helpful; [the] previous few weeks usually is sufficient" (Weintraub et al., 2010). Because the ED is such a significant source of admissions to other units, it needs to take part in those units' formulation of predictions.

At Northwest Community Hospital, each unit coordinator can see the ED's electronic tracking board, which helps project demand later in the day. Special situations—where patients are being held in the ED in the early morning because beds are not available, for example—can be added to the historical prediction of demand.

As with predicting capacity, prediction of demand occurs at the morning bed meetings, and at both the individual units' huddles and the hospital-wide meeting. The hospital-wide meeting is important in this step as a central station for coordinating communication and actions across units. And as with predicting capacity, flow teams and unit staff should test their predictions, assess them, and refine their methods, learning from inaccurate predictions.

PLAN FOR MISMATCHES

So, you've gathered information, compiled a list of available beds and known admissions, and projected likely discharges and likely admissions. The results tell you that you will probably face a shortage of beds by 2 pm. Now what?

Now it's time to form a plan to deal with the demand-capacity mismatch. Here again, specificity and detail are essential components. Vague statements such as "we will try to get another discharge" do not help. The plan should focus on specific patients and specific actions. For example, Mrs. Jones can be discharged at 10 am, but her husband cannot pick her up until 4 pm; someone in the unit becomes responsible for contacting a transportation company and arranging transport at 10:30 am. Or: Mr. Smith is ready to go home, but he needs medication for which there is not yet a prescription; someone becomes responsible for making sure the prescription gets to the pharmacy by noon.

Plans should not be based on an abstract possible action in response to general situations; they should be based on what is occurring in specific units with specific patients on this day. In the early years of responding to the Joint Commission standards, many hospitals implemented such methods as using color-coded indicators (e.g., green, yellow, red) to indicate when units were approaching full capacity, with hospital-wide attempts to mitigate the crowding.

The problem with such systems is that they are reactive, calling for action when units are already stressed. Additionally, they typically call for generic actions throughout the hospital. RTDC, on the other hand, is proactive, anticipating mismatches and detailing specific actions in a particular unit tied to conditions as they are developing that day.

Because of the need for specificity and monitoring, the plan should be written. In fact, in our experience, staff members in units tend to feel more invested in a written plan. Additionally, evaluation of success is easier with a written plan. As with predicting capacity, the specific patient, action, person responsible, and time frame should appear in the written plan. Staff attending the bed huddle should concentrate first on overall time frames, such as 8 a.m. to 2 p.m., and then refine the plan by attending to specific details, as in the examples above.

In regard to planning how to manage anticipated demand-capacity mismatches, the individual unit and the hospital as a whole have particular roles to play. Each unit needs to formulate its own plan, based on the specific details we've outlined here. In formulating the plan, managers need to involve frontline staff members. They are better acquainted with specific details of particular patients' cases and conditions in the unit than managers, and their involvement is likely to lead to a more accurate, more effective plan.

But a unit may be unable to plan effectively when needs exceed its own resources, and at this point, system-level planning becomes necessary. At Shadyside, the flow team considers any resource shared by more than one unit, such as lab testing and x-rays, a system-level resource. Thus, a system-level plan (or adjustment to a unit plan) might include coordinating with the director of the radiology department to expedite an x-ray for a specific patient.

Suppose a unit needs two additional discharges before noon to manage a projected shortage of beds. A system-level response developed at the morning bed meeting might be a request for the nursing supervisor to contact a hospitalist to round on that unit first that morning.

Our description of system-level planning here implies several considerations for the hospital wide bed meeting. Each unit's predictions of capacity and demand and plans to manage mismatches should be displayed. Participants in the meeting should focus on determining which units need plans, whether those plans seem adequate, whether any require system level actions, and if so, what specific actions are needed and who specifically should carry them out, and specifically by when. And as with unit plans, the system wide plan should be in written form. Figure 9.4 provides a sample of a worksheet for this purpose:

Unit	Available Beds	Discharges	Discharges by 2pm	Admissions	Admissions by 2pm	Surplus or Deficit	Plan

Figure 9.4 A system-level worksheet for managing demand-capacity mismatches

EVALUATE THE PLAN

For those people involved in the unit meetings and the hospital-wide meeting, once they've developed plans, their work is not done. The final step is equally as important as the others: evaluating the plans and how well they worked, or did not work. As with the other components of real-time demand-capacity management, this step happens daily. Each day, unit personnel involved in the process should review the plan from the day before. At Shadyside, each unit asks this question:

Did what we plan to happen really happen?

If the unit has a written form similar to the system worksheet in Figure 9.4 but tailored to it, it has a tool for evaluation ready at hand. If the plan did not enable the unit to manage the mismatch, the unit team should examine the adjustments called for in the plan to learn how to produce a better plan the next day, and then evaluate that next plan to learn how to improve it.

The accuracy of predictions of capacity and demand should also be evaluated. At Shadyside, participants in the project realized when they evaluated their plans how much easier recognizing why plans did not work is when the actions called for become more specific. When plans work, noting which actions made them work and why is equally useful in learning and adjusting day by day.

GETTING RESULTS

The Shadyside experience illustrates how effective implementing the methods of real time management can be. The flow team measured various indicators of flow before and after the project began and found clear evidence of improvement. For example, in regard to flow between units, overnight holding of patients in the PACU that had been occurring weekly was eliminated. Transfer times between the CT ICU and general inpatient rooms dropped from more than 100 minutes to less than 70 minutes within two years. Additionally, the percentage of patients who left without being seen in the ED dropped from 1.5 to 0.5.

Figure 9.5 shows how the aggregate length of stay in the hospital—which had been steadily increasing because of overcrowding—declined once the project began:

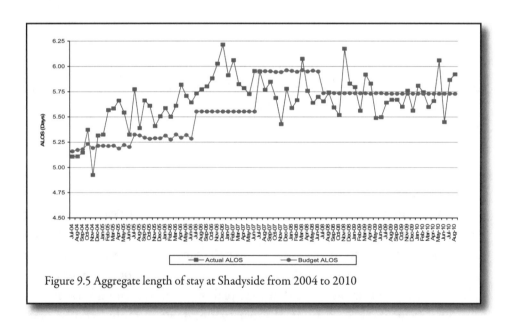

Figure 9.5 Aggregate length of stay at Shadyside from 2004 to 2010

Evaluating the success of plans has another benefit in addition to learning and fine tuning future predictions and planning. In the course of evaluating the success or failure of the plans, flow teams uncover specific barriers to patient flow, in that particular hospital. They also determine which barriers are common and frequent and which are not. They then know where to focus their efforts in future flow improvement projects. Making barriers visible, where they might not have been grasped or may have been poorly understood before, often leads to quick, targeted changes that can remove those barriers. Like resistance and aerobic training, the more you do it, the better you become, leading to impressive gains over time.

HARDWIRING FLOW™ FOCUS: USING REAL-TIME DEMAND-CAPACITY MANAGEMENT TO IMPROVE FLOW

- While flow is a complex adaptive system, real-time demand capacity (RTDC) management begins at the unit level and then builds out to address system implications and ramifications.
- Three reasons underlie the lack of progress in hardwiring flow over the years: (1) Improvement projects often did not connect to true bottlenecks holding up flow at the time; (2) Changes improved conditions in one or more units, but did not optimize flow throughout the hospital; and (3) hospitals tried to implement more projects than they had the resources to devote to them.
- The four steps of RTDC management are simple, but the devil is in the details with respect to how each step is implemented, and in assuring that the definitions are used accurately and consistently. The steps are to first predict capacity then predict demand. Next, address demand-capacity mismatches. Finally, continuously adapt and refine processes.
- Morning bed huddles at the unit and system levels are an integral part of RTDC.
- Definitions matter immensely if RTDC management is to work, including: *available bed, discharge, capacity,* and *admission.*
- Many instances of failure occur when different hospital units assume that they have the same definitions when they do not!

- Predicting expected capacity begins with those in the unit bed huddle listing potential discharges. The morning bed huddles should address six important questions.
- Once multiple units have engaged in real-time management, the hospital-wide bed meeting can be very useful.
- As with predicting capacity, prediction of demand occurs at the morning bed meetings, at both the individual units' huddles and the hospital-wide meeting. The hospital-wide meeting is important in this step as a central station for coordinating communication and actions across units.
- Planning for demand-capacity mismatches requires a detailed, specific, and written plan. "We will try to expedite discharges" isn't sufficient. "John will call by 10 a.m. to get a physical therapy appointment for Mr. Smith by noon so he can be discharged by 2 p.m." is what is needed.
- Formulating the plan with input by frontline staff members is important, as is evaluation of the plan to assess whether what was planned actually occurred.
- Continuously re-evaluating and adapting the RTDC plans and their outcomes allow for understanding common causes of constraints, bottlenecks, and both value-added and non-value added variation.

Chapter 10

Hardwiring Critical Care Flow

by Thom Mayer, MD, Jason Vourlekis, MD, and Kirk Jensen, MD

Critical care is the provision of life-saving interventions to patients at high risk of immediate, life-threatening deterioration, typically due to major organ failure. While most critical care is provided in the Intensive Care Unit (ICU), critical care is initially provided outside the ICU, either in the ED when the patient first presents to the hospital, the operating room in a trauma requiring emergency surgery, the medical floor for a rapid response or "Code Blue", or even in the patient's home when the Emergency Medical Services (EMS) team arrives and begins cardiopulmonary resuscitation for sudden cardiac death.

Similar to our insight regarding ED Fast Tracks, the same is true of critical care: "Critical care is not a noun; it is a verb." Thus, critical care is the highly evidence-based provision of care to profoundly sick patients and is something we *do* for the good of the patient, not simply a *place* where that care occurs. Further, as we discuss creative options to improve capacity, it becomes even more clear that it is the care provided, not just where it is provided that is important.

> Critical care is the highly evidence-based provision of care to
> profoundly sick patients and is something we *do* for the good
> of the patient, not simply a *place* where that care occurs.

Nonetheless, under "normal" conditions where capacity exceeds or meets demand, critically ill patients, "the sickest of the sick" are cohorted in the

ICU. Critical care adds value since we take desperately ill and injured patients and steadily, if sometimes slowly, take them from the "horizontal to the vertical" as we seek to return them to health and independence.

Conversely, value also can be added by providing frank, compassionate assessments of the potential for recovery to patients and their loved ones and at times, by making decisions to limit or even remove therapies and allow natural death when this best serves the patient's pre-stated healthcare goals (typically expressed via a living will or through a medical proxy).

In EDs and critical care units, it is increasingly recognized that a protocol-guided approach to palliative care is no longer a luxury, but a necessity (Cornell et al., 2010; Nelson, 2010; Norton, 2007). Additional palliative care resources for critical care units are available at http://www.capc.org/ipal/ipal-icu/monographs-and-publications.

Critical care and ICU care, by its very nature, is multi-disciplinary and is most effective when flow is maximized through a combination of efficient teamwork and the elimination of waste. Teamwork is essential to good ICU care and begins with the first signal of a possible admission. Each team member plays a "critical" role in the management of a patient, which is determined by the care plan.

BUNDLES OF FLOW ENHANCE FLOW

Technical advances in the care of the ICU patient have been nothing less than stunning, and are clear examples of the value of evidence-based medicine. (Chalfin et al., 2007; Hall, 2012). Work by the Institute of Healthcare Improvement (IHI) Idealized Design of the Intensive Care Unit (IDICU) project developed the concept of "bundles" of care, which are small sets of evidence-based interventions for defined patient populations in specific care settings. When implemented together, they have resulted in significantly better outcomes than when implemented individually (Resar et al., 2012).

Bundles also reinforce the multi-disciplinary nature of critical care and enhance flow by ensuring that each member of the care has a defined role that serves as an important link in the chain. At Inova Fairfax Medical Center, the ventilator bundle ensures that a nurse carries out a daily patient awakening (i.e., spontaneous awakening trial or SAT) based on predetermined patient criteria.

If the patient "passes" this test, the nurse passes the baton to the respiratory therapist to perform a spontaneous breathing trial (SBT). If passed, then the physician is contacted with the information and the request for an order to extubate the patient. By automating these processes, efficiency—or flow—is enhanced and waste—particularly the time waiting for a physician to round and provide patient orders for the day—is eliminated.

Therefore, bundles provide value in many different ways. These include: defining the goals of care for a disease state; standardizing care for a disease process; and frequently clarifying roles and responsibilities.

1. Elevation of the head of the bed to between 30-45 degrees

2. Daily "sedation vacations" and assessment of readiness to wean and extubate

3. Peptic ulcer disease prophylaxis

4. Deep venous thrombosis (DVT) prophylaxis

5. Daily oral care with chlorhexidine

Figure 10.1 IHI ventilator or 'bundle'

1. Mandatory ultrasound-guided placement

2. Hand hygiene

3. Maximal barrier precautions

4. Chlorhexidine skin antisepsis

5. Optimal catheter site selection with avoidance of the femoral vein in adults

6. Daily review of line necessity with prompt removal of unnecessary lines

Figure 10.2 Central line bundle

Surviving Sepsis Campaign Bundles

To be completed within 3 hours:

1. Measure lactate level

2. Obtain blood cultures prior to administration of antibiotics

3. Administer broad spectrum antibiotics

4. Administer 30 mL/kg crystalloid for hypotension or lactate ≥4mmol/L

To be completed within 6 hours:

5. Apply vasopressors (for hypotension that does not respond to initial fluid resuscitation) to maintain a mean arterial pressure (MAP) ≥65mm Hg.

6. In the event of persistent arterial hypotension despite volume resuscitation (septic shock) or initial lactate ≥4mmol/L (36mg/dL)
     -Measure central venous pressure (CVP)*
     -Measure central venous oxygen saturation (Scvo$_2$)*

7. Remeasure lactate if initial lactate was elevated*

*Targets for quantitative resuscitation included in the guidelines are CVP of ≥8 mm Hg, Scvo$_2$ of ≥70%, and normalization of lactate

Figure 10.3 Surviving sepsis bundle

The concept of bundles has spread rapidly, to the point that virtually every ICU currently uses some form of bundles to guide protocols for patient care. These are classic examples of using an evidence-based approach to add value and eliminate waste by improving reliability in ICU patients.

With five percent of patients consuming up to 80 to 85 percent of resources (often in the last days/months of life in ICUs), assessing value added versus eliminating waste is at the core of resource utilization in critical care as we seek to become the high quality, low cost provider of care. Further, we are striving to improve the costs of poor ICU flow, which cut across every dimension of patient care. These include efforts to improve safety through reduced errors, attain high reliability, increase patient satisfaction, provide a better patient experience, improve employee satisfaction, demonstrate more efficient resource utilization, and reduce the reputational cost of poorly managed care.

But, just as we have advanced the horizons of possibility in clinical care, there have also been important advances in Evidence-Based Leadership[SM] concepts driving improved flow in ICUs across the country. The ability to lead and manage the resources of the ICU, its team members, and the technology which supports them in ways that increase value and reduce waste is the source of an emerging literature based on innovative approaches (O'Brien et al., 2013; McCauley and Irwin, 2006; Seymour and Kahn, 2012).

Let us turn to a deeper look at how these approaches are being utilized in each of the seven Hardwiring FlowTM strategies that we outlined earlier.

1. DEMAND-CAPACITY MANAGEMENT (DCM)

Similar to the ED, ICU leaders are beginning to embrace and adopt the principles of demand-capacity management early, as they seek to hardwire flow in their units. Because critical care units have a fixed number of beds with fairly clear staffing patterns, the DCM questions are both clear and largely answerable and predictable over time. While overutilization is largely an economic and management responsibility, underutilization is largely a medical one, which in many cases can affect outcomes.

Who's coming? Where do these patients come from?

When are they coming? Arrival times are largely predictable

What are they going to need? How sick are they? What resources do they need? ICU Admitting Criteria

Are we going to have it? Matching their demands with our capacity

What will we do if we don't? What are our surge capacity plans and are they effective? Have they been effective in the past? What needs to be improved?

Figure 10.4 ICU demand capacity questions

Who's coming? ICU flow lends itself well to the input-throughput-output model of hardwiring flow. The inputs are the sources of ICU patients who are admitted to the unit, which include: ED, operating suite, transfers (e.g., internal, within the hospital floors, IMC, PACU) and external (transfers from other hospitals). Transfers may come from within the hospital or from outside hospitals lacking ICU resources.

Given both the cost and scarcity of ICU beds as a resource, most medical centers require that potential ICU patients meet predetermined admitting criteria. Such criteria typically are based on historical admitting patterns and informed by published guidelines from professional organizations such as the Society for Critical Care Medicine (American College of Medicine Critical Care Medicine, 1999).

Many organizations also follow either the McKesson Interqual Level of Care Criteria or the Milliman guidelines for ICU admission, both of which serve as screening tools for utilization review and case management. As the era of electronic medical records and real time metrics evolves, the use of patient acuity scoring systems to risk stratify and calculate disease-specific 30-day mortality in real time will also help determine which patients most need and would benefit from ICU admission (Seymour and Khan, 2012).

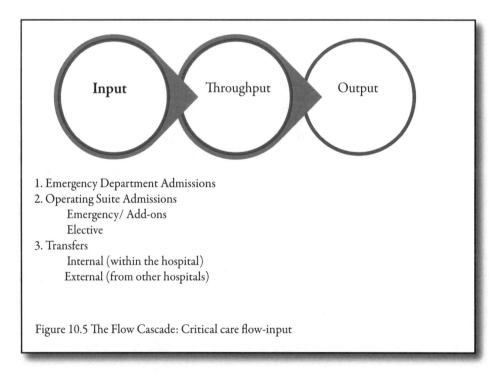

1. Emergency Department Admissions
2. Operating Suite Admissions
    Emergency/ Add-ons
    Elective
3. Transfers
    Internal (within the hospital)
    External (from other hospitals)

Figure 10.5 The Flow Cascade: Critical care flow-input

Random variation adds to the complexity of managing input. We have previously noted that variation is intrinsic in healthcare and that, while we strive to reduce variation when and where it adds value and reduces waste, the paradox of variation is that, in some cases, increasing process variation may actually add value.

Because random or natural process flow variability cannot be eliminated or even reduced to significant degrees, it must, therefore, be **managed**. The rate at which patients become ill enough to need ICU care, the number of admissions from the ED and floors, and the number of transfers are examples of random variability that must be managed. But, as we have seen in other hospital areas, this does not mean that they are completely unpredictable if the DCM tools are appropriately used. The relative number of patients and source of the inputs should be followed on an ongoing basis to tell us who is coming and where they are coming from.

Non-random or scheduling variability is a type of artificial variability often driven by individual priorities, particularly those driven by surgical scheduling, as we have discussed in detail in Chapter 11. Non-random variability should not be *managed*; it should be eliminated through effective leadership. The elimination of artificial, non-random variability is clearly an example of eliminating unnecessary waste.

Non-random variability should not be *managed*;
it should be eliminated through effective leadership.

It requires **leadership** precisely because it disrupts the *status quo ante* of taking current practices and changing them to meet the needs of the patient. Dr. Eugene Litvak and others have shown how dramatically changes in elective surgical block scheduling can change ICU utilization. Indeed, some believe that such programs will distinguish viable from non-viable hospitals in the future (Litvak and Fineberg, 2013).

Given the explosion of technology in critical care, coupled with the shortage in intensive care physicians, regionalization of critical care services has been advanced as a way to improve flow, both by increasing value and eliminating waste by reducing duplication of unnecessary services. Effectively designed and implemented, regionalization cohorts have selected ICU patients at more centralized medical centers based on the patient's medical acuity as well as the needs and availability of the referral medical center to provide the necessary technology and medical expertise.

For example, during the 2009 H1N1 influenza pandemic, patients with advanced respiratory failure who required extracorporeal membrane oxygenation (ECMO) to adequately oxygenate their blood were cohorted at regional medical centers that had this expertise. In fact, effective regionalization dates back to the last century, when, for example, burn centers were developed on a regional basis, both to assure that sufficient expertise in this highly specialized branch of trauma surgery was available and to assure that those centers had a sufficient number of patients to continuously develop and hone evidence-based care.

When are they coming? Understanding the inputs to the ICU and either managing or eliminating their variability includes inevitable consideration of the second DCM question: When are they coming? Certainly for non-random variability, we can predict and control when such patients will come to the ICU due to surgical scheduling of those cases whose post-operative care will require ICU resources at times when those resources (capacity) are maximized. (Or, at the very least, we can avoid scheduling them when they are minimal or non-existent.)

But even that ICU patient flow that is subject to non-random variability has some level of predictability if the data regarding these patients' arrival is studied closely. Increasingly, the use of EMRs and data systems allows us to track the sources and times patients arrive. For cardiac care units, this predictability is increased somewhat by the fact that episodes of acute chest syndrome are more common in the morning hours. The size and complexity of an ICU and hospital also impact patient flow.

At Inova Fairfax Medical Center, the majority of patient admissions to the ICU arrive between 4 pm and midnight. However, as discussed later, our intensivist staffing model also must take into account the needs of the patients already in the ICU. Therefore, given the fact that our program manages between 50 to 60 ICU patients on any given day, our staffing model must allow for adequate intensivist time to provide care for new patients as well as extant patients. This is accomplished by dedicating an intensivist to consult on all new potential admissions during daytime hours when ICU rounds are occurring.

What are they going to need? The next step is to consider what *specific* resources these patients will need. This requires a certain degree of patient segmentation, since not all ICU patients will need the same resources. Large tertiary medical centers typically cohort their ICU patients based on the primary medical condition for their admission. For example, patients with acute neurological issues will go to a neuroscience ICU; patients with traumatic injuries may go to a trauma ICU; and pediatric patients are taken care of in pediatric critical care units, with nurses and physicians specifically trained in the care of each of such patients.

In addition to segmentation of resources for patients with certain clinical entities, consideration should be given to *how long* they are likely to need these resources, based upon historical data and severity scoring systems, such as the proprietary Apache IV (Vasilevskis, 2009). This has important implications for forecasting demand, which is addressed below. As the number of evidence-based protocols increase over time, the ability to predict which resources will be needed and for how long will undoubtedly continue to improve.

Further, as we move rapidly from a fee-for-service to a value-based purchasing/population health model, insurers will be a key force guiding an approach that thoughtfully matches demand with capacity. Given the expensive nature of ICU care, we should expect careful scrutiny of how the care provided relates to cost-accountable outcomes (O'Brien et al., 2013).

Are we going to have what they need? Once we have as clear a picture as possible on the demand side of the equation, we need to assess whether we will have the capacity to meet that demand. Perhaps the simplest part of the calculus is whether we will have an available bed in the ICU for the patient. As we discussed in Chapter 7, an available bed has a clear definition, which must be consistently applied: a bed that has been cleaned, for which staff is present, and which is ready for a patient to occupy.

This leads to the second part of the equation, which is: Is there adequate physician and nurse staffing in the ICU to handle the patient? If a bed is empty, but there are inadequate nurses to staff the unit, the bed should not be considered "available" until nurse staffing matches the demand. Thus, both the bed and the staffing comprise capacity and neither should be considered without relating it to the other. These issues should be assessed and monitored as a part of real-time demand-capacity management and clinical bed huddles.

The "Are we going to have what they need?" question is changing somewhat as the roles and responsibilities within critical care units continue to change. With the shortage of critical care-trained physicians in many areas of the country, a number of ways of increasing capacity have developed.

These include the development of tele-ICUs/eICUs, training of nurse practitioners and physician assistants (now referred to as Advanced Practice Providers or APPs) in critical care medicine, and so-called optimal physician programs, all of which are intended to assure that the resources of the critical care units and the physicians and nurses responsible for staffing them are maximized. Telemedicine for critical care unit patients also represents another type of regionalization of care (Nguyen et al., 2010).

The ability to assess how the critical care physician best adds value and eliminates those tasks that can be done by APPs or non-critical-care trained physicians is a key example of how the Lean principles of hardwiring flow can be put to work (McCauley et al., 2006). As the contemporary ICU evolves, it is increasingly becoming a place where multi-disciplinary teamwork is the standard.

Our ICUs utilize a combination of providers from multiple disciplines including physician, nursing, advanced practice providers, pharmacy, social work, case management, nutrition, physical therapy, occupational therapy, and spiritual counseling to provide an integrated and holistic approach to patient management. To quote a former first lady, "it takes a village." While the physician maintains overall responsibility for the patient and particularly for diagnosis and development of the care plan, it is no longer realistic to think that the physician can be the context expert for all clinical matters. The challenge is integrating this expertise in a way that adds the greatest value.

What will we do if we don't have what they need? There will inevitably be times when the demand for critical care exceeds our capacity to provide that care. The critical issue is: What plans will be in place to deal with those eventualities? Developing a culture of leadership for hardwiring flow is an essential factor, since charge nurses and critical care physicians should be empowered to work with corresponding input and output units to adapt processes to meet patient needs at times when demand exceeds capacity.

As we've mentioned previously, the true test of leadership for critical care medical and nursing directors is not how well the unit functions when you are there. We know it will run smoothly then. The larger and more important question is, "How will it run when you are not there?" Or as Dr. Samir Fakhry, chief of general surgery at Medical University of South Carolina likes to ask, "Is the care provided at 2 am equally as good as the care provided at 2 pm?" Empowerment of those in charge on a real-time basis is a core value of high-performing critical care units (Mayer, 2014).

While in the past, simply going on "critical care re-route" was the only option, the system nature of flow is such that effectively closing the ICUs to new patients will immediately and inevitably result in back-ups, delays, and boarders in the ED and most importantly may have adverse consequences on patient outcomes (Chalfin et al., 2007). Most ICUs have created policies to determine which patients can be moved to step-down units on a real-time basis, and have changed the elective operative schedule to smooth critical care flow.

However, some studies have shown that the likelihood of return admissions to the critical care units (ICU "bounce-backs") can increase if such programs are not carefully conceived, implemented, and monitored (Hall, 2012). Fundamentally, these programs are a part of the hospital and healthcare system's surge capacity. Surge capacity is often interpreted to mean an aspect of disaster planning, but it actually should be considered a part of what we routinely do when the ICU's resources have been exceeded.

An additional aspect of managing demand and capacity when the number of patients exceeds the available resources is "after-action reviews" (AARs). Originally developed by the Department of Defense for use by combat teams, after action reviews have been extended to multiple industries, including healthcare. AARs seek answers to the following questions: What happened? Why did it happen? How can we sustain strength and improve identified weaknesses? The final step is to plan, prepare and execute the AAR results.

AARs answer these questions using this format:

After Action Report Format	ICU Example
What was supposed to happen?	ICU remains open
What did happen?	ICU closed for 18 hours
What needs improvement?	Communication among team and step-down units
What needs sustaining?	Accurate assessments
What can be done to improve?	Acting on assessments to transfer lower acuity patients
Plan, prepare, execute	Medical and Nursing Director will provide training and simulations

Figure 10.6 After Action Reports in the ICU

2. FORECASTING DEMAND

As we discussed earlier, asking and answering the demand-capacity questions and using the tools of RTDC are critical first steps towards being able to apply the second strategy of hardwiring flow: the ability to reliably forecast demand. This includes a thorough understanding of all aspects of the "input" side of the ledger regarding where our patients come from, when they are coming, and what they are going to need. As the old adage states, "Don't let life be a surprise to you." Forecasting demand is simply the best way to assure that ICU leaders and their staff aren't surprised by the type, acuity, and number of patients entering and being cared for in their units.

However, forecasting demand also involves consideration of the "throughput" phase of care as well. Using evidence-based clinical protocols and evidence-based leadership should allow us to predict not only how many patients we will see, but which resources will be necessary, how we will care for them, and how long those resources will be needed, as move them along on their journey from horizontal to vertical.

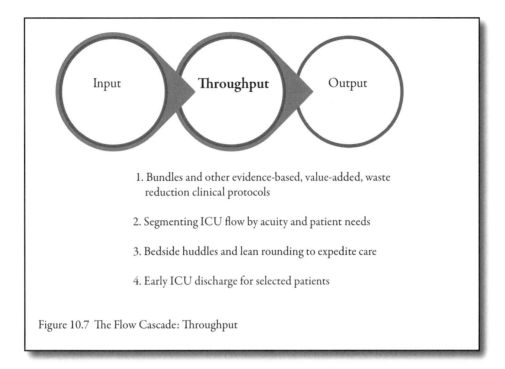

1. Bundles and other evidence-based, value-added, waste reduction clinical protocols

2. Segmenting ICU flow by acuity and patient needs

3. Bedside huddles and lean rounding to expedite care

4. Early ICU discharge for selected patients

Figure 10.7 The Flow Cascade: Throughput

3. REAL-TIME MONITORING OF FLOW

Perhaps no area of hardwiring flow is more poised for meaningful expansion and widespread applicability than real-time monitoring of flow data. Currently, while most critical care units attempt to have a sense of the current status of their patients' course, very few units have developed electronic tracking tools to measure current flow status, compliance with evidence-based guidelines, progression of patients towards discharge, or other critically important flow data. To be sure, many EMRs have tracking boards and can be used to extract data for analysis; however, most of these systems are used more retrospectively than proactively to identify existing flow problems.

Bed and shift huddles are extremely helpful ways in which to monitor flow on the macro level and their use should definitely be encouraged. Nonetheless, we expect creative critical care units to develop and implement much more sophisticated ways in which to use technology to provide real-time monitoring of actionable data on flow. As these are developed, they will be able to provide the ability to anticipate back-ups at unexpected times, warning signs that the unit will be full, and ways to keep referring units informed of that status.

4. QUEUING THEORY

As we've said repeatedly, anytime you wait in line, you are experiencing a queue, whether at Starbucks or the grocery store. But the original application of queuing theory to healthcare is illustrated in this graph plotting medical ICU (MICU) percentage utilization against waiting time and the likelihood of rejections or delays. Recall that at low rates of utilization, delays are short and predictable and the risk of bed unavailability is low.

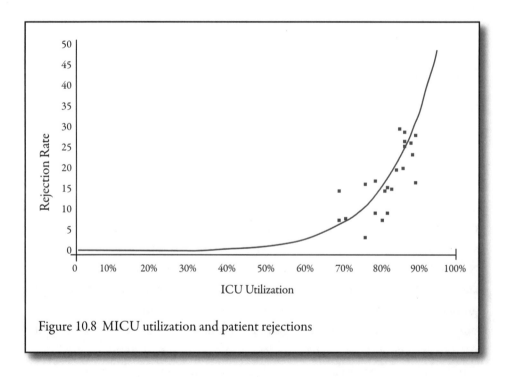

Figure 10.8 MICU utilization and patient rejections

However, as the critical care unit fills to around 85 to 90 percent, delays and rejections increase exponentially on this "steep" end of the curve. Fortunately, even relatively small changes on the steep end of the curve typically have a dramatic effect on creating additional capacity to meet demand.

Here are several ways in which this insight from queuing theory can affect critical care capacity at crucial times:

- Real time clinical huddles can identify patients who can be transferred to intermediate care units (IMCs) or "step-down" units.
- Clinical huddles can identify patients who might be transferred to other units or to critical care units at their local hospitals (also known as "back-transfers" for patients who need some level of critical care, but not those of a level I trauma center, for example).
- Standing protocols can be developed for using post-anesthesia care units (PACUs) as critical care holding areas.
- Similar protocols can be implemented for the use of ED beds for the same purpose (although this clearly affects the overall demand-capacity equation in a negative fashion).
- If IMC beds are available, they can also be used to care for critical care unit patients under the right circumstances.
- Telemedicine can be utilized to extend physician expertise outside the hospital walls in lieu of transferring patients into the hospital.

As we will see in the following, these types of changes are also examples of eliminating bottlenecks and constraints as well.

5. MANAGING VARIATION

Managing variation to maximize value and eliminate waste is a concept several progressive critical care units have used very effectively. For example, at Northwest Community Hospital near Chicago, a "critical care alert policy" was developed and implemented in order to improve outcomes and expedite transfer of critically ill or injured patients from the ED to the critical care units:

POLICY:

A Critical Care Alert can be called for patients meeting the following inclusion criteria:

1. Sepsis/Sepsis syndrome
2. Acute respiratory failure requiring mechanical ventilation
3. Resuscitation post-arrest
4. Unstable hemodynamics requiring vasopressor intervention
5. Intracranial hemorrhage with evolving neurological deficits or airway compromise

Figure 10.9 Critical care ' fast tracking' at Northwest Community Hospital

Patients with any of these criteria are candidates for a critical care alert:

- Sepsis/Sepsis syndrome
- Acute respiratory failure requiring mechanical ventilation
- Resuscitation post-arrest
- Unstable hemodynamics requiring vasopressor intervention
- Intracranial hemorrhage with evolving neurological deficits or airway compromise

Once these clinical entities are identified, the following process is followed:

- Patients meeting inclusion criteria will have a critical care alert called at the time they are recognized to meet inclusion criteria;
- A 30-minute response time (from notification to arrival in ED) is required from the patient's physician or the intensivist;
- The critical care unit will respond within 30 minutes of notification with both a bed assignment and a team for transporting the patient to critical care;
- All immediate diagnostic radiology needs should be completed prior to transport; and
- The patient's ED nurse will accompany the team to the critical care unit to give a bedside report.

Intermountain Health Care in Salt Lake City developed a similar program, called "Priority One":

1. Patient intubated
2. Respiratory extremis pending intubation
3. Persistent hypotension
4. Need for vasoactive infusions (pressors, inotropics)
5. Serum lactate > 4 mmol/L
6. Major bleeding
7. Physician discretion

Figure 10.10 Critical care 'fast-tracking' at Intermountain Health Care

These are both excellent examples of managing variation to increase value and eliminate waste by identifying subpopulations of patients who clearly need critical care resources, will definitely benefit greatly from application of those resources, and assure those resources reach the patient in the most timely fashion possible.

Perhaps one of the most quintessential examples of managing variation is in the daily management of critical care patients. It relates to one of the principles of high reliability organizations (HROs): preoccupation with failure. Weick and Sutcliffe delineated five principles of high reliability organizations, which operate in potentially dangerous environments, yet maintain extraordinarily high success rates, despite seemingly being surrounded by the possibility of failure. Of these five HRO principles, three guide anticipation and two guide containment of identified problems (Weick and Sutcliffe, 2007):

3 Principles of Anticipation

<u>Preoccupation with Failure</u>- Regarding small, inconsequential errors as a deeper symptom

<u>Sensitivity to Operations</u>- Paying deep attention to the front lines

<u>Reluctance to Simplify Operations</u>- Engaging diversity of perspective and expertise

2 Principles of Containment

<u>Commitment to Resilience</u>- Developing capabilities to detect, contain, and recover from negative events

<u>Deference to Expertise</u>- Pushing decision-making down and around to the person with most specific knowledge and expertise to solve the existing problem

Figure 10.11 5 principles of high reliability organizations

Preoccupation with failure is the capacity to regard even the smallest and seemingly inconsequential error as a symptom or trend of a potential problem. In HROs, this preoccupation with failure is a learned and cultural commitment to regard small deviations from the expected norm as harbingers of a negative trend, if not doom itself.

Far from being an innate pessimism that things will get worse, "preoccupation with failure" is actually a form of trained optimism that sees in any deterioration an opportunity for intervention and improvement.

Critical care professionals repeatedly use this HRO principle of anticipation every day, whether consciously or not. The constant, almost incessant, monitoring of physiologic data leads to a barrage of information, yet critical care nurses and physicians routinely act swiftly and decisively when the data deteriorates, often leading to interventions to slow or reverse the negative trend. Far from being an innate pessimism that things will get worse, "preoccupation with failure" is actually a form of trained optimism that sees in any deterioration an opportunity for intervention and improvement.

6. ELIMINATING CONSTRAINTS AND BOTTLENECKS

As we mentioned in the section on queuing theory, there are multiple steps that can be taken to reduce or eliminate bottlenecks to improve access to critical care units and their focused, expensive, and precious resources. Many of those solutions focus on the "output" aspect of flow:

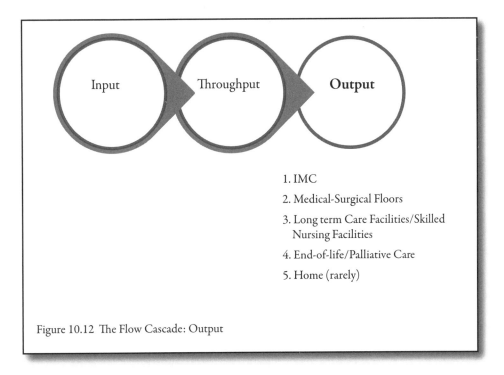

1. IMC
2. Medical-Surgical Floors
3. Long term Care Facilities/Skilled Nursing Facilities
4. End-of-life/Palliative Care
5. Home (rarely)

Figure 10.12 The Flow Cascade: Output

This includes developing mechanisms in which patients can be transferred directly from the critical care unit to long-term care facilities, skilled nursing facilities, and, for patients with tracheostomies or other ventilator needs, specific facilities geared to match the patients' demands with facilities with capacity. These types of care transitions are likely to become more common in the future as specialty hospitals such as long-term acute care facilities (LTACs) are better designed to accept improving ICU patients and offer the more intensive rehabilitation services and opportunity for care progression that these patients require.

Further, should the Center for Medicare and Medicaid Services move forward with public reporting of ICU-risk adjusted mortality and length of stay as recommended by the National Quality Forum, referring hospitals will have greater incentive to transfer patients to LTACs as such propensity significantly correlates with reductions in ICU mortality and length of stay (Hall et al, 2012).

It is also worth noting that there has been a major movement in healthcare to assure that appropriate palliative care resources are available, including not only personnel, but also evidence-based pathways to ensure that critical care professionals know how to access data and resources to care for patients whose needs have evolved from critical care to end-of-life issues, including appropriate resources for the family. Current efforts have targeted patients and their proxies who have an anticipated ICU stay of at least five days.

The palliative care communication bundle has nine domains with targeted interventions for days 1, 3, and 5. Day 1 objectives focus on six major domains: identification of proxy medical decision maker; investigation of advanced directives; addressing cardiopulmonary resuscitation status; distributing a family information leaflet regarding ICU care; assessing pain; and managing pain optimally.

Day 3 objectives include the two domains of offering both spiritual and social work support. The day 5 objective focuses on the single domain of a multi-disciplinary family meeting to address the current status of the patient with the medical proxy and family, prognosis, and to further define goals of care, including review of resuscitation status and use of life support.

Families of ICU patients have identified the following four areas as the most important: timely, clear and compassionate communication; clinical decision making focusing on patient preferences, goals, and values; patient care maintaining comfort, dignity, and personhood; and open access and proximity of families to patients and care givers. These findings reinforce the high value provided by effective and compassionate communication between caregivers and patients and how often this leads to greater efficiency through elimination of undesired, and therefore, unnecessary services (Nelson, 2006; Nelson 2010; Norton 2007).

As mentioned earlier, the use of severity scoring systems such as APACHE (acute physiology and chronic health evaluation), MPM (mortality probability model), and SAPS (simplified acute physiology score) is another mechanism to identify bottlenecks, especially when managing specific diseases. These scoring systems, particularly APACHE IV, have the capacity to provide risk-adjusted mortality and length of stay estimates, which when combined with actual data, can be converted into standardized ratios (Breslow et al., 2012a; Breslow et al., 2012b).

Ratios less than one indicate better than predicted results while ratios greater than one may indicate opportunity for improvement. Using these systems to look at specific patient populations in the ICU, which can be stratified by primary diagnosis or diagnosis related grouping (DRG), allows assessment of performance and serves as a first pass to discover where disease-specific bottlenecks may occur.

For instance, if Sepsis mortality is within a predicted range, but length of stay is excessive, there may be an issue with adequately triaging patients for ICU discharge. Or perhaps there is a shortage of appropriate beds to transfer such patients to when their overall condition stabilizes.

Other potential bottlenecks and constraints in the ICU include the coordination of imaging and lab studies, delays in preparing beds for new admission, or failure to adjust nursing ratios when patients are able to transfer but must stay in the ICU until a bed is available. In the latter example, nursing to patient ratios may be decreased for such patients as they no longer require high acuity staffing. As the staff becomes proficient with the principles of hardwiring flow, it becomes easier to identify constraints and bottlenecks, and a passion develops for aggressively eliminating them, whenever they are found.

FLOW AS A COMPLEX, ADAPTIVE SYSTEM

Perhaps no other area of the healthcare system better demonstrates its fundamental system nature than critical care units, since they occupy a highly focused yet capacity-constrained locus where demand often exceeds capacity and creative strategies to hardwire flow have both upstream and downstream impacts. Data from across the country verify that critical care unit closures and delays have an immediate and dramatic impact on the hospital's ED, with waits, delays, and diversions common (EDBA, 2014). This creates a "ripple effect," in that patient experience, flow metrics, patient safety, and reputational costs are all affected when critical units close.

However, if the critical care unit is in a referral or tertiary care medical center, this ripple effect can extend throughout the region, with the impact of ambulance diversion causing further waits, delays, and patient safety problems throughout the entire regional healthcare system. This often means that patients are provided care in hospitals that are not their primary healthcare institution or "medical home."

Examples of the problems from patient diversion abound, but perhaps none are more dramatic than when post-operative patients are forced to go to an ED other than the one in which their surgery was performed, without access to medical records or even the surgical specialists who performed the surgery.

Hardwiring critical care flow has a system impact within the hospital itself in that utilization of their resources not only has an impact on the ED, EMS, and the local and regional healthcare systems, it has a cascade-like impact in its interrelationships with the medical-surgical floors, operating suite, PACU, imaging services, and even laboratory. Thus, the more carefully we can hardwire critical care flow, the larger our positive impact will be on the hospital and healthcare system.

The complex adaptive system nature of critical care units will be further accentuated as we hone our responses to these questions:

- Does this patient need the resources of a critical care unit bed?
- If so, how does ICU admission specifically add value?
- How long, based on data from previous patients and using evidence-based treatment guidelines, is it likely that the patient will need to be in the critical care unit?
- If the patient's status changes, how will we adapt our monitoring of flow to best direct resources at the right time in the right setting for that patient?

Critical care units, including the ED, are a clear example of operations which function at a high level 24 hours per day, seven days a week, 365 days per year. But they rely on resources from the support systems of hospitals that operate at peak capacity much differently—in the range of 18 hours per day, 5 days per week—since staffing almost universally decreases in the afternoon, weekend, and holiday hours. Recognizing this fact and assuring that the system nature of hardwiring flow is dealt with effectively is key to improvement efforts.

HARDWIRING FLOW™ FOCUS: HARDWIRING FLOW IN CRITICAL CARE

- Critical care is not a noun; it is a verb. It is something we do for the good of the patient, not simply a *place* where that care occurs.
- Critical care and ICU care are multidisciplinary and most effective when flow is maximized through a combination of efficient teamwork and elimination of waste.
- "Bundles" of care (small sets of evidence-based interventions) result in significantly better outcomes than when implemented individually for defined patient populations.
- Assessing value added versus eliminating waste is at the core of resource utilization in crucial care.

Strategies to Hardwire Flow:
- **Demand-capacity management**—Ask the same questions: Who's coming? When are they coming? What are they going to need? Are we going to have it? What will we do if we don't? (See chapter for specific application to critical care.)
- **Forecasting demand**—Once you understand the "inputs" based on the above questions, consider the "throughput" phase of care to understand which resources will be necessary and for how long to move patients on their journey from horizontal to vertical.
- **Real-time monitoring of flow**—Monitor real-time flow data with bed and shift huddles, while continuing to seek out creative and sophisticated technology solutions over time to provide actionable data.
- **Queuing theory**—While delays are short and predictable with low rates of utilization, delays and rejections increase exponentially as the critical care unit fills to around 85 to 90 percent. However, even small changes on this "steep end of the curve" dramatically create additional capacity to meet demand.

- **Managing Variation**—Programs like Northwest Community Hospital's critical care alert policy and Intermountain Health Care's Priority One program offer excellent examples of how to manage variation to increase value and eliminate waste by identifying subpopulations of patients.
- **Reducing constraints and bottlenecks**— Focus on the "output" aspect of flow by developing mechanisms to assist the direct transfer of patients from the critical care unit to other types of facilities.
- **Flow as a complex, adaptive system**—Critical care unit closures and delays have an immediate and dramatic impact on the hospital's ED, creating a "ripple effect" that adversely impacts patient experience, flow metrics, safety, and reputational cost.

CHAPTER 11

SMOOTHING SURGICAL FLOW

by Kirk Jensen, MD and Thom Mayer, MD

"Before beginning, plan carefully."

—*Marcus T. Cicero*

"…For the secret of the care of the patient is in caring for the patient."

—*Paul Ogelsby,* The Caring Physician: The Life of Dr. Francis W. Peabody

Here are two statistics and a question: ED cases typically constitute 50 percent of hospital admissions and elective, scheduled surgical cases constitute 30 percent. So which one is the largest source of hospital census variability?

Logically, the ED, right? The answer is counterintuitive: They contribute equally. Both contribute to patient flow and patient waiting to the same extent. The reason they do so is because there are two kinds of variation: natural and artificial. The kind that occurs in the ED is natural. The type of variation that can often happen in the operating room (OR) is artificial variation… variation based on late starts, poor scheduling, inaccurate assessment of case lengths, poor use of block time, failure to complete pre-operative screening work-ups, and other factors that are artificial and not natural.

227

This leads to a cascade of negative consequences, including case cancellations, holes in the OR schedule, patient dissatisfaction, delays in scheduling elective cases, high OR nursing turnover and dissatisfaction, and surgeon dissatisfaction. Indeed, Dr. Eugene Litvak has stated that the single most distinguishing feature of successful hospitals will be their ability to smooth surgical flow. (Litvak and Fineberg, 2013; Litvak, 2013). And another counterintuitive point about these two kinds of variation is that the natural variation of unscheduled ED cases is easier to predict than the artificial variation of the OR. In other words, it's easier to predict when someone will break a leg than it is to predict when an elective procedure will occur.

By making use of the flow toolkit described in this book, you can deal with these two kinds of variation and improve flow through your OR. Patient flow through these two areas of the hospital are interrelated in some important ways, so some of the steps you can take to improve flow through the OR will improve flow through the ED as well. In this chapter, we'll look at the tools your flow toolkit provides to do so. First, let's look at the two kinds of variation more closely.

NATURAL VARIATION

One way to grasp the difference between these kinds of variation is to imagine the idealized healthcare facility. In this imaginary place, all the patients have the same disease, to the same severity. All the patients arrive at the same rate: every 10 minutes. All physicians, nurses, and physician assistants have the same abilities in providing care to those patients. Such a facility could theoretically operate at 100 percent efficiency. It would resemble a Toyota production line.

Is such a scenario likely to happen in any hospital? Obviously, no. It won't, because none of these imaginary circumstances is ever going to occur. The unscheduled patients who arrive at any healthcare facility have different diseases, with differing levels of severity. They arrive when they need to, not a rate convenient to the facility. The doctors, nurses, and mid-level providers have different abilities and work at different paces. This is natural variation (Litvak, 2003).

The ED deals with natural variation every day. For instance, if you examine ten consecutive patients with congestive heart failure who enter the department, you realize that not all such patients are the same in their condition; there is variation in the severity of their illnesses. If you examine five consecutive patients with the same grade ankle sprain, you realize all ankle sprains are not identical. There is variation in the severity of their ankle injuries, not to the same extent, perhaps, as identified in the CHF patients, but differences just the same.

Natural variation is just that—natural. You cannot eliminate it. You cannot reduce it. It is random, and it is going to happen. What a hospital can do to improve flow is manage natural variation optimally. The other chapters in this book provide the flow toolkit for optimal management of natural variation, while this chapter focuses on application of those principles to the surgical service.

What a hospital can do to improve flow is
manage natural variation optimally.

In regard specifically to surgery, emergency or urgent surgery is an example of natural variation. As with the other kinds of natural variation, it will happen and you cannot avoid it; to keep flow smooth, you must manage it optimally. Analyzing the historical data will give you the foundation to predict the volume and types of emergency cases so that you can plan and staff accordingly. This is an example of using demand-capacity management questions to understand flow. We'll look at some other ways to manage natural surgical variation later in the chapter.

ARTIFICIAL VARIATION

Now consider the operating room with its series of elective, scheduled surgeries. On the face of it, we might expect flow to be smooth when hospitals schedule surgeries. But take a closer look. Say a hospital's cardiovascular surgeons are allowed to choose to operate only on Mondays, Tuesdays, and Wednesdays. What happens? The intensive care unit starts to fill up by the end of the week with post-op patients, and ED patients and potential transfers are forced to wait for ICU beds.

Backlogs begin to build and flow decreases, as queuing theory clearly predicts they would. (See Chapter 1.) Performing many complex surgeries two consecutive days a week and not the other days is an instance of artificial variation. Artificial variation is neither necessary nor random. It is driven by largely unknown, ignored, or unchallenged individual priorities. And it is within hospitals' control; we can identify it and eliminate it, thereby smoothing flow. Figure 11.1 makes clear how artificial variation contributes to bottlenecks:

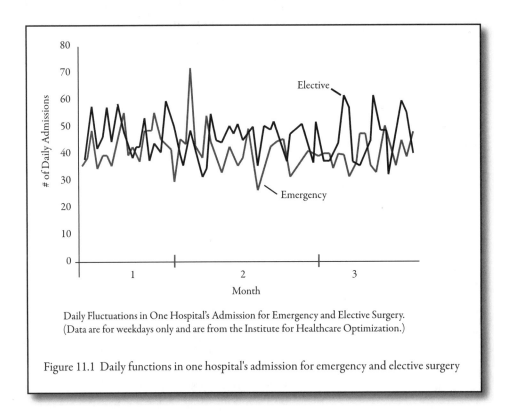

Daily Fluctuations in One Hospital's Admission for Emergency and Elective Surgery.
(Data are for weekdays only and are from the Institute for Healthcare Optimization.)

Figure 11.1 Daily functions in one hospital's admission for emergency and elective surgery

Here's an example from our experience: A hospital we worked with went on bypass every Thursday. When hospital management examined why this was happening, it discovered that it was not random; it occurred because the cardiovascular surgeons operated only on Mondays and Tuesdays. The solution was simple (though it wasn't easy, as we'll discuss later). Management scheduled one surgeon to operate on Mondays and one on Wednesdays. Under the new schedule, the need to go on bypass disappeared. Making this one change smoothed flow sufficiently to remove the bottleneck.

Artificial variation can easily lead to the unreliable matching of service staff or capacity to patient demand. Under artificial variation, the operating room can experience significant peaks and valleys, ranging from unused ORs and beds to a unit that is over capacity and accompanying patient diversions. Patients experience delays in care as surgeries are postponed. Patient satisfaction then declines, and so does that of the staff. Eventually surgical throughput and hospital throughput decrease, as does revenue. As deferred surgeries increase, surgical errors are also more likely to occur.

Here's yet another counterintuitive point: In regard to diversions, one study found (Litvak et al., 2001) a much stronger correlation between scheduled admissions (under conditions of significant scheduled demand) and diversion than between ED demand and diversion. In other words, scheduled admissions are a key driver of ED diversion. Artificial variation causes more diversion than natural variation. Figure 11.2 highlights some of the problems that artificial variation can cause.

Scheduled admissions are the key driver of ED diversion.

The Negative Impact of Artificial Variation
- Decreased access for patients (particularly the sickest ones)
- Extended delays in delivering care
- Diversion of patients (both internally and externally)
- Nurse understaffing and overloading, leading to lower quality of care and less safe conditions
- Decreased staff satisfaction, leading to poorer retention
- Underutilization of assets, leading to reduced revenue and higher costs

Figure 11.2 Problems that artificial variation can cause hospitals

On the other hand, smoothing elective surgeries can have a dramatic impact. One of us participated in a study of a multidisciplinary ICU that experienced approximately equal demand from the ED and the OR and found that the number of patients diverted from the ICU because of excessive demand was 25 to 30 percent, externally or internally (McManus et al., 2003). The study found that in some months, more than 70 percent of those diverted would not have been diverted if elective surgical procedures were smoothed. Obviously, that percentage equates to a large number of patients who could have been accommodated if throughput was smooth.

KNOW WHO IS COMING—AND WHEN

Individual elective surgeries are predictable, and as with other types of flow elsewhere in the hospital, the patterns of scheduled flow through the OR can be monitored, analyzed, and used to predict general trends. The added complexity is accounting for the impact of the artificial variation, as previously described. The demand-capacity management principles discussed in Chapter 8 will be useful: Match capacity to demand; use a dashboard to monitor flow and to measure demand and capacity in real time; establish back-up plans and triggers to put them into effect; and predict demand based on historical data.

SEGMENT PATIENT FLOW

Another tool we've discussed earlier that is useful in the surgical context is segmenting patient flow. Specifically in regard to the OR, the first step is designing processes separately for inpatients and outpatients. The second step is focusing on individual specialties and different case mixes, and tailoring processes that are optimal for each. Tracking patient flow through the use of a dashboard makes this process easier and more effective.

Figure 11.3 illustrates a useful procedure for this purpose, particularly for forecasting:

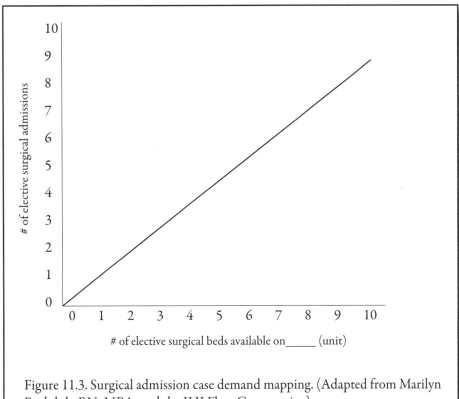

Figure 11.3. Surgical admission case demand mapping. (Adapted from Marilyn Rudolph, RN. MBA, and the IHI Flow Community.)

Use it at the bed huddle at the beginning of each day. The diagonal line marks the intersection of patients and beds as those numbers rise, the latter corresponding with the former. By putting a dot where the number of available beds and number of elective admissions actually intersect, labeled by date and weekday, you see clearly when there are more patients than beds (dot above the diagonal line) and when there are more beds than patients (dot below the line).

A separate line joining all the dots gives a graph of demand versus capacity over time, both a general pattern as well as the specific pattern for each weekday. Armed with this knowledge, you are better able to place patients in real time, and you are also better equipped to make forecasts.

Another significant aspect of unpredictable surgical flow, which we can both control and use to our advantage, is that we know when we're starting. These patients have scheduled times for surgery, and they arrive on time (generally). Your staff knows those starting times. And yet, in many hospitals, surgeries do *not* start on time.

There are various reasons: The surgeons don't arrive on time. Anesthesia isn't ready. Staff members treat posted schedules as rough approximations… more as suggestions than firm deadlines. Or different team members have different notions of what a start time actually means. These various reasons have a cumulative effect that leads to the artificial variation that hinder flow in many facilities.

But there are concrete steps your hospital can take to smooth this flow. To begin with, here are some key principles to keep in mind for smoothing surgical flow. Most reiterate the general principles of flow we discuss throughout this book in the surgical context:

- The goal should be to optimize surgical throughput for all patients, not just for one patient segment or for one surgeon, group, or specialty.
- The OR start time should not cause a bottleneck.
- Patients who need few resources (simple cases) should not routinely wait behind patients who need many resources (complex or difficult cases).
- Working on your processes on the front end of the OR will help identify significant bottlenecks.
- Focus on improving the bottlenecks on the front end of the OR and those bottlenecks or choke points under your control or influence.

By attending to these principles, you can do much to hardwire surgical patient flow. Figure 11.4 provides a more specific set of methods to enhance flow in the OR. We'll look at these next in detail. They fall into several groups of related actions:

1. Prepare a complete, timely preoperative work-up

2. Clearly define the start time

3. Start on time

4. Plan for and accommodate variations in surgical case length

5. Ensure reliable, effective scheduling of and communication with surgeons

6. Plan for and manage surgical cases with unpredictable lengths

7. Use an RN perioperative facilitator to coordinate overall flow

8. Refine postoperative patient placement

Figure 11.4 Ways to optimize surgical flow

OPTIMIZE MANAGEMENT OF THE START TIME

As Figure 11.4 makes clear, smoothing surgical flow requires an overall perspective and approach. A hospital must work on both OR processes and perioperative processes. And so your work of optimizing flow begins before the beginning, so to speak, with the procedures that precede the start time for surgery.

Preparing a timely work-up. The key to optimizing flow is starting on time. Late starts throw off the entire OR schedule and lead to diminished flow in other processes in the surgical unit too. An unfortunately common reason for delayed start times is incomplete work-ups. Thus, one important way to ensure that you do start on time is to complete the preoperative work-up well in advance of the scheduled start time. (See Chapter 13.)

Work-ups need to be completed far enough ahead of the schedule to be sure critical members of the surgical team have results in plenty of time. Accordingly, tests need to be scheduled and performed in time to get the results to those critical members, and instead management must put in place procedures to coordinate this activity.

This means that preoperative testing and service protocols that surgeons and anesthesiologists agree on must be established. In carrying out this coordination, management should make sure that anesthesia staff is assigned to the OR to help plan start times, that anesthesia preparation time is included in preoperative processes, and that anesthesiologists and surgeons exchange information.

The established procedures should spell out that surgeons order the appropriate tests as soon as the decision is made for surgery, and they should follow the established, mutually agreed upon protocols and order only necessary tests. For this purpose, preoperative order forms should be available for surgeons to use. As part of the established process, the surgical team should review test results immediately and take any necessary follow-up actions at least two to four days before scheduled surgery.

Our group has developed a formal pre-operative program to assure screening tests are performed in a timely and effective fashion. One of the vagaries of current CMS and commercial insurance regulations is that pre-operative screening is not reimbursed if performed by the anesthesia team, but is if it is performed by another service, providing an important disincentive. We have addressed this in EmCare Anesthesia by developing and implementing a service where our hospitalists or advanced practice providers from either the hospital medicine or emergency medicine program facilitate the screening examinations and testing. This provides a cost-effective and efficient means of assuring cases are not cancelled or postponed because of failure to complete needed screenings.

Defining the start time. The start time seems self-evident: You schedule a specific time and that's when surgery begins. But as we saw, different members of the surgical team often have different ideas of what start time means, and not all members treat the time as definite. So the first step in establishing a firm start time is ensuring everyone agrees on what "start time" in fact means.

And there's a handy way to achieve that agreement: It's not an arbitrary time on the clock but an action. *That action is the incision, and the starting time should be the exact moment when the team plans for the incision to occur.* By establishing a clear action as the starting moment, you enable everyone on the team to know what that time is, plan toward it, and work toward it. As we've said earlier: All language has meaning and all behavior has meaning. In this case, "start time" is the language meaning "time of incision" and the behavior is "on time, every time."

Here is where studying historical patterns will help. Variation in different surgical processes can be planned for by studying the data. This analysis will help you predict the length of various procedures and the length of time for different surgeons doing the same procedure. Again, establish procedures in advance—understood and agreed upon by all involved—to ensure that any work necessary to achieve the incision at the scheduled time is completed. Post the start time in the OR and communicate that this is the genuine time, based on the incision occurring at that exact moment, with all work completed so it actually is.

By establishing the principle that the incision does not occur until all necessary work has been completed, you enhance patient safety as well. If a surgical team knows that all preparatory processes have been completed before the scheduled time for incision, then a patient has been properly anesthetized and is ready for surgery. Under such procedures to improve flow, the provision of safer care is more likely.

Starting on time. Since late start times have a negative cascading effect in the surgical unit and beyond (because of the complex adaptive system nature of surgical flow), ensuring that surgeries do in fact start when they're scheduled to is critical to maintaining smooth flow. We've looked at how procedures need to be in place to ensure that processes are completed before the scheduled start time.

One method in the flow toolkit for efficiently preparing for the start time is to standardize room setup, with staff members cooperating to establish the best ways to set up for different kinds of cases. These standardized procedures should be familiar to all appropriate staff, and they should be reviewed regularly at staff meetings to reinforce that familiarity and to consider whether they need modification. A method closely related to standardization is routine preparation of commonly used drugs, equipment, and supplies well in advance of the start time, ensuring that preparation is an established process well understood by everyone involved.

An effective approach to coordinating the processes that must be completed before surgery can begin is to count backward. If the point of incision defines the starting time, then take that point and work backward from it for each process that must be finished for it to happen when it's scheduled. The point on the other end of this kind of time line is the patient's arrival.

So if the incision is scheduled for 9:00 am and the patient will arrive at 7:30 am, plot each stage to begin in relation to the start time based on how much time your protocols have set for that stage to take, and make sure that each person involved knows when his or her stage is supposed to begin and how much time the schedule permits. Figure 11.5 shows how a timeline based on this concept works:

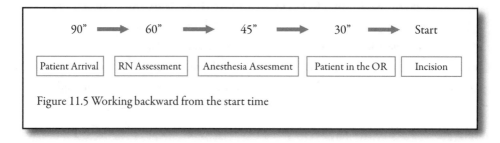

Figure 11.5 Working backward from the start time

In this example, the preoperative nurse knows in advance that he or she can begin assessment of the patient at 7:30 am but that in any case, assessment should be finished by 8:00 am. The anesthesiologist knows his or her time begins at 8:00 am and must be completed by 8:45 am. If the nurse or anesthesiologist knows that the preparatory work will not take all of the allotted time, arriving later than the beginning point on the timeline is well and good, as long as the work is complete by the scheduled point. You should monitor results and keep track of data, and communicate repeatedly, making sure everyone is clear on what should happen and what has happened. These are examples of both real-time monitoring of patient flow and managing variation.

Once you establish procedures and make sure everyone on the team understands them, plot out a timeline based on intervals from the patient's arrival to the incision, and complete all necessary preparation so that the surgeon can make the incision right at the scheduled time, flow is smooth, and bottlenecks are avoided. You are eliminating artificial variation. However, all of this requires managing processes across boundaries and stakeholder groups. Each area needs to establish a system of real-time monitoring and accountability for this to be effective.

USING VARIATION TO ADD VALUE

We have said that to effectively smooth surgical flow, you need to identify the causes of artificial variation and eliminate them. An effective approach is to *manage* natural variation and *eliminate* artificial variation. This adds value to our processes rather than resulting in bottlenecks. This approach involves taking into account variations in cases and when possible, taking advantage of that variation. We'll look at how to do that next.

> An effective approach is to *manage* natural variation
> and *eliminate* artificial variation.

Accommodating variations in case length. Not all surgical cases are the same. As is true anywhere in the hospital, different cases take different amounts of time to treat. Surgical cases differ in complexity and acuteness. Such variation—natural variation—can disrupt schedules, cause bottlenecks, and decrease flow. But you can manage this kind of variation, and doing so effectively increases your likelihood of scheduling properly. As with managing flow through the hospital in general, management of elective surgical flow begins with keeping track of what has happened in the past and what is currently happening.

The tools in your kit that you will use for this purpose should be familiar. First, collect historical data for the unit. Second, analyze how long various types of cases have taken. Third, use the results of your analysis to forecast case length. Fourth, schedule different cases based on your predictions. This is a simple example of using demand-capacity tools to predict performance accurately.

The forecasting and consequent scheduling will include the time that preparation and transition after surgery require. And your analysis should not be limited to just type of case in a generic sense, though it should certainly break down case length by type of procedure; this analysis also presents an opportunity to specifically analyze length of case for individual surgeons and to predict future length for each surgeon based on the analysis.

You then are equipped to schedule accordingly by type of procedure and for individual surgeon. Keep in mind that you are not tracking and predicting in order to rush surgeons through their work and patients through their care.

You are gaining a realistic idea of how long Dr. Jones typically takes to perform a specific type of hip surgery, for instance, so you'll have a better idea of how to schedule such an operation for Dr. Jones and his patients.

Armed with this knowledge, you can manage variation by, for example, staggering start times for the first cases each morning, coordinating the staggering with case complexity. Figure 11.6 is a simple chart showing how this basic process works, with different times and rooms. As the chart indicates, the surgical team must coordinate with schedulers to match the available time slots based on expected case length and staff availability. As we discussed in Chapter 4 on "Lessons from Other Industries," this is precisely how restaurants schedule arrivals in a staggered fashion, so the kitchen is not simultaneously inundated with large numbers of orders.

Patient	Surgeon	Room	Starting Time
Branson	Melnick	1	7:00
Horton	Van Dever	2	7:15
Reynolds	Smithson	3	7:30

Figure 11.6 Managing variation by staggering starting times

Scheduling and communicating with surgeons. As you might expect, surgeons are a key component of smoothing surgical flow. They must be involved in scheduling for two reasons. First, as participants on the front line of flow through the unit, they contribute valuable information that management needs to consider in order to achieve effective scheduling. They also have individual preferences, and achieving smooth flow requires taking those into account. Second, if they are not persuaded of the soundness and necessity of changes in scheduling to smooth flow, those changes are not likely to work as intended.

Involving surgeons in scheduling takes two forms. The first is part of your data analysis and forecasting. As we've seen, by tracking the work of individual surgeons, you gain a more realistic view of how to schedule those surgeons effectively. The second is communication: Make sure you know their preferences for scheduling, and make sure your schedulers check with surgeons on their availability for upcoming scheduled surgeries. Communication should flow both ways: Surgeons should keep schedulers informed of anything that may affect later scheduling as the day proceeds, and similarly, schedulers should keep surgeons informed.

Surgeons need to be involved as well in designing the processes to implement the new scheduling practices. (Remember: "If they're not with you on the takeoff, they won't be with you on the landing!") These processes need to enable effective two-way communication on scheduling and ongoing updates. They must also ensure sufficient and reliable information from surgeons to make effective scheduling possible in the first place. Forms, checklists, and preference cards help you gather that information. The processes should include a predetermined method for reviewing problems in scheduling as they arise.

Keep in mind that you are smoothing overall flow through scheduling. This does not mean that you schedule surgeons uniformly. Surgeons differ in their capacity to perform cases and procedures. Knowing these individual patterns and taking them into account will help you keep throughput smooth in times of high demand.

Managing cases with uncertain length. If you are unsure of how long a procedure will require, and it will very likely take a long time, you face a potential problem in planning and implementing schedules, one that can lead to delays that ripple out beyond the surgical unit through the hospital as a whole. There is, however, a way to manage this uncertain type of surgery.

In fact, there are two ways to do so, and they are both surprisingly simple actions that can have a significant impact on flow. The first is to set aside a separate room for cases with uncertain length. By assigning those cases to a separate room, you enable your unit to adhere to the elective schedule of cases with predictable length much more effectively, unaffected by how long an uncertain procedure takes. Flow is smoother, and you minimize the effects of those uncertain cases.

The second way is to schedule your cases of uncertain length as the last cases each day in the unit. This step has the same effect as the other; you are better able to manage your predictable schedule and maintain flow smoothly.

Any cases that take longer than expected do not disrupt your schedule of predictable elective surgeries.

Either of these methods allows you to contain potential disruptions of the schedule by confining likely cases to a specific, separate space or time. The chair of surgery and the surgical committee should choose which method your unit will use. They should also ensure that procedures are established to identify cases that should be selected for the separate room or time and then schedule them, making sure these schedules are coordinated with the relevant surgeons and any other personnel who should be involved. Our experience is that, despite their intelligence and expertise, many surgeons are highly inaccurate in predicting the length of unpredictable cases, especially those that are done rarely or infrequently. Thus, using historical data is imperative.

Using these methods manages natural variation (the cases of uncertain length) and eliminates artificial variation by smoothing flow through the OR of elective scheduled surgeries. The latter become more predictable and sustaining flow becomes easier. The impact on units beyond the surgical unit improves overall flow as well. If there is a designated room for uncertain and unexpected cases from the ED, for instance, then backups in that unit are less likely. This ripple effect leads us to the next set of tools.

COORDINATING OVERALL FLOW

One of the central principles of smoothing flow, as we've said before, is that units in a hospital cannot isolate themselves in their projects to improve flow; all the units are related, and what one does affects flow in others. This principle is in force in the surgical unit as with any other. Smoothing elective surgical flow depends not only on taking the steps we've outlined here to maintain schedules effectively but on coordination with areas beyond the OR itself, which is another example of flow as a complex adaptive system. Two types of coordination in particular stand out in this regard, and we'll examine them in here.

Using a perioperative facilitator. We said earlier that everyone should be clear on what start time means. But if surgeons, nurses, and anesthesiologists all show up on time, but the patients do not, schedules are still thrown off. Transporting patients must be both timely and efficient; if it doesn't, not only are operating schedules going to be disrupted, but postoperative placement is likely to be as well.

And what about cleaning the OR and turning it around for the next kind of procedure? To take these sorts of details into account, you need established procedures in place, such as anticipating and handling different kinds of transport to and from different units. You also need a perioperative facilitator to coordinate such activities—all activities related to the surgical unit—to keep schedules flowing smoothly.

The facilitator ideally should be an RN, preferably with substantial experience in dealing with operative suites and processes. The facilitator coordinates patient transitions into and out of the OR and on to destination units after surgery. This coordinator also ensures clear communication among the various staff members involved in surgical procedures as well as preliminary and postoperative activities. The facilitator monitors flow in the OR and in preoperative and postoperative areas, circulating through those areas repeatedly and equipped with a cell phone. The facilitator adjusts schedules as needed, remaining in touch with leaders of day-to-day operations.

This person functions much like an air traffic controller, in that they must have situational awareness on a real-time basis for all of the myriad factors affecting surgical flow, as well as the training and skill set to make changes "on the fly," as the situation dictates. This person must see the big picture, guide team members in effective decision-making, and convene stakeholders to develop and implement real-time solutions. This position is one in which the use of "after action reviews" (see Chapter 4) can be very helpful in analyzing situations where flow breaks down in order to identify what can be done better in the future.

Having established processes in place to ensure coordination of all these activities is a necessary first step; having a facilitator in place on staff helps your unit attain and maintain optimal flow.

Refining post-operative placement. A specific type of coordination involves patient placement after surgery. The fact that elective surgeries are scheduled and many procedures are predictable in length can become an advantage rather than a source of artificial variation. Using the tools in your flow toolkit, such as compiling and analyzing historical data, forecasting, demand-capacity management, and real-time tracking, you can anticipate with high accuracy when patients will be ready to transfer from the PACU to inpatient units. Accordingly, you should plan ahead of each day's schedule the transfers of patients after surgery to the appropriate units.

A staff member from the PACU should be involved in daily bed huddles and take part in the forecasting to single out beds that will be needed each day. Ideally, those bed huddles and safety rounds should occur on the frontlines, with executives coming to the units, instead of taking team members out of the frontlines to convene. A coordinator in the PACU helps with this process as well. (An obvious candidate is the charge nurse.) The coordinator monitors PACU flow and facilitates transitions of patients to inpatient units.

An additional tool in the flow kit in this regard is use of established admission and discharge criteria. Clinicians should set up these criteria and day-to-day leaders should have authority to ensure their efficient use. Using such criteria both smooths flow and enhances patient safety. As with the other tools, monitor the procedures on an ongoing basis and in real time, and have review procedures in place to deal with problems.

Using the tools of queuing theory and eliminating bottlenecks, it is critical to recognize and act when ICU and inpatient beds are getting scarce. This keeps the system running well. PACU holds are one critical indicator that the entire system is in jeopardy of failing to keep flow moving. An important principle in this process is having a system of communication *before* PACU holds are in place, so that leadership can intervene and troubleshoot the bottlenecks causing the potential holds.

Another tool is developing a discrete Phase II recovery area, where patients who will be discharged can be moved to a chair and family members can be brought into the discharge process earlier. Evidence-based use of anesthetics that are intended to reduce recovery time are also critically important. Finally, some hospitals with large numbers of operating rooms have developed "Go Teams" of nurses who can be deployed to wherever they are needed, based on volume and acuity; a clear example of demand-capacity management, managing variation, and real-time monitoring of flow.

BRINGING THE SURGEONS ON BOARD

Surgeons are necessary to efforts to smooth flow, as we noted. Not only are they important participants, but they can also become a barrier to the initiative if they are not persuaded of its value. So management must take the initiative to persuade them. They may be reluctant to alter their schedules to smooth the elective surgery case load throughout the week rather than on operating on two or three consecutive days early in the week. The key to convincing surgeons of the wisdom of smoothing elective surgical flow is to show them the benefits: to prove that it's in their own self-interest to do so.

In that regard, here are some of the benefits that smoothing the elective surgical schedule bring, using the tools we've discussed here:

- increased surgical capacity and, thus, greater patient volume,
- fewer delays of elective surgery and consequent backups,
- less nursing stress and a consequent decrease in nursing vacancies,
- fewer medical errors and lower patient mortality,
- higher staff and patient satisfaction, and
- greater revenue from greater volume.

When your ability to forecast accurately improves and you spread out the elective schedule, you can better predict staffing needs. This leads to less overtime and smoother flow; throughput will improve. When it does, surgeons can take on increased volume. Being able to show them this benefit is key to persuading them to join the improvement effort willingly, or indeed, in some cases, enthusiastically. It may take some experience to convince them, but when these benefits become apparent, they will see them.

And our experience does indicate that these benefits are realized. The *Wall Street Journal* reported that at Boston Medical Center, "delays and cancellations of elective surgeries were nearly eliminated" after surgeons agreed to stop block scheduling in the middle of the week and dedicate one operating room for urgent or emergency cases (Landro, 2005). In fact, from April through September 2004, the hospital had three cancellations, compared with 334 during the same period the previous year. At St. John's Regional Health Center in Springfield, MO, surgeons agreed to spread elective OR time over five days instead of two and designated one room for unscheduled surgeries. As a result, OR overtime was the lowest in the facility's recent history; surgeons' revenue increased by 5 percent; and the number of surgeries performed after 3 pm. because of delays dropped by 45 percent (Landro, 2005).

More recently, at the Patient Flow Summit 2013, Eugene Litvak, PhD, of the Institute for Healthcare Optimization, presented several case studies on optimizing patient flow in the OR. A case study of Boston Medical Center found smoothing surgical flow increased surgical throughput by almost 10 percent, decreased delayed elective surgeries by 99.5 percent, and cut ED waiting time by 33 percent. Another case study at the Summit, of Cincinnati Children's Hospital, found that surgery volume had grown 7 percent each year for the previous two years, OR overtime had decreased 57 percent for an annual savings of about $559,000, and weekday surgical volume increased by 24 percent while waiting time decreased by 28 percent.

Many of the changes we discuss in this chapter seem simple. These changes, however, can result in reductions in throughput time that can significantly improve flow. When they do, a hospital experiences improvements in safety, patient satisfaction, and staff morale.

HARDWIRING FLOW FOCUS™: SMOOTHING SURGICAL FLOW

Strategies to hardwire flow:
- **Demand-capacity management**—Use the demand-capacity questions (Who's coming, when are they coming, what are they going to need, are we going to have it, what will we do if they don't) to fully delineate both elective and emergency surgical cases. Segment flow further by looking at historical data on inpatients versus outpatients, surgical sub-specialties, and case mix.
- **Forecasting demand**—Use the data generated above to plot a clear guide to volumes and acuities by day of the week, month and yearly trends. Forecast case length for each category. Establish a clear definition of "start time" as "incision time." Use staggered start times to smooth flow. Assure that pre-op work-ups are completed in a timely and systematic fashion by developing a system with assigned personnel.
- **Real-time monitoring of flow**—Monitor whether the predicted case length data are holding. If not, why not and what needs to be done to fix it? Develop and empower an air traffic control peri-operative facilitator to act on real-time sources of delay and bottlenecks.
- **Queuing theory**—As ICU and inpatient bed placement utilization increases, the number of cancelled surgeries rises, resulting in a negative

cascade of quality, safety, and dissatisfaction. Implementing effective communication systems to assure that perioperative leadership is aware and can troubleshoot and intervene to avoid PACU holds is a critical step. Implementing a Phase II recovery area to increase flow of patients preparing to go home and engaging family members early in the discharge process is also key.

- **Managing variation**—Variances in case length by surgeon, by procedure, by acuity, by age of patients, and by teaching vs. non-teaching cases should be plotted and followed over time. Best practices must be shared. Assuring there is an air traffic control perioperative facilitator on duty to manage variation improves flow. As the system nears capacity, different processes may be needed to avoid cancellations.

- **Eliminating bottlenecks and constraints**—Start time should rarely be a bottleneck and can be eliminated by having a clear definition and accountability system in place. Staggered OR starting times and improving processes on the front-end are key to smoothing OR flow. Patients who need few resources (simple cases) should not routinely wait behind patients who need many resources (complex or difficult cases).

- **Flow as a complex, adaptive system**—Surgical flow has a dramatic effect on flow throughout the hospital, including inpatient units, outpatient surgery, and the ED (when ICU flow is affected). Poor surgical flow poses major reputational risks for the hospital, including elements of nursing retention, patient, surgeon, and nursing dissatisfaction, quality, and safety.

CHAPTER 12

ACUTE CARE SURGERY AND FLOW

by Thom Mayer, MD, John Josephs, MD, and Kirk Jensen, MD

"Surgeons must be very careful
When they take the knife!
Underneath their fine decisions
Stirs the Culprit-Life!"

—*Emily Dickinson,* Surgeons Must be Very Careful, *1860*

"Surgeons must have three essential qualities: ability, affability and availability. The first is assumed, the second is sometimes considered optional, and the third is increasingly critical."

—*Donald Trunkey, MD, Chairman of the American College of Surgeons Committee on Trauma, 2000.*

Healthcare leaders are in search of emerging, innovative solutions which increase quality and decrease cost by adding value and decreasing waste in their systems. Acute care surgery is just such an emerging and adaptive solution, born initially out of the need to provide in-house or immediately available surgeons for hospitals which pursued trauma center designation or verification. However, one of the most dramatic effects on hardwiring flow is the expansion of acute care surgery beyond simple trauma coverage into general surgical coverage, as we will explain in some detail.

DEFINING ACUTE CARE SURGERY

Acute care surgery (ACS) is an evolving specialty comprising the intersection of three essential concepts: trauma surgeon coverage, emergency general surgery coverage, and surgical critical care (variably applied, as we will discuss).

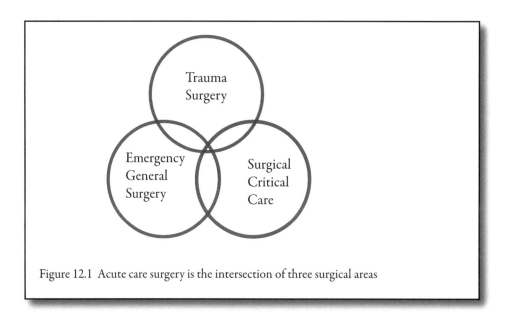

Figure 12.1 Acute care surgery is the intersection of three surgical areas

Verification or designation as a level I or level II trauma center by the American College of Surgeons or states require trauma surgeons to be in-house or immediately available to respond to trauma patients, who are defined by strict physiologic or mechanism of injury criteria as described here:

Level I Activation	Level II Activation

1. Multisystem trauma with:
   - BP < 90 torr
   - GCS < 12
   - Sustained HR > 140 bpm
	1. 2 or more long bone fractures

2. Intubated Patients	2. Head Injury requiring neurosurgical care
3. Penetrating injury to the head, neck, torso or genitalia	3. Burns > 20% TBSA
4. Flail Chest	4. High energy impact
5. Amputation other than digits	5. Falls > 2 stories or twice the patient's height
6. Arterial laceration	6. Ejection from vehicle
	7. MVA > 20 inch intrusion
	8. Ejection from bike/ATV > 20 mph

Figure 12.2 American College of Surgeons trauma activation criteria

Level III trauma centers provide definitive initial trauma care and have the capability to care for most trauma victims, with the exception of multiply injured or extremely complex trauma patients, who are referred to a level I or II center after initial stabilization. Level III centers also require coverage by general surgeons who are dedicated to the care of trauma patients, but are not required to be in-house. Level IV trauma centers provide evaluation and resuscitation of trauma patients using advanced trauma life support guidelines, with cases transferred immediately afterward.

Acute care surgery adds, at a minimum, the more efficient use of trauma surgeons by extending their capacity to provide ED and inpatient consultative general surgery coverage. In some cases, the practice of acute care surgery may also extend to surgical critical care coverage.

THE DISRUPTIVE NATURE OF TRAUMA AND ED SURGICAL COVERAGE

Even before healthcare reform, value-based purchasing, and managed care, the practice of office-based general surgery and the subspecialties thereof (i.e., breast, colorectal, vascular) required surgeons to be able to focus on performing surgery or having non-disrupted office hours in order to practice most efficiently. Trauma is perhaps the most disruptive disease for ED operations and for general surgeons in the community who are not solely contracted and responsible for trauma coverage.

From the perspective of ED operations, the trauma patient requires highly-focused resources, including at least 2 ED nurses, an emergency physician, an ED tech, radiology, laboratory and, very often, STAT CTs which disrupt the radiology flow, forcing other ED patients to wait while the trauma CTs are completed and read. Because of the relatively unpredictable arrival times of trauma patients, ED flow "grinds to a halt" or slows appreciably when trauma patients arrive.

In effect, they "compete" for the already scarce resources for other ED patients. It is also disruptive for surgeons in community practice, as it draws them away from the office or from their homes on nights and weekends, and they cannot schedule surgery or, in general, be on-call for any other hospitals or EDs while on trauma call.

Without question, the speed of having dedicated acute care surgeons solely responsible for trauma, ED and hospital general surgical consultations and, in some cases, surgical critical care is better. It smooths flow at all levels and better uses OR capacity. Even in those hospitals where general surgeons on trauma call are compensated, many surgeons feel that the "cost" of disruption exceeds the benefits of on-call compensation.

However, non-trauma ED surgical call for an office-based general surgeon is often also highly disruptive to the flow of the surgeon's practice, causing them to cancel office visits and sometimes elective cases in order to deal with surgical emergencies and consults from the ED. Further, in most cases, the surgeon on-call for the ED is also on call for medical-surgical floors and may be called for consults, central line placement, and other surgical procedures.

Frankly, in most hospitals and healthcare systems, trauma and emergency department call for a surgeon is much more of a burden than it is a blessing. As a highly respected general surgeon once said to us, "I love you guys. I really do. But somehow it doesn't seem like 'good news' when I hear from the ED."

> Frankly, in most hospitals and healthcare systems,
> trauma and emergency department call for a surgeon
> is much more of a burden than it is a blessing.

Given this disruptive nature, it is extremely common for surgeons to delay their response to the ED and/or the floors, with those surgical cases starting much later in the day than occurs with an acute care surgery program (examples of which we present below). It is extremely common for surgeons to "finish the office" prior to responding to the ED, unless the case is a true surgical emergency.

This not only backs up the ED and floors, resulting in longer length of stay, but can also devolve into clinical issues, unless timeliness of response is monitored closely. It also results in a less collegial relationship between on-call surgeons and the ED staff when the ED has to monitor and report variances in response times.

This inefficiency also spreads to the operating rooms. Since the on-call surgeon has an office full of patients or an elective schedule to run, the patients are typically seen after office hours and then scheduled in the evening, placing a demand on a less than fully staffed operating room or scheduled the next day, thereby delaying the care for multiple hours.

In the setting of an acute care surgery program, the on-call surgeon is readily available since he or she is not trying to see elective patients or operating on elective cases. Instead, the surgeon responds quickly to the ED and schedules the patient in the next available slot in the operating room. This speeds up the definitive treatment of the problem and shortens the overall length of stay.

Since most operating rooms are scheduled in "blocks" for each individual surgeon, and many surgeons do not fill their blocks, there are almost always gaps in the OR Schedule that can accommodate an emergency add-on. When these cases are scheduled during the standard hours of the OR, they improve efficiency and off-load the frequently overwhelmed evening and night operating room team, thus lowering the cost of care and streamlining OR efficiency.

Acute care surgery improves but never fully eliminates the fundamentally disruptive nature of the trauma patient to an ED's operations. However, having immediately available surgeons who routinely and regularly work with the emergency physicians and nurses using evidence-based protocols to evaluate and treat patients can dramatically improve ED flow. (The Dutch philosopher Baruch Spinoza famously said, "Excellence is what we strive for, but consistency is what we demand.")

With multiple general surgeons taking ED and inpatient surgical call, there is understandably a great deal of variation in how clinical problems are evaluated and treated. This results in staff who are unclear exactly how a given problem will be handled. However, with a dedicated group of acute care surgeons in a group practice, it is much easier to adopt and promulgate evidence-based protocols, as well as adapt those protocols over time, based on evidence and experience. This is a classic example of using acute care surgery to manage variation, improve reliability, and reduce bottlenecks through evidence-based medicine.

ADVANTAGES OF EFFECTIVE ACUTE CARE SURGERY PROGRAMS

An effective acute care surgery program affects virtually every aspect of surgical flow in the hospital. It is quite a bold statement to make, but Figure 12.3 shows the advantages of an ACS program:

An effective acute care surgery program affects
virtually every aspect of surgical flow in the hospital.

- Improved timeliness of response to ED and floors
- Improved, closer working relationship with ED physicians and nurses
- More predictable, evidence-based clinical protocols
- ED/emergency call becomes much more elective and less burdensome for non-ACS surgeons
- Fills holes created by block scheduling
- "Load-levels" entire general surgery schedule by filling slots previously beset by delays or after-hours scheduling
- Faster turn-around-times in ORs
- Eliminates or reduces long (1-1 ½ hour) gaps in OR scheduling
- Dedicated surgeons on call with general surgery commitment as opposed to sub-specialty surgeons (breast, colorectal, vascular, etc.) with limited or competing interests during daytime hours
- Creates loyalty of surgeons to hospitals with acute care surgery programs
- Potential to segment surgical flow
- Allows demand-capacity management for emergency surgical cases, consults, line placement, and other procedures
- Allows the ability to forecast demand for surgical services
- Eliminates/reduces surgical bottlenecks and constraints
- Less activation of on-call/after-hours surgical teams

Figure 12.3 Advantages of acute care surgery programs

Because ACS surgeons do not depend on a primarily consultative practice, they are able to respond far more quickly to ED and floor consults; they are not constrained by an office-based practice. Simply stated, they are not only emergently, but *imminently available* for consultation. This results in a much more collegial and cooperative relationship with the ED staff, since they work so closely together on so many cases.

In fact, the ED becomes the front door to their practice. As the ancient adage states, "Quality time comes from quantity time." Because the ACS surgeons are so frequently on call, and therefore spend a great deal of time with the ED staff, they become, effectively, members of the ED team.

The same becomes true, albeit to a lesser extent, with the medical-surgical personnel, who also become familiar with the surgical staff. This should result in surgeons in the acute care practice who are much more focused on customer service to the hospital and its staff. It also can result in improved HCAHPS scores, reflecting improved patient satisfaction…and, in the value-based purchasing era, improved reimbursement.

As we mentioned above, a predictable and positive result of all of this is the development of established and reliable patterns of evidence-based practice, where ED and other staff have a clear understanding of how certain cases will be handled and even how their work-up will proceed, including which imaging studies and labs will be utilized. This increases reliability and in the best of circumstances results in clearly defined and evidence-based clinical protocols, which improves patient safety.

While more difficult to quantify, all of the acute care surgery programs with which we have been associated have found that the decreased frequency of ED call for responsible general surgeons or sub-specialty surgeons results in a higher standard of performance among the non-acute care surgeons.

It is clear that the decreased frequency of the disruptive stress of the "call burden," as we have discussed above, results in an overall higher level of performance. In almost all cases, the implementation of an ACS program allows being on-call to become optional. For surgeons in a mature practice, the ability to off-load this burden allows them to focus on their practice and increase their own efficiency, which results in higher physician satisfaction and higher utilization of the facility with the program.

This creates much stronger surgeon loyalty towards the hospital, since the ease of his or her practice improves at the hospital due to an acute care surgery program. In addition, as the evidence-based protocols used by the ACS surgeons become widely adopted, the other surgeons on call find adoption of these protocols increasingly easy, particularly for the specialty-based surgeons who less frequently take general surgical call.

Acute care surgery adds value and decreases waste by effectively "load-leveling" the entire general surgical schedule. This occurs through a simple and logical, yet ultimately elegantly important mechanism. As we noted in the previous chapter, surgical flow is a critical area in which hardwiring flow can leverage increased capability for hospitals and healthcare systems.

Acute care surgery adds value and decreases waste
by effectively "load-leveling" the entire general
surgical schedule.

Because of the current inefficiencies of OR scheduling and operations, the timely response of surgeons dedicated to ED and emergency floor consultations allows for much faster evaluations; patients are ready for the OR much more quickly than when surgeons have to respond from their offices. ACS thus 'fills the gaps" inherent in current OR scheduling, resulting in the "load-leveling" effect we mentioned previously.

Since the acute care surgeon is "in-house," his or her ability to fit into the OR schedule is much improved. For example, a patient with acute cholecystitis needs a laparoscopic cholecystectomy. Acute care surgeons can see the patient immediately and get them into the OR at the next available time, which results in shorter lengths of stay. With the advent of the "2 Midnight Rule," this timeliness of response not only increases patient satisfaction, but also improves the hospital's bottom line.

This also allows for use of classic demand-capacity tools to answer these questions:

DCM Question	Acute Care Surgery Correlate
Who is coming?	Who are the patients?
When are they coming?	When do they arrive?
What will they need?	What resources are needed, including surgery?
Will we have it?	Will we have the capacity?
What will we do if we don't?	What are our contingency plans, back-up call, etc.?

Figure 12.4 Demand-Capacity management and acute care surgery

Using historical data from the acute care surgery program, all of the demand-capacity questions can be answered, bringing a previously unavailable level of predictability to emergency surgical consultation and response. This further allows the ability to forecast demand for such services in a highly predictable fashion. While forecasting trauma patients has always been theoretically predictable, very few trauma programs have taken the time to do so.

Extending forecasting to non-trauma emergency consults and surgeries is a powerful planning tool to further "load-level" surgical flow. All of this serves to reduce or eliminate bottlenecks and constraints in the system by having dedicated surgeons available to care for ED and inpatients. Because of all of the effects mentioned above—particularly the timeliness of consults and surgeries—the hospital's on-call surgical teams are called in less frequently, saving money. And by reducing the variation in the utilization of the OR and smoothing the flow, flow is enhanced for all surgical patients and surgical teams.

Finally, an increasing body of literature indicates that surgeons who perform certain procedures more frequently than those who don't have improved outcomes and lower costs. This is a clear example of adding value and eliminating waste, and therefore hardwiring flow into the system. When breast, colorectal, vascular and other sub-specialty general surgeons are asked to do appendectomies, laparoscopic cholecystectomies, and laparotomies, they are doing procedures with which they have less experience than dedicated general surgeons who perform these procedures routinely. In fact, in some cases, such specialty surgeons ask for acute care surgeons to scrub with them.

SURGICAL CRITICAL CARE AND ACUTE CARE SURGERY

Some acute care surgery programs also offer surgical critical care as a part of their service, ranging from consultation to running discrete surgical critical care units. However, to date, in the majority of hospitals and healthcare systems, the existing intensivists or pulmonary critical care physicians provide this service, which is generally a highly profitable part of their practice.

How this evolves over time will vary from community to community, but acute care surgeons understand the importance of maintaining a collegial and cooperative relationship with the ICU/critical care physicians in the community. In some cases, the acute care surgeons augment or share call with the community intensivists, making their call burden easier in those hospitals where 24/7/365 coverage is difficult. Finally, some communities have developed a model where the intensivists are responsible for call, but have the ability to consult the acute care surgeons in specific cases where their expertise is helpful.

IN SUMMARY

Acute care surgery is an emerging and innovative form of surgical practice, which can be a major advantage for hospitals that have pursued trauma center verification. Acute care surgeons are hospital-based surgeons with expertise in trauma surgery, trauma program development and management, and emergency/acute surgery. Adding acute care surgeons can offer an attractive platform to broaden surgical offerings to retain patients for the hospital, instead of having to transfer them.

Although subsidies are generally required, hospitals recoup these costs through new billings for trauma activations and trauma patients' ICU, operative, and surgical floor billings. Increased revenue is also generated by freeing up the non-acute care surgeons and surgical teams to operate on non-acute care surgical patients. For many institutions, this produces at least some level of "halo effect," since trauma centers are often referral centers for other, non-trauma services.

Acute care surgeons should also have a focus on customer service and fulfilling the changing service needs of the hospital, since they are directly or indirectly hospital-based physicians by nature. They are therefore dedicated to the hospital in a way that most surgeons traditionally have not been. They also provide a platform for more effective recruitment of specialty surgeons, because they either will not have to take general surgical call or will do so far less frequently than when acute care surgeons are not available.

It is important to recognize that each acute care surgery program is, by nature and necessity, different, precisely because each community and each hospital will have vagaries associated with implementation of such a program.

The adage that, "If you've done one of these, you've done one of these" is certainly true in the case of acute care surgery.

It is essential that those who are asked to implement these programs have experience in having done so, since there is inherent complexity in understanding the unique factors that guide success. However, acute care surgery offers a very powerful tool to improve surgical flow. Moreover it utilizes all of the strategies we have outlined to hardwire hospital-wide flow.

HARDWIRING FLOW™ FOCUS:
ACUTE CARE SURGERY AND FLOW

- **Demand capacity management**—Who's coming? Plot the number of trauma patients, including severity. When are they coming? Take the analysis further by plotting hour of the day, day of the week, and seasonal variations to improve predictability and reliability of trauma responses. What will they need? Use severity of trauma response to predict which resources will be needed, including trauma surgeon response (versus ED resuscitation followed by trauma consult). Layer in use of essential services. Will our service capacity be sufficient? Match demand and capacity to assure resources are available in a timely fashion. What will we do if we don't have capacity? Prepare for multiple trauma patients at the same time (i.e., disaster planning, regional trauma responses).

- **Forecasting demand**—Determine the timing and acuity of CT scans, plain films, other imaging studies, laboratory use, OR activations, other ED general surgical consults, consults from the medical-surgical floors, and consults from the ICUs. Use this data to forecast demand for the acute surgery service and to help essential services plan staffing and utilization appropriately.

- **Real-time monitoring of flow**—Use simple IT tools to monitor current flow in the acute surgery service. Use seasonal variation to forecast and monitor flow (weather variations). Factor in other variants (e.g., athletic events, tailgating at colleges and professional events).

- **Queuing theory**—SICU and OR rejections increase as utilization rates rise above 80 to 90 percent. However, small changes make huge and important differences on the "steep end of the curve."

- **Managing variation**—Eliminate variation that doesn't add value. Encourage variation that does add value. Determine the positive and negative predictive values of CT studies. Develop age-specific criteria for scans. (e.g. chest CTs are rarely needed in pediatric trauma victims except when signs of great vessel disruption or tracheobronchial disruption are present.)

- **Eliminating constraints and bottlenecks**—Avoid the rate-limiting step of CT scans. Remember that timely consults result in earlier surgeries. "Load-level" the OR schedule by smoothing surgical flow. As call becomes more elective and less frequent for non-acute care surgeons, time and quality of performance increases, both for acute care and non-acute care surgeons.

- **Flow as a complex adaptive system**—Acute care surgery operates across all the boundaries of hospital-wide flow, including ED, OR, essential services utilization, discharges, case management, and length of stay. HCAHPS scores improve as a flow-directed system is put in place. Trauma and acute care surgery reputation improves as the system becomes more focused on flow.

CHAPTER 13

INTEGRATING ANESTHESIA SERVICES INTO THE FLOW EQUATION

by Michael Hicks, MD, Kirk Jensen, MD, and Thom Mayer, MD

"Here the most sublime scene ever witnessed in the operating room was presented when the patient placed himself voluntarily upon the table, which was to become the altar of future fame…The heroic bravery of the man who voluntarily placed himself upon the table, a subject for the surgeon's knife, should be recorded and his name enrolled upon parchment, which should be hung upon the walls of the surgical amphitheater in which the operation was performed. His name was Gilbert Abbott."

—Washington O. Ayer on the first public demonstration of ether at the Massachusetts General Hospital on October 16, 1946 (from The Semi-Centennial of Anesthesia, Massachusetts General Hospital (1897), Source Book of Medical History

INTRODUCTION TO PERIOPERATIVE FLOW

Few areas within healthcare are more well suited to realizing the benefits of using the flow toolkit than the perioperative experience of surgical patients (Litvak and Fineberg, 2013; Institute for Healthcare Improvement, 2003). Busy operating rooms contribute to the financial performance of hospitals both in terms of revenue as well as cost. Surgical cases generate large percentages of hospital admissions, revenue and profits as well as consuming large amounts of resources, such as labor and equipment.

Thoughtful and deliberate management of perioperative processes can provide opportunities to advance a facility's mission, not only in caring for the surgical needs of the community, but also in ensuring the continued viability of many other programs throughout the hospital and community. Much attention is given to the care and processes within the surgical suite itself and appropriately so.

Interestingly, and often underappreciated, however, is that the performance of surgical services and the satisfaction of the patient and the surgical team is frequently dependent upon managerial and operational decisions made at times and places distant from the surgical suites themselves. Surgical scheduling, the preoperative preparation process, choice of anesthetic technique, and management of patient flow in the post-anesthesia care unit and elsewhere in the hospital all contribute to surgical department performance.

While hospital leaders have long appreciated the financial contributions derived from providing surgical care, many have viewed their surgical suites—while housed within their hospitals—as physically, even culturally, isolated and self-contained businesses and clinical units. Operating rooms typically have been seen as profit centers for the facility, since surgical cases generally provide more revenue than they consume in cost.

In fact, taken as a whole, the contribution margin generated in caring for surgical patients has in many cases been sufficient to provide much of the operational funding needed by hospitals to fulfill their other non-surgical missions. This level of profitability, while generally easy to achieve historically, has unfortunately led the surgical suite to become immune to focused approaches in operations management and flow improvement. The one notable exception to this is the extent that OR operations has negatively affected facilities' ability to attract referring surgeons due to real or perceived lapses of efficiency and satisfaction.

Healthcare reform and changing market conditions, however, continue to apply new financial and operational pressures to all healthcare facilities. This is increasingly true in the management of the perioperative experience. Margin erosion for procedural care, the decreasing ability of facilities and clinicians to cost-shift, and the continued growth of alternatives to the historical fee-for-service and cost-plus reimbursement systems are now forcing leaders to drive rigorous financial and operational management of all aspects of their facilities, including the perioperative continuum.

Indeed, managing quality and cost—the essence of value-based purchasing—and the coming changes in how care delivery is funded increasingly force us to view the surgical suite as a cost center where revenues are fixed and the sound management of scarce and valuable resources becomes the predominant mindset. This changing perspective requires administrative and clinical leaders to seek and embrace opportunities to create efficiencies, better utilize capacity, and drive value creation.

Fortunately, this hits at the heart of the conceptual framework of flow and provides hospital leaders opportunities to create needed value and to attain the efficiency and cost effectiveness necessary to remain financially viable and relevant (Litvak and Bisognano, 2011; Litvak and Fineberg, 2013).

THE PERIOPERATIVE CONTINUUM

The perioperative continuum is a complex, fragmented, and insular system. And for most patients, the surgical experience consists of a series of largely isolated interventions whose aggregate intended goal is the production of a successful and safe surgical procedure with minimal risk, inconvenience, and cost. Unfortunately, these interventions typically have a high degree of variability in how, what, where, and when they are scheduled and actually occur.

In addition, these interventions are punctuated by physical and communication transitions that are often not well coordinated. They result in a system that is not designed to maximize flow (i.e., value) for the patients who are the major consumers of the ultimate product. Instead, the perioperative process is frequently more like a disjointed sequential piecework manufacturing process whose inherent design is predicated not on the needs, convenience, safety, and burden of the patient, but instead on the workflow and financial needs of those providing the services.

The typical surgical experience for patients is that they are moved like inventory in a poorly designed manufacturing process that was created to maximize the efficiency of individual clinicians and departments, with little thought to the experience of patients, the overall efficiency of the system, or whether value is being created for all stakeholders. Even aside from the unappealing burden placed on patients, both temporally and psychologically, the typical perioperative process has profound ramifications for the overall performance of the surgical system and even the facility as a whole.

This process can even compromise patient safety. Not surprisingly, much attention is focused on the technical and intellectual skills of the clinicians providing care, in particular those of the surgeon. However, it should be argued that the more likely threats to patient safety do not involve these individual skill sets, but rather, the design and performance of the system in which the clinicians are operating. The perioperative system can be viewed in this regard as a confluence of all of the necessary components of care (e.g., people, equipment, processes, information) all delivered in the right measure, place, condition, and time to optimally meet the needs of the patient.

As an example, consider the nature of patient information that is needed to provide surgical care. In most hospital surgical routines, patient data is collected, recorded, and distributed downstream (frequently incompletely and sometimes incorrectly) to the next processing point, where in many cases, the data process begins again. (The theory, of course, is that each progression or iteration of information gathering is an opportunity to add more value).

This *should* be true. Each step should build on the previous ones, validating and further refining the information gleaned earlier. However, each step along the way also introduces opportunities for inefficiency, miscommunication, waste, and even direct patient harm. Attempts to overcome or reconcile the resulting inefficiencies, miscommunications or errors can lead to rushed workflows, inappropriate shortcuts, and increased waste. All too frequently, what we see as opportunities in workflow become all too real burdens on patients and staff (Classen et al., 2011; Landrigan et al., 2010).

Fortunately, the surgical continuum can be viewed from a flow and systems thinking perspective. Applying the concepts of flow provides very real opportunities to create value (Chassin and Loeb, 2011; Reid et al., 2005; Kaplan et al., 2013). Certainly many of the steps in the perioperative continuum, such as case scheduling, patient preparation, or postoperative disposition have intrinsic value and are important in their own right. However, viewing the perioperative process as a series of isolated steps can and does reduce our opportunity to use the flow toolkit to fully enhance patient flow and create and capture value.

Maximum value is created for all participants (e.g., patient, surgeon, nursing staff) only when the patient flows through a perioperative process where all phases are tightly coupled and interventions are focused on delivering high quality care and services while minimizing costs and other burdens to the greatest extent possible (Healthcare Financial Management Association, 2003). When done properly, the benefits of flow accrue to patients and other stakeholders, as well as to the system as a whole.

This is possible, however, only when there is commitment on everyone's part to do so (Sevdalis et al., 2012). When flow is a fundamental part of an organization's surgical care culture, the perioperative process—the system bound by original diagnosis and decision for surgical intervention through full post-operative recovery—can be measured, analyzed, and managed both in its totality as well as its discrete but interdependent units (Malangoni, 2006). With this approach, the surgical experience for both patients and staff becomes a series of opportunities that can create value for all of the participants within the surgical system.

THE VALUE OF ANESTHESIA IN IMPROVING FLOW

Successful and optimized flow of surgical patients, however, requires successful and optimized management. In this regard, the anesthesia department can provide a great source of clinical and operational leadership. Indeed, much of the preoperative preparation of surgical patients is performed in order to optimize the patient's condition for the surgical and anesthetic experience. Forward-thinking anesthesia departments are increasingly extending their medical care and management further and deeper into the perioperative continuum.

This allows better coordination and resource utilization in terms of case scheduling, laboratory and imaging needs, anesthetic and post-operative pain management planning, and the rational allocation of the highly capital intensive surgical suites themselves. Furthermore, there is the added benefit for the surgical team of anticipatory planning for those patients and procedures that fall outside of normal workflow and routine.

The anesthesia team can also contribute much to the daily management of the surgical suite. Successful management of operating rooms and all those who work within them requires skill, patience, foresight, and far too often, a thick skin. Anesthesiologists and CRNAs who are well versed in the principles of flow will be valuable contributors to every OR management team. Management of the OR experience itself is clearly a collaborative process. Prudent allocation of staff and equipment and superb communication with surgical team members, families and other facility departments is paramount. The rewards for doing so are impressive.

There are many real benefits to patients and their families when they experience care that is highly focused, efficient, and personalized to meet their individual needs. This is precisely the kind of experience delivered when the concepts of flow are part of an organization's culture. Anesthesiology should be an important leader in these efforts.

Well-managed surgical flow increases the likelihood that patients are optimized for their surgical and anesthetic experiences and this has a direct bearing on quality and safety metrics. Errors are more frequent and more serious when the staff are hurried and disorganized by poor patient flow (Cima et al., 2011). Likewise, improved efficiency results in the facility's reduced financial subsidization of the anesthesia department.

Unfortunately, anesthesia services have increasingly required ever greater financial support from facilities for a number of reasons, including the relative shortage or maldistribution of anesthesia clinicians, poorly utilized operating rooms, inefficient scheduling of elective cases, and poor management of the surgical staff and resources at the daily operational level (Girotto et al., 2010). Improvements in these areas can directly affect anesthesia department efficiencies and required staffing levels. This, in turn, can lead to lower financial assistance.

Just as we have discussed with respect to the ED, patient flow improvements in the perioperative process can have a dramatic positive impact on flows throughout the hospital. Patients admitted electively for surgery compete for bed space with all of the other patients coming to the hospital for inpatient care (Litvak, 2010; Litvak and Bisognano, 2011).

Since elective surgical cases are key drivers of many hospitals' financial performance, it is not surprising that hospitals are reluctant to delay or cancel these cases. Elective surgical patients (and most importantly, their admitting surgeons) frequently have options on where to perform cases, and most hospital administrations know this all too well. Typically then, this results in patient backlogs in other areas of the hospital, most notably the emergency department, as staff and administration work to keep the electively scheduled surgical cases on time and the surgeons happy.

For example, patients are "boarded" in the ED because med/surg beds are occupied or have been reserved for surgical patients. Similarly, ICU bed availability can also be subject to the scheduling vagaries of the elective surgical cases. Departments blessed with anesthesia leaders possessing both operational and political talent can address these problems through a "smoothing" process designed to address the artificial variability involving demand for elective surgical cases (Litvak, 2010). Demand capacity management, as we have discussed, provides an important approach and tool set to allow well-managed surgical departments to address problems presented by variability in scheduling.

VARIABILITY IN PERIOPERATIVE FLOW

Variability in perioperative flow, like elsewhere in the healthcare system, is a result of both natural and artificial causes. Just as in the ED, natural variation is a result of patient disease processes and the need for emergency or urgent procedures. Management of this natural variability, particularly when due to the need to perform emergency surgeries, is best handled by separating the emergency cases from the elective schedule (Litvak et al., 2013; Institute for Healthcare Improvement, 2003). (See chapter 11.)

On the other hand, artificial variation in the operating room is largely driven by the elective scheduling process. All too often this process is inefficient and occasionally even haphazard. Surgical time is typically allocated largely by surgeon demand and only marginally by the resulting effects on other facility resources. While the scheduling process manages to assign a date, time, and place for the procedure, it frequently does little to help manage the documents and information needed to care for the patient on the day of surgery.

As a result of this approach to scheduling, it is not uncommon for case delays and cancellations to routinely occur. Interestingly, the great majority of these inefficiencies are not the result of inadequate resource availability, excess demand, or a lack of process, but rather, are due to a relative and frequently artificial mismatching of available capacity to demand for surgical services and a lack of appreciation for the logistical advantages of a properly constructed surgical patient flow experience. To correct this mismatch for improved patient and information flow, the use of specific quality management and process improvement tools is recommended.

SIMPLIFYING THE PERIOPERATIVE CONTINUUM

All participants in the perioperative continuum—from the scheduler and surgeon in the office to the nursing staff in the PACU—can make meaningful contributions to patient flow and benefit from its successful implementation. However, key drivers in enhancing flow within the perioperative continuum are the anesthesiologists and the anesthesiology department.

Anesthesiologists are uniquely suited to leading flow improvement, particularly to the extent that the scope of their care and management extends beyond the four walls of the operating room. In fact, a skilled anesthesia leadership team within a flow-attentive department can drive processes that result not only in enhanced throughput, improved access for patients and surgeons to the OR, and improved quality in surgery, but also in other seemingly unrelated areas of a hospital.

An example of this is the implementation of a well-designed preoperative patient preparation process. Teams led by physician anesthesiologists and medical hospitalists that optimize the physical condition of patients for their surgical and anesthesia experience are becoming more common. These teams serve to smooth the patient flow experience by aggregating actionable patient data and coordinating and streamlining care. In an important sense, the preoperative preparation process can be seen as an aggregating, coordinating, and optimizing function that can be conceptually framed by the "complete kit" concept (Ronen et al., 2006).

The "complete kit" concept. At its essence, a "complete kit" for a planned surgical experience consists of all of the required components and material (e.g., labs, medical documents, imaging results, equipment, staff) needed to complete the planned procedure for a patient. In its more complete form, a "complete kit" for a surgical procedure would be the timely and accurate aggregation and optimization of all things related to the complete care of the surgical patient.

Done correctly, this approach can result in significant reductions in laboratory and imaging screening encounters with subsequent reductions in direct patient care cost.

In addition, and most importantly, there will be a marked decreases in case cancellations, particularly those cancellations that occur so late that the now unscheduled OR time cannot be filled with alternative cases, as well as case delays that create schedule inefficiencies due to unused OR time.

Unused OR time can affect the perioperative system in several ways, particularly in those facilities with open surgical staff models and those in which the surgeons have a choice about where they provide surgical care. First, since OR time is another manifestation of a perishable service or good, any unused OR time cannot be inventoried or used at a later date. In other words, today's vacant OR time cannot be recouped at a later date. In theory, cancelled cases can be rescheduled and 100 percent of the revenue recouped. However, this is not always the case in practice.

Second, because of the late nature of the cancellations or unexpected and significant delays in case starts, the surgical suite schedule can appear artificially full, resulting in cases being lost to other facilities whose schedules appear more accommodating. (Anecdotally, this form of OR "time shopping" is more commonplace than many appreciate. In fact, most experienced anesthesiologists are familiar with variations of the phrase, "I wanted to do the case there, but there wasn't any OR time.")

Interestingly, very few facilities actually track OR requests that go unfilled, making quantification of this phenomenon difficult, despite the fact that it is relatively easy to incorporate this type of data query in demand capacity management tools. Similarly, surgical scheduling has been a function usually performed without significant input from most of the participants in the perioperative care continuum.

Questions of where and when cases should be performed
will become much more important as pressures to
educe cost and maximize value begin to take precedence
over convenience.

Anesthesiology certainly has not played a significant role in addressing this issue. Instead, decisions as to where and when cases are performed has been left to surgeon and facility office and nursing staff who seek to optimize the experience of the surgeon and fill available time at the facility. Increasingly, however, questions of where and when cases should be performed will become much more important as pressures to reduce cost and maximize value begin to take precedence over convenience.

It should be of no surprise that it is difficult for facilities to excel in all areas of surgical care. The abilities of surgeons and nursing staff vary considerably, as does the underlying cost structure when providing care. As facility integration continues, it will be increasingly legitimate to incorporate information about these factors into the logistical decisions about where and by whom surgical cases are performed, possibly even down to the level of specific procedures themselves.

Herzlinger and others have written about the concept of the "focused factory" approach to healthcare (Herzlinger, 1997). Although this approach has yet to become mainstream in American healthcare—with the possible exception of the ambulatory surgery center environment—one can certainly argue that it is consistent with a focused patient flow paradigm.

Given the elective nature of much of surgical services, one would logically expect a great deal of expertise in the ability to forecast demand for surgical resources and for it to be applied to the scheduling process. Unfortunately, this is not the case in most facilities. Many facilities, hospitals in particular, face the all too familiar issue of mismatches in operating room availability and the attendant staffing required to cover the actual demand for surgery.

Hospitals, and to some extent surgery centers, typically staff a fixed number of rooms for a defined number of hours for each week of the year regardless of the actual real time case load. On general analysis, it is relatively easy to demonstrate wide variation in demand for operating room time that has only minimal relationship to the actual surgical volume or functional capacity of the facility. This leads to excessive operating costs at one extreme, or artificially created lack of capacity on the other. Either way, the end result is dissatisfaction, margin erosion, and declining performance.

Advancing skills and abilities of perioperative care providers. One aspect that will allow these types of questions to be considered more fully is the continuing advances in the skills and abilities of those providing perioperative care. For example, anesthesiology continues to experience improvements in training, pharmacology, clinical monitoring, and advanced pain management techniques that are allowing surgical procedures to migrate out of traditional higher acuity hospital inpatient venues.

Likewise, the skill sets of perioperative nurses also continue to evolve, allowing members of the nursing profession to assume greater roles in caring for surgical patients. In addition, as traditional hospitals increasingly coalesce into integrated delivery networks with multiple nearby surgical suites (i.e., hospital and ambulatory surgery centers) there will be added opportunities for anesthesiology leadership, in theory at least, to participate in and contribute to more aspects of the care of the surgical patient.

This may well extend into how and where cases are scheduled, since members of the anesthesia department are likely the only caregivers routinely providing care in all of the available delivery areas. Anesthesiologists can assist with scheduling of elective cases by offering guidance on the best venue for the surgery, and even possibly whether inpatient care is required. This type of collaboration can contribute to managing at least some of the variability around the elective surgical schedule, which will drive improvements in patient flow.

Utilization of operations management and patient flow science. Finally, there is a growing body of research and case reports on the benefits to be gained by utilizing operations management and patient flow science on the perioperative process (Dexter and Epstein, 2012; Buchanan and Wilson, 1996; Cohen et al.,1997; Dexter and Traub, 2002; Dexter et al., 2012; Heslin et al., 2008; Jeang and Chiang, 2010).

Surprisingly, despite the growing body of literature supporting the use of these tools, little actual progress has been made in most surgical facilities to alleviate such problems, even as pressure increases to deliver surgical care from a value-based perspective. Fortunately, in recent years, progressive anesthesia and surgical leaders have begun to embrace opportunities to redefine the surgical care delivery system. Efforts such as the American Society of Anesthesiologists' proposed perioperative surgical home are but one example of how anesthesia clinicians can improve the flow of the surgical patient. By utilizing patient flow techniques and operations management science, anesthesiology departments can be at the forefront of improving safety, cost, and ultimately value in the care of the surgical patient.

HARDWIRING FLOW™ FOCUS:
INTEGRATING ANESTHESIA INTO FLOW

- There is great opportunity for organizations that use the flow tool kit in perioperative care to realize gains in revenue, market share, quality, safety, and improved physician and patient satisfaction. In fact, due to new financial and operational pressures to deliver value-based care, there will be increasing urgency to adopt tools that speed flow in this area.

- The perioperative continuum is a complex, fragmented, and insular system with typically isolated and poorly coordinated physical and communication transitions that impede flow. This system is frequently designed to meet the needs of individual clinicians rather than teams or patients.

- When flow is part of an organization's surgical care culture, the perioperative process can be measured, analyzed, and managed to create a series of value-added opportunities for patients, staff, and providers.

- Anesthesiologists are uniquely suited to extend their medical care and management further into the perioperative continuum to maximize flow for better coordination, resource utilization, and anticipatory planning. Likewise, the anesthesia team can be a strong contributor to the efficient daily management of the surgical suite for improved access and more efficient throughput.

- The "complete kit" for a planned surgical experience consists of all the required components and material needed to complete a planned procedure for a patient. It improves flow by reducing lab and imaging screening encounters, while also decreasing direct patient care costs and cancellations that leave unused and unfilled OR time.

- Anesthesiologists and perioperative nurses are advancing their skills and abilities in providing perioperative care, which creates new opportunity for anesthesiology leadership and could extend into how and where cases are scheduled.

- There is a growing body of research on the benefits to be gained by utilizing operations management and patient flow science on the perioperative process. However, little actual progress has yet been made in most surgical facilities to alleviate such problems and redefine the surgical care delivery system.

- Improving flow in perioperative care through better distribution of anesthesia clinicians, optimization of operating rooms, and efficient scheduling of elective cases can reduce the need for organizational financial support for this group of specialists.
- Improvements in patient flow for perioperative care can dramatically improve patient flow throughout the hospital by reducing artificial variability for elective surgical cases.

Appendix: A Tactical Approach to Integrating Anesthesia into Flow

1. **Evaluate the current workflow and processes.**
   a. What is the current performance?
      i. Overall satisfaction of surgeons, anesthesiologists, staff and patients?
      ii. Case cancellation and delay rates? Room turnover rates? Percentage of time cases pulled correctly? Room utilization rates including block and unassigned time?
      iii. Number of cases scheduled at first desired time and date?
      iiii. Estimation of cases lost to other facilities? Reasons why?
2. **Map the current scheduling process (from surgeon office through procedure start).**
   a. How many steps are involved? Assess each step for opportunities that allow incomplete, missing, or incorrect information.
   b. Are there unnecessary redundancies, routine rework, etc.? (Think about the "complete kit" concept.)
   c. How easy is it for the surgeon to bring patients to the facility? Are the process, surgeon, and staff friendly?
      i. What are the obstacles or difficulties in scheduling a case at the facility?
      ii. What attempts have been made previously to improve the process, how successful were they, and what were the limitations that prevented achieving better results?
      iii. How often are cases scheduled at competing facilities due to scheduling or workflow issues?
      iv. What changes are required to capture more of that surgeon's case volume?

v. How much intervention in the preoperative process is required of the surgeon's staff once cases are scheduled?

vi. Are there repeated data requests?

vii. Is paperwork lost frequently or misplaced?

d. Are surgical patient preparation requirements clearly communicated and consistently applied (e.g., the requirements for testing and evaluation from the preoperative nursing and anesthesia staffs)?

3. **Assess pre-admission and pre-anesthetic evaluation issues.**

a. How is required patient information (clinical as well as financial) received and managed at the facility? (Evaluate the processes in place to collect and collate patient information.)

b. Is there a central organized process for patient information and coordination?

c. Who manages the process?

d. Does the process provide for adequate and appropriate review by the nursing, anesthesia, materials management, and bed control staffs?

e. Is critical information completed with adequate time for review by nursing and anesthesia staff?

f. What is the process for supplementing any deficiencies in preparation that may be noted?

g. Is there a formal review process to verify that charts are complete and that patients are cleared for the procedure?

h. Does the scheduling process signal that preparation for scheduled cases is complete or incomplete?

i. Is there an existing preoperative evaluation or screening clinic? If yes, assess its performance in terms of the questions. (Answer questions listed above—questions a through h—to assess performance.)

j. What is the current role of the anesthesia department in preoperative process?

i. Does it provide leadership?

ii. How many issues are within the control of the anesthesia department?

iii. Are the anesthesia clinicians engaged in the preoperative preparation process beyond the day of surgery?

4. **Evaluate global "governance" issues.**
   a. What is the current process for governing and coordinating the surgical continuum?
   b. What is the role of the nursing, surgery, and anesthesia departments in managing the surgical patient continuum?
   c. If a committee structure is used, how effective is it currently? Is there a dominant "voice" in the process?
   d. If the facility uses a "block time" program, how is managed from the standpoint of utilization goals, governance, and review of individual block time utilization?
   e. What methodology is used to predict case duration? How is its validity reviewed on a surgeon-specific basis? Are predictive revisions made in a timely fashion?
   f. Are there relevant utilization, quality, and satisfaction metrics? Are they valid? Are they actionable and does action occur in a timely and data-driven fashion?

5. **Consider day of care and post-operative issues.**
   a. What is the process for managing the daily schedule? When does it begin (e.g., same day, day before)?
   b. How are changes from the schedule communicated? Who has decision authority? Is there a tracking process?
   c. What constraints exist elsewhere in the facility? Med/Surg or ICU bed occupancy? Radiology, laboratory issues or equipment issues? Policy issues? Personnel issues such as inadequate transportation or housekeeping staff?

Next, use the Flow Toolkit to modify or redesign the patient flow process to address issues identified by the above analysis. The exact solutions will vary between facilities, but in general, the following are likely to be needed:

1. Create a robust perioperative governance structure.
   a. Ensure all constituencies are represented.
   b. Develop and adhere to clear rules of engagement and governance.
   c. Monitor performance and modify operations accordingly.

2. **Streamline information and document handling.**
   a. Create a centralized repository for patient and procedure information. As part of the system, designate clear responsibility for collecting information easily, correctly, and completely the first time.
   b. Include a "flagging" system to signal whether charts are incomplete or complete and reviewed by the anesthesia staff.

3. **Implement a patient screening and evaluation tool to help determine the level of patient interaction required** (e.g., no further evaluation needed ▶ proceed to surgery, telephone call for more information, formal preoperative assessment).

4. **Implement a comprehensive preoperative or pre-anesthetic clinic, ideally with care managed and coordinated by the anesthesiology department.**

5. **Continually monitor system performance for opportunities to improve and signals that performance may be deteriorating!**

CHAPTER 14

THE ROLE OF IMAGING SERVICES IN EXPEDITING FLOW

by Thom Mayer, MD, Greg Rose, MD, and Kirk Jensen, MD

"Think where man's glory most begins and ends
And say my glory was I had such friends."

—William Butler Yeats, *"The Municipal Gallery Revisited"*

IMAGING AS AN "ESSENTIAL" SERVICE

Imaging services are fundamental, not "ancillary," to adding value, reducing waste and improving reliability of the care we provide to our patients. Radiologists have increasingly taken on a key role as consultants in the care of our patients, guiding which studies are most likely to provide the information clinicians need to move their patients through their healthcare journey most efficiently.

Try this experiment with anyone in your hospital: Simply ask him or her what term they use to describe laboratory and radiology services. Almost without exception, they will cheerfully answer, "Ancillary services!" As we have said before, we believe that all language and all behavior have meaning. As dedicated students of the derivation and meaning of words, this is curious language to use for critically important members of the healthcare team. The word "ancillary" derives from the Latin *ankilla*, which literally translated, means "female slave."

While we are quite sure that no one means any disrespect by using the word "ancillary," the fact is, it connotes a sense of marginal or limited value that is completely inaccurate. These services, far from being ancillary, are *essential* to hardwiring flow into the hospital at every level.

Thus, the first step in assuring that radiology and imaging services (terms we use interchangeably in this chapter) are integrated into the flow equation is to assure that the term "ancillary" is banned and replaced by "essential services." Hardwiring flow requires us to utilize our "friends" (to use Yeats' words) in radiology to best assure we are moving the patient through the service transitions and queues in the most effective fashion, as judged by the "treasure hunt" to add value and the "bounty hunt" to reduce or eliminate waste.

RADIOLOGY AS A SERVICE BUSINESS

The days when a radiologist was perceived as a "denizen of a dark room" are fortunately long since gone. Radiology has evolved into a specialty founded on service, service not only to the patient but also to the physicians caring for the patient. Indeed, the trend toward referring to radiology as "imaging services" is testament to the changing role of service in the specialty. The radiologist's interpretation of the imaging study performed is a critical piece of information which will not only guide patient flow, but in some cases also change the lives of the patient and his family.

When a 62-year old man with a history of heavy chronic smoking presents with a two-week history of blood-streaked sputum, the chest radiograph has locked within it the answer to the mystery of whether this man and his family will face a battle with lung cancer or dodge the bullet. So a timely and accurate reading of that study will change the patient's and family's lives forever. The same is true of numerous other types of studies, including CT scans, PET scans, stress echocardiograms, nuclear medicine studies, and arteriograms.

One of the most important aspects of flow is assuring that the results of those studies are communicated in an accurate and timely fashion. And it is almost always most beneficial for the clinician to be available to actually communicate the news to the patient once the results are available. Nonetheless, in cases where the study is negative, our view is that radiologists should not hesitate to communicate the good news to the patient.

The growth of interventional radiology has turned those specialists into treating physicians, whose contact with the patient provides not only critical therapy, but service as well. The strides which have been made in interventional radiology have been no less than stunning and continue to evolve over time. Moreover, radiologic technicians are increasingly viewed as a fundamental part of the patient experience.

The process of obtaining imaging studies can be uncomfortable, unpredictable or even scary (particularly when the patient fears that a life-changing diagnosis may emerge from the results of the study). Many hospital radiology departments teach all of their radiologic technicians to sit down at eye level with the patient, explain what will happen during the imaging process, and ask if the patient has any questions about the process. This provides a radically different patient experience and level of service than one in which the technician simply says, "I'm Thom and I will be taking your x-rays. Hold still. Don't move!"

Finally, some teleradiologists have taken service to an extremely high level by allowing the radiologist to create an audio/video radiology consult at the time of the interpretation. VidRay® presents the salient points and critical images (including prior images for comparison) with the radiologist speaking in real-time concerning the findings. As technology improves, we expect to see many more service-oriented solutions such as these. As the world becomes progressively digital and perhaps less personal, it is critical that we continue to preserve and support the day-to-day crucial interactions among radiologists, clinicians, and patients. With the aid of technology, we can now enhance and even record these interactions.

IMAGING AND VALUE-BASED PURCHASING

One of the most important aspects of healthcare reform has been the move from volume-based purchasing to value-based purchasing, which has effectively moved healthcare from a "cost-plus" reimbursement system to one in which an evidence-based approach must be taken to decide which studies can best guide the course of patient care and flow.

An increasing amount of work will go into using EBM tools to guide which studies will yield the best results, but there are already many examples of how these approaches have focused the approach to certain decision-making algorithms.

Clinical Entity	EBM Imaging Approach
Pulmonary Embolism	PIOPED Study
Pediatric TBI	PECARN Guidelines
Pediatric Trunk trauma	PECARN Guidelines
Testicular Torsion	Color Doppler Flow Study

Figure 14.1 Focused imaging in the VBP era

This has moved the position of radiology from simply taking the films which are ordered into a fundamental consultant role, in which the radiologist helps the clinician determine which imaging studies have the best ratio of sensitivity and specificity to answer the questions at hand. This has moved us from "We can image anything" in volume-based purchasing to "We know *what and how* to image only what needs to be imaged" in value-based purchasing.

As the healthcare financing paradigm continues to shift towards doing more with less, and rewarding those who successfully do so, clinicians will inevitably be drawn back to performing a much more thorough history and nuanced physical examination to guide their care, selecting only those imaging studies that clearly add value. Radiologists will therefore have a much more involved consulting role than in the past. Equally important, radiologists will be key participants in establishing clinical guidelines.

An example of a digital clinical decision support tool to potentiate clinician knowledge and the vast wealth and experience of years of radiology experience (using the ACR Appropriateness Criteria®) is a consultative, real-time product called ACR Select. This online service assists the ordering clinician at the point of ordering by assessing the patient's symptoms together with the requested study to generate an "appropriateness" score for conducting that test. This is like an instant radiology consult. The clinician is given a variety of feedback, such as other more appropriate studies to order, other symptoms that might improve the appropriateness, and the option to directly consult the radiologist for further discussion.

It is estimated by the ACR Select staff that proper use of ACR Select leads to at least a 10 percent reduction in radiology studies ordered (www.acrselect.org). Not only does this improve the efficiency of the ordering clinician, reduced wasted time and radiation for the patient, and costs, it serves as an example of addressing the two major drivers of ACO reimbursement, namely improving quality and reducing costs. Studies over the years have estimated inappropriate radiology ordering in the range of 35 percent (Hettrich et. al, 2013).

During an international meeting in Brussels, it was stated that, "Appropriateness criteria and referral guidelines are tools available to a physician when deciding whether or not a particular imaging study is justified for a patient with a specific set of conditions. Experience in the USA and the United Kingdom underscore the advantage of using such tools to arrive at the correct choice of imaging, and indicate that the number of radiological investigations can potentially be reduced by up to 44%" (Zachariasova, 2009).

Taking all of this into account, radiology is rapidly evolving to a much more flow-directed, service-oriented, cost and dose-conscious specialty than ever before. With that introduction, we turn to a consideration of how radiology can impact the seven strategies of hardwiring hospital-wide flow.

DEMAND-CAPACITY MANAGEMENT

The fundamental questions of demand-capacity management are the same for the essential service of radiology as for all other areas of hardwiring flow.

- Who's coming?
- When are they coming?
- What will they need?

- Will our service capacity be sufficient?
- What will we do if we don't have capacity?

As radiology services become more attuned to hardwiring flow, they should routinely track the answers to these questions and display them in a simple straightforward fashion:

Demand-Capacity Questions	Radiology Correlates
Who's coming?	What studies can we plan on doing?
When are they coming?	What times of the day?
What are they going to need?	What radiology resources will be needed to complete the required studies?
Are we going to have it?	Will we have the staff?
What will we do if we don't have the capacity?	What surge/call-in capacity plans are in place?

Figure 14.2 Demand-Capacity in radiology

The demand-capacity curve in radiology is much different than that seen in the emergency department. DCM curves in radiology compared to ED are fundamentally shifted "to the left," with many more studies done during the morning hours. This is to be expected, since it reflects the large number of scheduled studies performed early in the course of the day, at least on a weekday and non-holiday basis. If there is a sudden surge in demand, such as an outbreak of respiratory disease requiring chest radiographs, the demand may well exceed capacity, causing delays for non-emergency studies.

Calling in extra technicians might be one solution to this mismatch. Developing clinical guidelines to assist in reducing chest radiographs for only those patients who will benefit is another. We used such an approach successfully during the inhalational anthrax bioterrorism crisis and those algorithms became a part of the guidelines now used in suspected bioterrorism outbreaks (Mayer et al., 2003).

Without asking, answering, and displaying the answers to the DCM questions, radiology departments can't hope to hardwire flow. Fortunately, many if not most services have the capability to track and trend these data. In fact, some progressive radiology groups are moving to aggressively and proactively use such data to deploy resources to address constraints and bottlenecks.

FORECASTING DEMAND

A logical extension of DCM tracking and trending is extending it to forecasting reasonable demand in order to manage it effectively. An early example of forecasting demand was the Emergency Department Benchmarking Alliance (EDBA) program to determine the type and number of radiologic studies done in EDs of varying annual volumes (EDBA, 2014), including:

- Plain films
- CTs
- MRIs
- Ultrasounds
- Interventional Procedures
- Pediatric Studies

Looking at utilization of services as a function of ED volume bands (clustering EDs with closely related volumes and acuities into distinct subsets for analytic purposes) can be useful. It was apparent in one study, for example, that more CT scans were done in large volume\ trauma center EDs than in smaller volume non-trauma center EDs (EDBA, 2014).

Such forecasting data should also be extended to predict imaging volumes coming from other units, including ICUs, medical-surgical floors, operating rooms, and others. With respect to outpatient settings, the schedule is highly predictable. In fact, in most programs, there are a set number of "slots" for different imaging studies, which are simply filled. "Overflow" patients are slotted into a later day.

These forecasting data should be used to plan staffing and utilization to best meet or exceed the needs of their customers. The more forecasting data are used, the more helpful they are likely to be as experience with them expands.

Over the years, an experienced radiology department might evolve from reactivity to over preparation, but the most sophisticated departments are looking to business intelligence (BI) to help manage their practices and workflow. Anecdotally, radiology contains some of the most structured and "clean" data of all medical specialties. This sets it up for success in understanding past performance and predicting future needs. By processing this "big data" as it's called, trends can be identified and allow important questions to be reliably and consistently addressed. As departments consolidate and best practices are combined with universal protocols and sharing of workflow, efficiency should progressively improve.

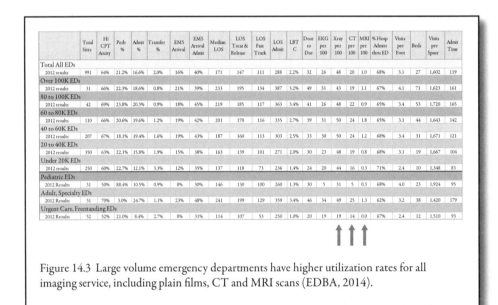

	Total Sites	Hi CPT Acuity	Peds %	Admit %	Transfer %	EMS Arrival	EMS Arrival Admit	Median LOS	LOS Treat & Release	LOS Fast Track	LOS Admit	LBT C	Door to Doc	EKG per 100	Xray per 100	CT per 100	MRI per 100	% Hosp Admits thru ED	Visits per Foot	Beds	Visits per Space	Admit Time
Total All EDs																						
2012 results	991	64%	21.2%	16.6%	2.0%	16%	40%	171	147	111	288	2.2%	32	26	48	20	1.0	68%	3.1	27	1,602	119
Over 100K EDs																						
2012 results	31	66%	22.3%	18.6%	0.8%	21%	39%	233	195	134	387	3.2%	49	31	43	19	1.1	67%	4.1	71	1,623	161
80 to 100K EDs																						
2012 results	42	69%	23.8%	20.3%	0.9%	18%	45%	219	185	117	363	3.4%	41	26	48	22	0.9	65%	3.4	53	1,720	165
60 to 80K EDs																						
2012 results	110	66%	20.6%	19.6%	1.2%	19%	42%	201	170	116	335	2.7%	39	31	50	24	1.8	65%	3.1	44	1,643	142
40 to 60K EDs																						
2012 results	207	67%	18.1%	19.4%	1.6%	19%	43%	187	160	113	303	2.5%	33	30	50	24	1.2	68%	3.4	31	1,671	121
20 to 40K EDs																						
2012 results	350	63%	22.1%	15.8%	1.9%	15%	38%	163	139	101	271	2.0%	30	23	48	19	0.8	68%	3.1	19	1,667	104
Under 20K EDs																						
2012 results	250	60%	22.7%	12.1%	3.3%	12%	35%	137	118	73	236	1.4%	24	20	44	16	0.3	71%	2.4	10	1,348	83
Pediatric EDs																						
2012 Results	31	50%	88.4%	10.5%	0.9%	8%	30%	146	130	100	260	1.3%	30	5	31	5	0.3	68%	4.0	23	1,924	95
Adult, Specialty EDs																						
2012 Results	31	70%	3.0%	24.7%	1.1%	23%	48%	241	199	129	359	3.4%	46	34	49	25	1.3	62%	3.2	38	1,420	179
Urgent Care, Freestanding EDs																						
2012 Results	52	52%	21.0%	8.4%	2.7%	8%	31%	114	107	53	250	1.0%	20	19	19	14	0.0	67%	2.4	12	1,510	93

Figure 14.3 Large volume emergency departments have higher utilization rates for all imaging service, including plain films, CT and MRI scans (EDBA, 2014).

REAL-TIME MONITORING OF FLOW

Dashboards that provide real-time monitoring of flow have been deployed in some sophisticated radiology services to give them a true sense of current performance of the system and its responsiveness to its customers. Establishing dashboards requires consideration of functionality, specific targets, clear messaging, and measurement of flow impact. Also, assuring functionality requires design, not just from imaging services but also by the clinicians requesting the study. Their input is critical to a functional dashboard and should be sought at the earliest stage of dashboard design.

Turn-around time and accuracy targets should be part of the dashboard design as well. For example, CT scans for trauma patients during their initial evaluation are time-limiting for flow and will have a different target than non-emergency scans done in follow-up on most medical-surgical patients. A fundamental part of effective dashboards is the ability to message the clinicians regarding the results of the study in a timely fashion. Finally, consideration must always be given to the overall flow impact that the dashboard has, both to justify its work and to continuously improve the utility of the dashboard.

These dashboards can be used to determine current demand-capacity curves for overall radiology services and even to segment demand and utilization by specific studies, which is a far more important and useful analysis. For example, overall radiology delays are much less helpful than real-time monitoring for ultrasound, plain films, CT, and MRI. As flow concepts spread through radiology services, we believe that real-time monitoring of flow will become an essential management tool.

QUEUING THEORY

As a reminder, anytime you stand in line for a service, you are in a queue, whether at Starbucks, an airline, a grocery store, or a bank. In a very real sense, anyone who waits for an imaging study is in a queue. Those queues themselves are unavoidable. But what is avoidable is having those queues constantly be a surprise to us and a source of delay to our patients. By using the tools of hardwiring flow, we can begin to anticipate the sources of waits and delays and progressively eliminate them. Recall this figure from Chapter 3, which shows that, as utilization increases into the 85-90 percent range, the percent and number of service rejections increases, not in arithmetic, but an exponential fashion.

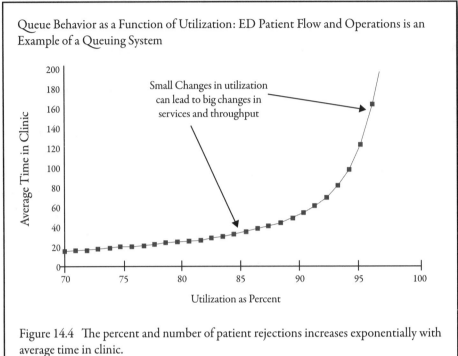

Queue Behavior as a Function of Utilization: ED Patient Flow and Operations is an Example of a Queuing System

Small Changes in utilization can lead to big changes in services and throughput

Average Time in Clinic

Utilization as Percent

Figure 14.4 The percent and number of patient rejections increases exponentially with average time in clinic.

But it is also important to recall that even small changes to improve processes in that steep, ascending portion of the curve result in dramatic changes in a positive direction, effectively moving the curve to the left, where delays and rejections are reduced. The same concept applies to areas such as CT scans, where routine usage at lower levels can be handled without delays. But as the usage approaches higher levels, the percentage of patients who wait—sometimes for long periods—increases dramatically. However, recognizing such delays can result in changing processes to increase turn-around times, by asking techs and transporters to stage patients more quickly, thereby decreasing delays on the "steep end" of the utilization curve.

A major transformation is underway in using these tools to use queuing theory in concert with the rest of our toolkit for hardwiring flow to change the face of the way radiology services make the jump to better understanding flow and improving the service we provide to our patients.

Managing Variation

As we've noted repeatedly, simply eliminating variation isn't our goal: eliminating non-value-added variation, while encouraging variation that does add value is the goal of hardwiring flow. Programs such as ACR Select and other clinical guidelines are all ways in which variation can be effectively managed to add value and eliminate waste (which, in this case, are radiographic studies that do not add value).

It will also be critical to educate patients about these changing standards of managing variation. Even the simplest of tools to manage variation, such as the Ottawa ankle and knee rules, require managing the patients' inevitable expectations. It is our experience that taking the time to appropriately educate patients with regard to dose strategies, the risks of radiation exposure, and the role of evidence-based clinical guidelines are highly effective in helping them to understand which studies are indicated, their value, and why.

ELIMINATING CONSTRAINTS AND BOTTLENECKS

There are many examples of ways in which bottlenecks and constraints can be reduced in radiologic studies. The use of standing physician orders for advanced triage of extremity injuries in EDs eliminates the bottleneck of requiring physician or APP examination at times when there are delays in getting patients to ED rooms.

Guidelines to reduce the number of head, chest, and abdominal CT scans in pediatric trauma and the routine use of "pan scans" in adult trauma patients have multiple benefits of reducing dosing, improving time to diagnosis, and bed placement for the trauma patients themselves. Such guidelines also reduce wait times for CT scan patients who are not trauma patients. More and more work will be done in eliminating or ameliorating these constraints and bottlenecks.

IMAGING SERVICES AS A "RATE-LIMITING STEP"

Because the results from radiologic studies often definitively determine the next steps in care, they frequently are a "rate-limiting step" in the flow equation. (See Figure 14.5.) A positive abdominal CT or ultrasound for appendicitis drives urgent if not emergency surgery. A negative chest CT for pulmonary embolism takes the clinician to another arm of the decision tree for acute chest pain, unless there is extremely high clinical suspicion for PE. A positive upper GI study in a neonate with bilious vomiting confirms malrotation and the need for immediate surgery. The list is lengthy and continues to be refined as we improve our understanding of how best to use imaging according to evidence-based guidelines.

Clinical Entity	Radiologic Study
Acute Appendicitis	Abdominal CT or Ultrasound
Testicular Torsion	Color Doppler Scan
Epidural Hematoma	Head CT
Ectopic Pregnancy	Pelvic Ultrasound
Acute Cholecystitis	Gall Bladder Ultrasound
Neonatal Malrotation	Upper GI
Pyloric Stenosis	Abdominal Ultrasound
Liver/Spleen Trauma	Abdominal CT or FAST
Extremity Fracture	Plain Film

Figure 14.5 Imaging studies as rate-limiting steps

One of the first steps towards including our radiologic colleagues in our efforts to hardwire flow is to proactively discuss with them which studies will best determine the next steps in the care of our patients. Those can be broken down into studies which are clearly the source of recognized decision points and those which are important, but less rate-limiting. For example, a follow-up chest radiograph (CXR) on a hospitalized patient with community-acquired pneumonia may not be a rate-limiting step if the patient is expected to be hospitalized for several more days. However, it can clearly be a rate-limiting step if the results of the film will be used to decide if the patient can be discharged *that* day.

This fundamental triage function is one in which the clinician needs to provide proactive input to the imaging service so they can be maximally responsive to the patient's needs.

All of this information can be used to help identify and eliminate bottlenecks where unnecessary delays occur and remove the bottlenecks and constraints. The American College of Radiology has also published a large number of guidelines to help improve predictability and appropriateness of radiologic studies, relying on an evidence-based approach. (These can be viewed at: http://www.acr.org/Quality-Safety/Appropriateness-Criteria/ACR-Select.)

FLOW AS A COMPLEX ADAPTIVE SYSTEM

Radiology, by the very nature of the specialty, exists to serve the patient and those who care for the patient, so it is quintessentially an example of the system nature of healthcare. It not only responds to the needs of the patients and the clinicians serving them, but its results drive decisions on the course of care which will be followed as patients continue their journey through the system. Thus, perhaps no part of the hardwiring hospital-wide flow equation is more emblematic or illustrative of flow as a complex adaptive system.

HARDWIRING FLOW™ FOCUS: THE ROLE
of Imaging Services in Expediting

- Imaging is a service that is "essential", not "ancillary" to adding value, reducing waste, and improving reliability of care. Also, it has evolved into a specialty founded on service to both patients and physicians.
- The advent of value-based care—from volume to value—has moved radiology from the simple taking of films into a fundamental consultant role to help the clinician determine which imaging studies have the best ratio of sensitivity and specificity to answer the questions at hand.

Strategies to drive flow:
- **Demand-capacity management**—The questions are the same for radiology as all other areas of hardwiring flow. However, the demand-capacity curve in radiology is much different than that of the ED, with many more studies done in the morning hours. Demand-capacity mismatches may be corrected, for example, by calling in extra technicians during these hours and developing clinical guidelines.
- **Forecasting demand**—Considering the utilization of imaging services as a function of ED volume bands can be useful. In outpatient settings, the schedule is highly predictable. The most sophisticated radiology departments are using business intelligence to manage practices and workflow for identifying trends and consistently and reliably address questions.
- **Real-time monitoring of flow**—Dashboards can offer a true sense of current performance of the system and its responsiveness to customers. They can be used to determine current demand-capacity curves for radiology services and to segment demand and utilization by specific studies.
- **Queuing theory**—While queues are unavoidable, they can be anticipated and eliminated using the tool kit to hardwire flow. As noted earlier with respect to the MICU, when utilization rises to the 85 to 90 percent range, service rejections increase exponentially. Yet, even small changes in improving processes result in dramatic positive improvements in flow.
- **Managing variation**—Programs such as ACR Select and other clinical guidelines can manage non-value added variation to add value and eliminate waste with radiographic studies. It's critical to educate patients about these changing standards of clinical care to manage their

expectations and help them understand the risks of unneeded studies.

- **Eliminating constraints and bottlenecks**—In radiologic studies, these can be reduced through the use of standing physician orders for advanced triage of extremity injuries in the ED; guidelines for head, chest, and abdominal CT scans in pediatric trauma; and avoiding the routine use of "pan scans" in adult trauma patients.

- **Imaging services as a rate-limiting step**—Because results from radiologic studies often determine next steps in care, they are a "rate-limiting step" in the flow equation. As a result, it's key to proactively discuss with radiologic colleagues which studies will best determine next steps of care for recognized decision points.

- **Flow as a complex adaptive system**—Radiology, by its very nature, is an example of the system nature of healthcare as it responds to the needs of both patients and clinicians, and its results drive decisions on the course of care.

CHAPTER 15

THE FUTURE OF FLOW: SOME OBSERVATIONS

by Kirk Jensen, MD and Thom Mayer, MD

---

*"If we open a quarrel between past and present,
we shall find that we have lost the future."*

—*Winston Churchill*

Why should hospitals focus on improving flow? In answering this question, two points are most salient. In coming years—it's happening now, in fact—the number of patients entering our hospitals will grow and their conditions will increase in complexity. The pace of those changes will accelerate. Given the budget realities of our day, hospitals are likely to prioritize efficiency and effectiveness over being able to expand facilities and implement significant increases in staffing. Providing excellent care to our patients and a rewarding environment for our people is the goal. Improving flow is a means to that end. Also, in the capacity and resource constrained environments in which we find ourselves, improving flow may be the only way to consistently and effectively improve value, reliability, safety, service, and quality.

This second point is important to keep in mind as a guiding principle in all efforts to improve flow. In working to smooth flow, the flow toolkit we've discussed in this book provides valuable methods and principles, but the focus should always be on the patient…on doing what's right and what's best for the patient. And we should never forget that the patient is both patient and customer.

That observation relates back to the first point above; increasingly, patients get to choose where they go for healthcare. How they are treated and how they perceive the care they receive and the caregivers who provide it affect the decisions they make on where to go. Equally important is the fact that, to an unprecedented degree, patients not only have the ability to rate the quality of care we provide to them, but to have those ratings posted publically—and in some cases, instantly—in this era of social networking.

One need only go to www.hospitalcompare.gov to see that reputation, which used to move at the speed of sound, now moves at the speed of electrons. The reputational cost of ignoring flow as a key tool in improving our patients' lives simply cannot be ignored.

HEALTHCARE IS A SCIENCE, AN ART, AND A BUSINESS

Healthcare is a science, an art, and a business, and an increasingly competitive and complex one. Accordingly, the quality of the customer service we provide has important bearing on what the hospital's bottom line will be. To many healthcare professionals in the front lines, concern about the bottom line may seem foreign or even objectionable, something other professions need to worry about, but a hospital that can't stay in business can't provide care.

Since resources for operating that business aren't likely to increase (and indeed may decrease) we must be more resourceful. Effective flow improves service and safety, while at the same time reducing operating costs. As we noted previously, it is important to create a culture where all of us in healthcare understand that we all have three jobs: doing our job, improving our job (making our job easier, better, and more productive), and leaving a legacy.

By focusing on the patient and delivering excellent customer service, we also do what is best for the healthcare team, too. Simply put, improving flow makes your job easier and more pleasant. When implemented effectively, steps to smooth flow enable the team to serve more patients and serve them better, while at the same time making the job easier.

> Improving flow makes your job
> easier and more pleasant.

In other words, creating this kind of environment serves self-interest as well as patients' interests. These two observations are powerful agents of self-motivation on the part of your team's members. Your team members most likely entered healthcare because they have a desire to serve others, and like everyone else, they want to work in an environment that everyone enjoys working in, with colleagues they enjoy working with. Using the tools in the flow toolkit makes these outcomes more likely. They also make it more likely that we can effectively leave a meaningful legacy, both in the confidence of a job well done and in leaving the system improved from the flow improvements embedded into it.

It is also important to understand that hospitals and healthcare systems that are successful at hardwiring flow throughout the hospital have a very substantial competitive advantage in a hidden, but critically important way: the recruitment and retention of employees. We believe that leaders and managers should consider themselves to be in the "talent arbitrage business," since our ability to recruit and retain the best clinicians and the staff who support them will be a key distinguishing factor for world-class systems.

As flow becomes embedded in the fabric of daily operations at every level, word will quickly get out that your organization is the best place to fulfill a satisfying career that not only better serves patients, but also those who serve patients. Where would you prefer to work? In a hospital full of waits and delays? Or one in which flow-driven leadership is apparent at every step? (In which environment are you more likely to leave the legacy you deserve to leave?)

A key part of the future of flow is therefore its role in the "talent arbitrage" aspect it will play. Flow-driven healthcare organizations will be able to recruit and retain talented physicians, nurses, and leaders, since they will be able to deliver better care in a more efficient environment (Mayer, 2014).

Another central principle you should use to steer by is the concept of enhancing flow by adding value and eliminating waste. In healthcare, adding value means increasing benefits (to the patients first, as well as to the team and the hospital), while eliminating waste means decreasing burdens for patients, which in turn decreasing burdens for the team and hospital.

Recall that we can "calculate" value in this sense through this equation: Value equals benefits received divided by the burdens endured. Adding to the top number (increasing value) or subtracting from the bottom number (decreasing burdens endured), or both, will produce greater value. In this context, that means better flow and better care for our patients.

SOME FINAL PRINCIPLES OF HARDWIRING HOSPITAL FLOW

At the heart of all the principles of flow and techniques for advancing flow that we've discussed throughout this book, there is one particularly important point: working to improve flow is a two-edged sword. You can study data and develop plans, appoint a committee, and attempt to implement those plans, but if that initiative is not done well, the efforts to improve flow will instead impede it.

The tools in the flow toolkit all work effectively—if they're effectively used. Some institutions bemoan that, "We tried the 'flow stuff' but it didn't work." In such instances, our experience is that they have neither understood the flow tools nor how to deploy them effectively. With this caveat in mind—at all times—here are some general principles to guide your project to improve flow:

To succeed, any flow initiative must be integrated hospital-wide. Silos are a natural occurrence in systems, including hospitals. If an initiative is launched in one department but not integrated across others, it's not likely to succeed in the long run, even if that department achieves some short-term gains. An inescapable implication of this fact is that top management must be committed to the initiative, must coordinate it, and must throw their collective weight behind it.

Ask: "What can *our* team do to make *your* jobs easier and *our* patients lives better?"

A patient flow coordinating committee should include representatives from throughout the hospital, especially the ED, since it is the front door of the hospital and the source of the majority of admissions in most hospitals. This group should develop procedures to ensure that members of different departments work together and understand the issues others face. Silos impede smooth transitions and inhibit flow, and the tendency to erect them must be countered. Leaders and managers instead should take the first step in flow by talking to others. Ask: "What can *our* team do to make *your* jobs easier and *our* patients lives better?"

Communication throughout the hospital and across silos is essential. It is equally essential within teams in the same department. The importance of clear communication manifests itself in virtually every aspect of a hospital's operations if it is going to attain smooth flow.

From what is happening to one patient in triage in the ED to what is going on with beds in multiple units, members of a small team of providers and representatives of different units must all make clear to each other what is happening and what is likely to happen, not only from their unit's perspective, but from the perspective of the system. For example, a program that focuses exclusively on decreasing ICU length of stay without involving the units to whom those patients are transferred to when the ICU accomplishes its goal may result in actually increasing total hospital LOS and the number of ICU "bounce-backs."

Top managers and the coordinating group should seek out, listen to, and act on information and assessments of processes and conditions provided by those team members working on the front lines. These include doctors, nurses, and others who are working with patients on a daily basis.

They know from experience what the current reality is, and it often is not what the processes are predicated on or supposed to produce... or what top management assumes it is. (As Chris Argyris described it, the "theory in action" is often different from the "espoused theory.") Their input is invaluable for any work to improve flow. This principle holds not just in the beginning stages when the coordinating group is gathering information and designing new procedures, but also throughout the initiative and beyond; it should be considered standard operating procedure.

Managers and other flow leaders should circulate. They should walk around their own department, or in the case of the top leaders, around the facility, observing what is happening. They should also talk with those involved: care providers and other staff as well as the patients themselves. Leaders and team members from one department should also visit other units with whom they interact regularly.

Observing their processes and their challenges provides perspective that leads to clearer understanding and more effective communication and coordination. We call this *"Rounding for Flow,"* in that it isn't just a social visit to the units but rather a rigorous approach to look for whether value is added and waste is eliminated or reduced by increasing benefits and decreasing burdens as the patient moves through the system.

When rounding for flow, look for "the seams," which are the transition points between systems, or hand-offs from one person to another. These seams are often where value can be added. Bedside sign-out rounds for hospitalists and emergency physicians are examples of how we can add value and make our jobs easier by assuring there is a systematic and personal transition both for us and for our patients.

When rounding for flow, look for "the seams."

Be proactive. Managers and clinical leaders of units should conduct rounds regularly and hold bed huddles at least daily, and more often if doing so seems helpful. Rounds and huddles provide valuable real-time information that enables staff to act in advance, based on what seems likely to happen, rather than reacting to what happens. The chances of flow proceeding smoothly are considerably higher when staff are proactive in this way.

Align incentives, understanding, and purposes throughout the system. Transparency is vital: Goals must be clear so that everyone understands what the goals are and how we will meet them. They must be intuitive; everyone should be able to see why these are good things, arising naturally from excellent healthcare, which makes widespread support of them more likely.

Expectations of staff must be equally clear to all, and incentives should align across the hospital so that all share the same goals and are accountable for achieving them. Shared expectations are not just overall general ideas; they can boil down to seemingly small details. As we saw in Chapter 7, if there is not agreement on what "available bed" means, disruptions to flow are likely. As we saw in Chapter 11, if there is not agreement on what "start time" means, flow can easily bog down.

Once you've established the groundwork for smooth flow using these principles:

Start small and tinker. Use trial and error (small tests of change, with a rapid-cycle testing approach). Conceptually small means *small*. Start with one doctor, one nurse, and one patient. (We recognize that often starting with a small step will involve more people in one unit!).

See what works and what doesn't work, and why. Refine the process, learning from testing, keeping what works and discarding or modifying what doesn't. Test again. When you're sure that the results are positive and are improving flow, expand the scope of the trial and go through the same process again. One thing we emphasize in this regard is that an idea to enhance flow may seem highly promising and may have delivered impressive results elsewhere, but it is imperative that you try it in your facility on a small scale first.

Testing prior to full-scale deployment is critical: It engages the staff, allows for needed modifications to your particular work flows, and enables one to determine if the changes being tested actually address a barrier to flow in your hospital under current conditions. Improving flow is seldom a process of "bolting-on" a solution imported from another hospital or even another unit in your own hospital. It requires adaptation and alignment to each unique healthcare environment and culture. (Or as former US House Speaker Tip O'Neill is reported to have said, "All politics are local.")

Real-time monitoring and mentoring. This is a central component of this trial-and-error concept in the hospital. Regardless of what your historical data trends show and your forecasts lead you to expect, and regardless of how well your tests of changes have worked, you must monitor what is happening as it unfolds. While your plans should be based on the data and analysis of the trends, and on results of testing and refinement of processes, real-time monitoring is necessary to make adjustments on the fly.

These will always be necessary no matter how smooth your flow. You will need to manage and measure flow to ensure that it remains smooth and that bottlenecks do not develop or are removed when they do. Real-time mentoring means not only tracking and trending data on a real-time basis, but also having the ability and the bandwidth to mentor the teams and the individuals on the consistent use of these skills to find solutions to your patient care work flow challenges.

Instill a culture of safety and accountability, not blame. This evolves from an approach that studies errors and near misses, learns from them, and works to avoid them. Errors can and will happen; a hospital committed to smooth flow and excellent patient care will have management that looks not for whom to blame but how to improve the process. As we saw in Chapter 2, those who are blamed frequently aren't primarily responsible. Your organizational culture should encourage the reporting of error (and "near-misses") as well as the analysis of why they happened, and then refine approaches to avoid them in the future. Inculcating a culture of safety and removing a culture of blame, as well as focusing intently on what can go wrong, is the path for smoother flow and safer care.

Figure 15.1 summarizes these general principles that we have touched on in preceding chapters:

1. Integrate improvements throughout the system

2. Communicate within teams and between units

3. Seek input from frontline staff

4. Round for Flow—walk around the unit and the facility

5. Be proactive

6. Align incentives, understanding, and purposes

7. Start small, test, and tinker

8. Install a culture of safety and accountability, not of blame

Figure 15.1 Eight general principles of hardwiring hospital-wide flow

THE TOOLKIT TO HARDWIRE FLOW

Throughout this book, we have illustrated how the following seven core strategies smooth flow:

1. Demand-capacity management

2. Forecasting demand

3. Real-time monitoring of flow data

4. Queuing theory

5. Managing variation

6. Reducing or eliminating bottlenecks

7. Flow as a complex adaptive system

Figure 15.2 The seven core strategies for hardwiring flow

In light of the increasingly complex operating conditions we face in healthcare as well as the increasing numbers of patients our hospitals will continue to see with finite resources, the ability to match demand and capacity are crucial parts of any flow initiative. It is the building block the other strategies rise from.

In fact, you will likely be unsuccessful removing barriers to flow until you can effectively forecast who is coming and when. When you know who those patients are, you also must ascertain where the beds are they will need, and when those beds will be ready. You must also predict which resources will be necessary to care for those patients.

Matching demand and capacity and forecasting demand are highly relevant in the environment of limited resources hospitals operate in now, and will most likely operate in tomorrow and next year, and the year after. This environment makes smoothing flow not only desirable, but also imperative.

As we noted in Chapter 2, flow involves streamlining processes, not necessarily adding resources, (even staff!). While we may be constrained in our ability to add resources, we may not actually need to. As we saw, for example, adding beds in the ED doesn't necessarily affect crowding there; improving the rate of discharge and admission to the hospital does.

Once you can effectively match demand and capacity, and are monitoring it in real time to smooth flow where needed and deal with unexpected bumps in demand or limitations on capacity, you can apply lessons other businesses have learned to adjust and refine your efforts. These are especially useful with regard to queuing, variation, and constraint management.

It is also important to understand the distinction between natural and artificial variation, so that you can act to predict the former to manage and smooth or eliminate the latter. It is important to learn to spot what the key constraints are at various times, to recognize bottlenecks that occur, and to ascertain which bottlenecks are critical. In this way, you'll distinguish between those that will affect the system as a whole and those that will not, due to their localized in impact. (Remember too, that bottlenecks and constraints not only can, but also frequently do, move, depending on demand-capacity mismatches, the effects of variation, and the consequences of working within a queuing system.)

Parallel processing. We should emphasize here a concept that comes into play in implementing several of these strategies: parallel processing. Often in processes within systems, actions occur sequentially (probably because they were developed in a logical order, and people have followed that order.) Sequential processing, however, can be a prescription for bottlenecks and backups.

In many cases, flow teams can examine processes and determine ways to carry out steps at the same time. (This is preferred to proceeding to the next one only when the previous one has been completed, when there is no reason they could not occur at the same time.) As we saw in Chapter 7, for instance, ED staff does not need to wait for a diagnostic evaluation to be completed to request a bed for a patient.

And as we demonstrated in Chapter 6, using team triage and fast tracks are effective methods to keep flow smooth in the ED. Recognizing and taking advantage of opportunities to implement parallel processing can be a powerful boost to flow. Be-A-Bed-Ahead programs, early notification of admitting teams, express admitting units, and ICU fast-tracking are all examples of using parallel versus sequential processing to benefit the patient, and the people who take care of the patient.

Because a hospital is a complex system, it's important to keep in mind that its various units are interrelated, and what affects one affects others as well. Our discussion of hospitalists in Chapter 8 illustrates this point well: Without a clear understanding of their role in the system as a whole, particularly how they relate to the ED and admission into inpatient units, they can impede flow.

When they do have that system-wide perspective, they can contribute significantly to smooth flow. The complex nature of systems influences the way to proceed with change, as well. Though we advised starting small, you can't make changes in one unit without causing effects in other units, so ultimately you need to coordinate change across units.

As we noted in Chapter 2, *optimizing subunits individually will lead to suboptimal performance for the system as a whole.* And bottlenecks can be more disruptive in complex systems because their effects beyond the immediate location can be hard to detect; this is also why some bottlenecks are critical and others aren't, because of their effects on flow system-wide.

SMOOTH FLOW: SOME FINAL THOUGHTS

In summary, all of the methods we discuss in this book are valuable for enhancing flow. But if we have to make our message as concise and as simple as possible, think of it this way: *Serve your patients' best interests first, but also your own.* The techniques we describe in these chapters are ways to accomplish those aims. To fulfill them, keep these seven points in mind on your journey to more efficient flow:

- Every patient has a clinical diagnosis and a customer service diagnosis.

- The more one needs a bed, the more one is a patient (though still a customer to some degree), and vice versa.

- Keep vertical patients vertical and in motion.

- Assure that your inpatient staff understand that they are serving the patient on their journey from horizontal to vertical each day.

- Keep patients moving forward through the system, with discharge as the clear end goal.

- Build and maintain an "A-team."

- Transformative long-term change must be self-motivated, so staff must see how changes benefit their both their patients and themselves.

Figure 15.3 Essential points to serve the best interests of patients (and staff)

We've made a number of key points throughout this book, which are important to keep top of mind as you strive to smooth flow and increase the quality of patient care in the future: the importance of Evidence-Based Leadership[SM] (rather than eminence-based leadership); ensuring specificity, use of metrics, and accountability in change initiatives; and getting physicians involved; as well as using standardization and checklists.

All can be tied in some way to those two essential aims of providing the best medical care and customer service that we can to our patients and providing the best environment we can for our staff to work effectively in so that they may motivate themselves to provide excellent care and excellent service. When you achieve those goals, you are well on your way to becoming a world-class facility.

THE FUTURE IS BRIGHT

The future is bright for flow and the role it will play as healthcare transforms itself from a volume-based reimbursement model to one in which population and value-based solutions are rewarded. The tools and strategies of flow are uniquely positioned to allow organizations to accelerate cultural change to one in which their patients recognize that those who care for them and the processes they utilize are geared to increase benefits and decrease burdens both for the patient and those who care for the patient.

Just as Amazon can anticipate what you will order and Hyperactive Bob at McDonald's can approximate the order based on the type of car and its occupants, so too will the precepts of flow help guide patients to ways in which we can not only anticipate their needs but also proactively meet and exceed them. Hospital inpatients will not only know what is happening to them that day, but also where they are with regard to their progression towards discharge and what they can do on that day, concretely, to move their care along most effectively.

Instead of waiting for bottlenecks, constraints, and rate-limiting steps to develop, we will be able to anticipate, mitigate, and even eliminate their effects, keeping the patient moving through the service transitions and queues of healthcare. Radiologists will be able to monitor waits and delays and mobilize their assets to keep patients moving through the system. Surgical suites will effectively assure more efficient use of the constrained resources of the operating rooms by addressing pre-operative evaluations, while acute care surgeons will be able to fill the slots of cancelled surgery with emergent surgical cases.

Critical care specialists will be able to not only anticipate ED and OR admissions, but also be able to watch statistical trends on emerging diseases to accurately predict when and where outbreaks will stress the system with surges. Inpatients whose care is not matching predicted progress towards health, mobility, and discharge will be monitored and appropriate resources mobilized to accelerate their progress. The various "pods" of emergency departments will not only be viewed as discrete product lines with differing metrics and missions, but also have discrete metrics, dashboards, demand-capacity curves, and deployment of resources to meet their respective needs.

Instead of patients entering their healthcare systems full of doubt, concern, and questions, they will approach their care with confidence that their expectations will not only be met, but exceeded in predictable fashion. Perhaps equally important, patients will be a part of the ongoing dialogue to revise and improve our healthcare systems to add value and reduce waste. They will then be not just patients, but also active participants in the creation of a healthcare system we can all be proud of.

A final thought is this: We are entering a new frontier in flow, where the ability to use *data* (which has previously been difficult to obtain) to drive deep *knowledge* of the system and how it interrelates can produce the *wisdom* of being able to use the tools of flow to know how to serve both our patients and ourselves. Not only do our patients notice flow and the benefits it brings, but so do our most talented leaders, managers, clinicians and support staff. Our hope is that these approaches and tools will make your journey toward optimal hospital-wide flow easier and more rewarding, contributing to a legacy we can all be proud of.

REFERENCES

CHAPTER 1

ACEP (American College of Emergency Physicians). 2010. "CDC: Two-Thirds of Emergency Visits Occur During Non-Business Hours; Percentage of Non-Urgent Emergency Patients Drops To Less than 8 Percent." Washington, DC: ACEP.

American College of Emergency Physicians. 2010. "CDC: Two-Thirds of Emergency Visits Occur During Non-Business Hours; Percentage of Non-Urgent Emergency Patients Drops To Less than 8 Percent." "Preliminary 2008 Data Indicate ER Visits Hit New High of Nearly 124 million." Press release. Retrieved from: http://www.acep.org/Legislation-and-Advocacy/Practice-Management-Issues/Access-to-Emergency-Care/CDC--Two-Thirds-of-Emergency-Visits-Occur-During-Non-Business-Hours;-Percentage-of-Non-Urgent-Emergency-Patients-Drops-To-Less-than-8-Percent.

Asplin, B., F. C. Blum, R. I. Broida, W. R. Bukata, M. B. Hill, S. R. Hoffenberg, S. M. Schneider, P. Viccellio, and S. J. Welch. 2008. *Emergency Department Crowding: High-Impact Solutions*. ACEP Boarding Task Force. Dallas, TX: ACEP.

Asplin B. R., and D. J. Magid. 2007. "If You Want to Fix Crowding, Start by Fixing Your Hospital." *Annals of Emergency Medicine* 49 (3): 273–74.

Barishansky, R. M., and K. E. O'Connor. 2004. "The Effect of Emergency Department Crowding on Ambulance Availability." Letter to the editor. *Annals of Emergency Medicine* 44 (3): 280.

Bellow. 1965. *Herzog*. New York: Ballantine Books.

Case, R., D. L. Fite, S. M. Davis, S. Hoxhaj, W. P. Jaquis, T. Seay, and C. S. Yeh. 2004. *Emergency Department Crowding Information Paper*. Emergency Medicine Practice Subcommittee on Crowding. Dallas, TX: ACEP.

CDC (Centers for Disease Control and Prevention), National Center for Health Care Statistics. 2006. National hospital ambulatory medical care survey: 2006 emergency department summary, no. 7. Atlanta, GA: CDC.

Davidson, S. 2011. "Multitasking in Emergency Medicine, presentation made at the Emergency Department Benchmarking Alliance National Meeting". Orlando, Fl.

Druckenbrod. 2004, Urgent Matters Team Triage Demonstration Project, personal communication to the authors.

Eckstein, M., and L. S. Chan. 2004. "The Effect of Emergency Department Crowding on Paramedic Ambulance Availability." *Annals of Emergency Medicine* 43 (1): 100–105.

Emergency Department Benchmarking Alliance. 2013. *EDBA Annual Report of Data: 2013*. www.edbenchmarking.org. Accessed December 12, 2013.

GAO (General Accounting Office). 2009. *Hospital Emergency Departments: Crowding Continues to Occur, and Some Patients Wait Longer than Recommended Time Frames*. Washington, DC: GPO.

Hollander, J. E., and J. M. Pines. 2007. "The Emergency Department Crowding Paradox: The Longer You Stay, the Less Care You Get." *Annals of Emergency Medicine* 50 (5): 497–99.

Institute for Healthcare Improvement Innovation Series White Paper. 2005. *Going Lean in Healthcare*. Cambridge, Ma. http://www.ihi.org/knowledge/Pages/IHIWhitePapers/GoingLeaninHealthCare.aspx, accessed December 12, 2013.

Jensen, K. 2012. The Emergency Department Autobahn, presented at the American College of Emergency Physicians Scientific Assembly.

Jensen, K. and D. G. Kirkpatrick. 2014. *The Hospital Executive's Guide to Emergency Department Management*. Marblehead, MA: HCPro. Second edition.

References

Kim, D. 2006. "Friday Night at the ER". www.fridaynightattheer.com. Accessed September 11, 2014.

Mayer, T. and R. Cates. 2014. *Leadership for Great Customer Service: Satisfied Patients, Satisfied Employees: 2nd Edition,* Chicago, Health Administration Press.

Mayer, T., and K. Jensen. 2009. *Hardwiring Flow: Systems and Processes for Seamless Patient Care.* Gulf Breeze, FL: Fire Starter.

McCarthy, M. L., Zeger, S. L., Ding, R., Levin, S.R., Desmond, J.S., Lee, J., and D. Aronsky. 2009. "Crowding Delays Treatment and Lengthens Emergency Department Length of Stay, Even among High-Acuity Patients." *Annals of Emergency Medicine* 54 (4): 492–503.

Schattner, E. 2012. "The Physician Burnout Epidemic: What It Means for Patients and Reform." *Atlantic Monthly*, Aug. 22, p. 1.

Schneider, S., M. E. Gallery, R. Schafermeyer, and F. L. Zwerner. 2003. "Emergency Department Crowding: A Point in Time." *Annals of Emergency Medicine* 42 (2): 167–72.

Senge, P.M. 2006. *The Fifth Discipline: The Art and Practice of the Learning Organization.* New York: Doubleday.

Studer, Q. 2013. *A Culture of High Performance: Achieving Higher Quality at a Lower Cost.* Gulf Breeze, Fl.: Fire Starter Press.

Sun, B., G. Gabayan, V. Chu, S. Yiu, and S. Derose. 2012. "Predictive Validity of Emergency Department Crowding Measures for Inpatient Mortality." *Annals of Emergency Medicine* 60 (4S): S72–73.

Sun, B. C., R. Y. Hsia, R. E. Weiss, D. Zingmond, L.-J. Liang, W. Han, H. McCreath, and S. M. Asch. 2013. "Effect of Emergency Department Crowding on Outcomes of Admitted Patients." *Annals of Emergency Medicine* 61 (6): 605–11.

Touissaint, J. S., and L. L. Berry. 2013. *The Promise of Lean in Health Care.* Mayo Clinics Proceedings, 88 (1): 74-82.

Watts, H., R. Sikka, and E. Kulstad. 2010. "Further Characterization of the Influence of Crowding on Medication Errors." *Annals of Emergency Medicine* 56 (3): S24.

Weber, P. 2013. "A Dissatisfied Customer? Do the Math." *First-Rate Customer Service: Tips for Taking the Best Care of Customers*: 352.

CHAPTER 2

Berry, L. L. 1999. *Discovering the Soul of Service: The Nine Drivers of sustainable Business Success.* New York: Simon and Schuster.

Berry, L. L., and K. D. Seltman. 2008. Management Lessons from Mayo Clinic: Inside One of the World's Most Admired Service Organizations. New York: McGraw-Hill.

Berwick, D. M., and A. D. Hackbarth. 2012. *Eliminating Waste in US Health Care,* JAMA 307; 362-367.

Black, J. R., and D. Miller. 2008. *The Toyota Way to Healthcare Excellence: Increase Efficiency and Improve Quality with Lean.* Chicago: Health Administration Press.

Emergency Department Benchmarking Alliance. 2013. *EDBA Annual Report of Data: 2013.* www.edbenchmarking.org, accessed December 12, 2013.

Greenleaf, R. K. 2010. *Servant Leadership: A Journey into the Nature of Legitimate Power and Greatness.* New York: Paulist Press.

Kokiko, J., and T. A. Mayer. 1997. *Advanced Triage/Advanced Interventions: Improving Patient Satisfaction.* Topics in Emergency Medicine 1997; 19: 19-27.

Mayer, T. 1991. "Continuous Quality Improvement: Passing Trend or Critical Tool for Emergency Department and Professional Survival." The James B. Mills Lecture. American College of Emergency Physicians, Scientific Assembly. Boston, Massachusetts.

Mayer, T. 2004. *Team Triage and Treatment Improves ED Outcomes.* http://urgentmatters.org/testnews/322847, accessed December 12, 2013.

Mayer, T., and R. Cates. 2014. *Leadership for Great Customer Service: Satisfied Patients, Satisfied Employees: 2nd Edition,* Chicago, Health Administration Press.

Mayer, T. A., K. Jensen, J. Howell, R. W. Strauss, and A. Lo. 2014. *Front Loading Flow: Team Triage and Treatment, Provider at Triage, and Other Creative Strategies,* in Strauss, RW, Mayer TA (Eds), *Emergency Department Management.* New York: McGraw-Hill.

Porter, M. E., and E. O. Teisberg. 2004. *Redefining Competition in Health Care.* Harvard Business Review, 82, no. 6 (June 2004).

Porter, M. E., and T. H. Lee. 2013. *The Strategy That Will Fix Health Care.* Harvard Business Review 91, no. 10 (October 2013): 50–70.

Studer, Q. 2004. *Hardwiring Excellence.* Gulf Breeze, Fl.: Fire Starter Press.

Studer, Q. 2013. *A Culture of High Performance: Achieving Higher Quality at a Lower Cost.* Gulf Breeze, Fl.: Fire Starter Press.

CHAPTER 3

Crane, J., and C. Noon. 2011. *The Definitive Guide to Emergency Department Operational Improvement.* Boca Raton, Fl., CRC Press.

Emergency Department Benchmarking Alliance. 2013. *EDBA Annual Report of Data: 2013.* www.edbenchmarking.org. Accessed December 12, 2013.

Graban, M. 2012. *Lean Hospitals: Improving Quality, Patient Safety, and Employee Engagement.* Boca Raton, Fl., CRC Press.

Jensen, K., T. Mayer, S. J. Welch, and C. Haraden. 2007. *Leadership for Smooth Patient Flow: Improved Outcomes, Improved Service, Improved Bottom Line.* Chicago, Health Administration Press.

Mayer, T., and K. Jensen. 2009. *Hardwiring Flow: Systems and Processes for Seamless Patient Care.* Gulf Breeze, FL: Fire Starter Publishing.

Resar, R., K. Nolan, D. Kazcynski, and K. Jensen. 2011. "Using Real-Time Demand Capacity Management to Improve Hospitalwide Patient Flow." *Joint Commission Journal on Quality and Patient Safety* 37 (5): 217–27.

Touissaint, J. S., and L. L. Berry. 2013. *The Promise of Lean in Health Care.* Mayo Clinics Proceedings, 88 (1): 74-82.

CHAPTER 4

Bilas, J. 2014. Toughness: Developing True Strength on and off the Court. New York: Penguin.

Brown, R. M. 1983. "Sudden Death." New York: Random House.

Brown, T. 2008. Retrieved from: http://redwood.colorado.edu/jkb/ geen1500/readings/Tim-Brown-HBR.pdf.

Ferguson, A. 2013. *My Autobiography.* London: Hodder and Stoughton.

Gawande, A. 2012. "Big Med." Retrieved from: http://www.newyorker.com/ reporting/2012/08/13/120813fa_fact_gawande.

Gawande, A. 2009. *The Checklist Manifesto.* New York, NY: Metropolitan Books.

Jennings, J. 2011. "Why TPS/Lean is Struggling in Most American

Hospitals." Western Pennsylvania Healthcare News. Retrieved from: Retrieved from: http://www.americanhs.com/Resources/articles/pdf/ TPS%20Lean.pdf.

Krzyzewski, M. 2012. Leading with the Heart. New York: Hachette.

Krzyzewski, M. 2014. Remarks made to the Duke University Health System Board of Visitors, personal communication to the author (TM).

Leape, L. 1994. "Error in Medicine." *Journal American Medical Association, Vol. 272*, (No. 23).

Mayer, T. 2010. Lessons from the Flight Deck: 10 Lessons for Patient Safety. Presented at the American College of Emergency Physicians 2010 Scientific Assembly. Las Vegas.

Nussbaum, B. 2004. "The Power of Design." *Bloomburg Business Week Magazine May 16.*

Sullenberger, S, B. III. 2012. *Making a Difference.* New York, NY: Harper-Collins Publishers.

Toussaint, J. and L. Berry. 2013. "The Promise of Lean in Healthcare." Retrieved from: http://www.mayoclinicproceedings.org/article/S0025-6196(12)00938-X/pdf.

Tyrrell, T. 2012. *Sir Alex Ferguson: The Official Manchester United Celebration of 25 Years at Old Trafford David Meek.* UK: Simon & Schuster.

Wooden, J. and S. Jamison. 2009. *Coach Wooden's Leadership Game Plan for Success.* New York: McGraw-Hill.

Wooden, J. and S. Jamison. 2007. *The Essential Wooden: A Life of Lessons on Leaders and Leadership.* New York: McGraw-Hill.

Wooden, J. and S. Jamison. 2005. *Wooden on Leadership.* New York: Mc-Graw-Hill.

CHAPTER 5

Asplin, B. A., D. J. Magid, K. V. Rhodes et al. 2003. "A conceptual model of emergency department crowding." *Annals of Emergency Medicine* 42: 173-180.

Emergency Department Benchmarking Alliance. 2013. Annual Report. Accessed online September 10, 2014.

Gummerson, K. 2012. Personal communication to the author (TAM).

Kokiko, J. and T. A. Mayer. 1997. Advanced Triage/Advanced Interventions: Improving Patient Satisfaction. *Topics in Emergency Medicine* 19 (2): 19-27.

Mace S. E., and T. A. Mayer. 2008. Triage. In: Baren, J. M., S. G. Rothrock, J. A. Brennan, L. and Brown (eds.). Pediatric Emergency Medicine. Philadelphia, PA: Sa.

Mayer, T. 2009. "Team Triage and Treatment." Presented at the American College of Emergency Physicians Scientific Assembly.

Mayer, T. 2014a. "Developing Effective Leadership and Communication Skills". *Emergency Department Director's Academy.* Dallas.

Mayer, T. 2014b. "Implementing Effective Peer Review and Physician Profiling" *Emergency Department Director's Academy.* Dallas.

Mayer, T. A. and R. J. Cates. 2014. *Leadership for Great Customer Service: Satisfied Employees, Satisfied Customers. 2ⁿᵈ Edition.* Chicago: Health Administration Press.

Mayer, T. A., K. Jensen, J. Howell et al. 2014. "Front-Loading Flow: Team Triage and Treatment, Provider at triage and Other Creative Strategies."

In: Strauss RW, Mayer TA (EDs). *Strauss and Mayer's Emergency Department Management.* New York: McGraw-Hill.

Mayer, T., and K. Jensen. 2009. *Hardwiring Flow: Systems and Processes for Seamless Patient Care.* Gulf Breeze, Fl.: Fire Starter Press.

Studer, Q., B. C. Robinson, and K. Cook. 2010. *The HCAHPS Handbook: Hardwire Your Hospital for Pay-for-Performance Success.* Gulf Breeze, Fl.: Fire Starter Press.

CHAPTER 6

Gummerson, K. 2012. Personal communication to the author (Thom Mayer).

Mayer, T. 2004. "Team Triage and Treatment Improves ED Outcomes." *Urgent Matters Newsletter.* www.urgentmatters.org/testnews/322847. Accessed September 7, 2014.

Mayer, T. 2009. "Team Triage and Treatment." Presented at the American College of Emergency Physicians Scientific Assembly.

Mayer, T.A., J. Howell, K. Jensen et al. 2014. "Front-Loading Flow: Team Triage and Treatment, Provider at triage and Other Creative Strategies." In: Strauss RW, Mayer TA (EDs). *Strauss and Mayer's Emergency Department Management.* New York: McGraw-Hill.

CHAPTER 7

Asplin, B., F. C. Blum, R. I. Broida, W. R. Bukata, M. B. Hill, S. R. Hoffenberg, S. M. Schneider, P. Viccellio, and S. J. Welch. 2008. *Emergency Department Crowding: High-Impact Solutions.* ACEP Boarding Task Force. Dallas, TX: ACEP.

Bernstein, S. L., D. Aronsky, R. Duseja, S. Epstein, D. Handel, U. Hwang, M. McCarthy, K. J. McConnell, J. M. Pines, N. Rathlev, R. Schafermeyer, F. Zwemer, M. Schull, and B. R. Asplin. 2009. "The Effect of

Emergency Department Crowding on Clinically Oriented Outcomes." *Academic Emergency Medicine* 16 (1): 1–10.

Chalfin, D. B., S. Trzeciak, A. Likourezos, B. M. Baumann, and R. P. Dellinger. 2007. "Impact of Delayed Transfer of Critically Ill Patients from the Emergency Department to the Intensive Care Unit." *Critical Care Medicine* 35 (6): 1477–83.

Druckenbrod. 2004. Urgent Matters Team Triage Demonstration Project. Personal communication to the authors.

Gavin, J. M. 1978. *On to Berlin: Battles of an Airborne Commander, 1943–1946.* New York: Bantam.

Hsiao, A. L., K. A. Santucci, J. Dziura, and J. Baker. 2007. "A Randomized Trial to Assess the Efficacy of Point-of-Care Testing in Decreasing Length of Stay in a Pediatric Emergency Department." *Pediatric Emergency Care* 23 (7): 457–62.

Innes, G. 2000. "Successful Hospitalization of Patients with No Discernible Pathology." *Canadian Journal of Emergency Medicine* 2 (1): 47–51.

Murray, R. P., M. Leroux, E. Sabga, W. Palatnick, and L. Ludwig. 1999. "Effect of Point of Care Testing on Length of Stay in an Adult Emergency Department." *Journal of Emergency Medicine* 17 (5): 811–14.

Peters, T. J., and R. H. Waterman, Jr. 1982. *In Search of Excellence: Lessons from America's Best-Run Companies.* New York: HarperCollins.

Roger Resar, via personal conversation. 2012.

Schneider, M. E. 2013. "Joint Commission Beefs Up Patient Flow Rules." *ACEP News,* January 14.

Welch, S. 2009. "'Priority One' Protocol Relieves ED of Critical Care Burden." *Emergency Medicine News* April: 15–18.

CHAPTER 8

Chadaga, S., et al. 2012. "Hospitalist-Led Medicine Emergency Department Team: Associations with Throughput, Timeliness of Patient Care, and Satisfaction." *Journal of Hospital Medicine* 7 (7): 562–66.

EmCare Holdings. "EmCare's Door-to-Discharge Service Provides Seamless Coordination of Care." 2011. In *Emergency Department and Hospital Medicine Outsourcing*, p.11. Danvers: Healthleaders Media, a Division of HCPro, Inc.

Hamm, W. M., R. W. Strauss, and T. A. Mayer. 2014. "Hospital Medicine." In *Emergency Department Management*, edited by R. W. Strauss and T. A. Mayer. p. 315–23. New York: McGraw-Hill.

Harbuck, S. M., A. D. Follmer, M. J. Dill, and C. Erikson. 2012. Estimating the Number and Characteristics of Hospitalist Physicians in the United States and Their Possible Workforce Implications. *Association of American Medical Colleges Analysis in Brief* 12 (3): 1–2.

Mayer, T. A., and R. Cates. 2014. *Leadership for Great Customer Service: Satisfied Patients, Satisfied Employees: 2nd Edition,* Chicago, Health Administration Press.

Society of Hospital Medicine. 2008. *Hospitalists: Leading the Way to More Effective, Higher Quality Health Care.* Philadelphia: Society of Hospital Medicine.

Studer, Q. 2008. "Manage Up To Improve Performance." In *Results That Last.* p. 35-54. Hoboken: Wiley & Sons.

CHAPTER 9

Resar, R., K. Nolan, D. Kazcynski, and K. Jensen. 2011. "Using Real-Time Demand Capacity Management to Improve Hospitalwide Patient Flow." *Joint Commission Journal on Quality and Patient Safety* 37 (5): 217–27.

Weintraub, B., K. Jensen, and K. Colby. 2010. "Improving Hospitalwide Patient Flow at Northwest Community Hospital." In *Managing Patient Flow in Hospitals: Strategies and Solutions,* 2nd ed., edited by Eugene Litvak, Ph.D., pp. 129–51. Oakbrook Terrace, IL: Joint Commission Resources.

CHAPTER 10

American College of Medicine Critical Care Medicine. 1999. "Guidelines for ICU Admission, Discharge, and Triage." Crit Care Med. 27(3): 633-638.

Breslow, M. J., and O. Badawi. 2012a. "Severity Scoring in the Critically Ill. Part 1: Interpretation and Accuracy of Outcome Prediction Scoring Systems." Chest. 141 (1): 245-252.

Breslow M.J., and O. Badawi. 2012b. "Severity Scoring in the Critically Ill. Part 2: Maximizing Value from Outcome Prediction Scoring Systems." Chest. 141(1): 518-527.

Chalfin, D. B., et al. 2007. "Impact of Delayed Transfer of Critically Ill Patients from the Emergency Department to the Intensive Care Unit". Crit Care Med. 35(6): 1477-1483.

Cornell, M., M. Levy, E. Martin, et al. 2010. "Rhode Island ICU Palliative Care Collaborative Toolkit". http://www.healthcentricadvisors.org/images/stories/documents/Palliative-Care-Collaborative-Toolkit.pdf. Accessed September 11, 2014.

Emergency Department Benchmarking Alliance. 2014. Annual Report of Emergency Departments. www.edba.org. Accessed September 11, 2014.

Hall, W. B. 2012. "The Implications of Long-Term Acute Care Hospital Transfer Practices for Measures of In-Hospital Mortality and Length of Stay." Am J Respir Crit Care Med. 185(1): 53-57.

Litvak, E., and H. Fineberg. 2013. "Smoothing the Way to High Quality, Safety, and Economy". *New England Journal of Medicine*. 369: 1581-1583.

Mayer, T. 2014. "Leadership, Management and Motivation." In: Strauss R.W. and Mayer, T.A. (EDs). *Strauss and Mayer's Emergency Department Management*. New York: McGraw-Hill.

Nelson, J. E. 2006. "Improving comfort and communication in the ICU Qual Safety Health Care". 15 (4): 264-271.

Nelson, J. E. 2010. "In their own words: patients and families define high-quality palliative care in the intensive care unit". Crit Care Med. 38(3): 808-818.

Norton, S. A. 2007. "Proactive palliative care in the medical intensive care unit: effects on length of stay for selected high-risk patients." Crit Care Med 35(6): 1530-1535.

McCauley, K., and R. S. Irwin. 2006. "Changing the Work Environment in ICUs to Achieve Patient-Focused Care: The Time Has Come." Chest. 130(5): 1571-1578.

Nguyen, Y., J. M. Kahn, and D. C. Angus. 2010. "Reorganizing Adult Critical Care Delivery: The Role of Regionalization, Telemedicine, and Community Outreach." Am J Respir Crit Care Med. 181(11): 1164-1169.

O'Brien, J. M., A. Kumar, and M. L. Metersky. 2013. "Does Value-Based Purchasing Enhance Quality of Care and Patient Outcomes in the ICU?" Critical Care Clinics. 29(1): 91-112.

Resar, R., F. A. Griffin, C. Haraden, and T. W. Nolan. 2012. *Using Care Bundles to Improve Health Care Quality.* IHI Innovation Series white paper. Cambridge, Massachusetts: Institute for Healthcare Improvement.

Seymour, C. W., and J. M. Kahn. 2012. "Addressing the Growth in Intensive Care." Arch Intern Med. 172(16): 1226-1228.

Vasilevskis, E. E. 2009. "Mortality Probability Model III and Simplified Acute Physiology Score II: Assessing Their Value in Predicting Length of Stay and Comparison to APACHE IV". Chest. 136(1): 89-101.

Weick, K., and P. Sutcliffe. 2007. "Managing the Unexpected: Resilient Performance in an Age of Uncertainty" San Francisco: Jossey-Bass.

CHAPTER 11

Litvak, E. 2003. Personal communication to the authors.

Litvak, E., M. C. Long, A. B. Cooper, M. L. McManus. 2001. "Emergency Room Diversion: Causes and Solutions." Academic Emergency Medicine. 8(11): 1108-1110.

Litvak, E., and H. Fineberg. 2013. "Smoothing the Way to High Quality, Safety, and Economy." New England Journal of Medicine. 369: 1581-1583.

Litvak, E. 2013. "Don't Get Your Operation on a Thursday". *Wall Street Journal Online.* http://online.wsj.com/news/articles/SB1000142405270 2303914304579194530055759414.

Landro, L. 2005. "Unsnarling Traffic Jams in the O.R." *Wall Street Journal Online.* http://online.wsj.com/articles/SB112362701513709147.

McManus, M. L., M. C. Long, A. B. Cooper, J. Mandell, D. M. Berwick, M. Pagano, and E. Litvak. 2003a. "Impact of Variability in Surgical Caseload On Access to Intensive Care Services." *Anesthesiology.* 98: 1491–96.

CHAPTER 13

Buchanan, D., and B. Wilson. 1996. "Re-engineering operating theatres: the perspective assessed." Journal of management in medicine. 10(4): 57-74.

Chassin, M. R., and J. M. Loeb. 2011. "The ongoing quality improvement journey: next stop, high reliability." Health Affairs. 30(4): 559-568.

Classen, D. C., R. Resar, F. Griffin, F. Frederico, T. Frankel, N. Kimmel, J. C. Wittington, A. Frankel, A. Seger, and B. C. James. 2011. "Global trigger tool shows that adverse events in hospitals may be ten times greater than previously measured." Health Affairs. 30(4): 581-589.

Cima, R. R., M. J. Brown, J. R. Hebl, R. Moore, J. C. Rogers, A. Kollengode, G. J. Amsutz, C. A. Weisbrod, B. J. Narr, C. Deschamps, and the Surgical Process Improvement Team (Mayo Clinic, Rochester). 2011. "Use of lean and six sigma methodology to improve operating room efficiency in a high-volume tertiary-care academic medical center." Journal of the American College of Surgeons. 231(1): 83-92; discussion 93-94.

Cohen, M. M., M. Wreford, M. Barnes, and O. Voight. 1997. "Re-engineering surgical services in a community teaching hospital. Cost & Quality Quarterly Journal. 3(2): 48-57.

Dexter, F., R. H. Epstein, and P. Shi. 2012. "Descriptive study of case scheduling and cancellations within 1 week of the day of surgery." Anesthesia and Analgesia. 115(5): 1188-1195.

Dexter, F., and R. H. Epstein. 2012. "Influence of staffing and scheduling on operating room productivity." In: A. D. Kaye, C. J. Fox, and R. D.

Urman (Eds.). Operating room leadership and management. p. 46-66. Cambridge: Cambridge University Press.

Dexter, F., and R. D. Traub. 2002. "How to schedule elective surgical cases into specific operating rooms to maximize the efficiency of use of operating room time." Anesthesia and Analgesis. 94(4): 933-942.

Girotto, J. A., P. F. Koltz, and G. Drugas. 2010. "Optimizing your operating room: or why large, traditional hospitals don't work." International Journal of Surgery. 8(5): 359-367.

Healthcare Financial Management Association. 2003. Achieving operating room efficiency through process integration. Healthcare Financial Management. 57: 1-7.

Herzlinger, R. 1997. "Market-driven healthcare: who wins, who loses in the transformation of America's largest service industry." Reading, MA: Addison-Wesley.

Heslin, M. J., B. E. Doster, S. L. Daily, M. R. Waldrum, A. M. Boudreaux, A. B. Smith, L. W. Rue. 2008. "Durable improvements in efficiency, safety, and satisfaction in the operating room." Journal of the American College of Surgeons. 206(5): 1083-1089.

Institute for Healthcare Improvement. 2003. "Optimizing patient flow: moving patients smoothly through acute care settings." IHI Innovation Series White Paper.

Jeang, A., and A.-J. Chiang. 2010. "Economic and quality scheduling for effective utilization of operating rooms." Journal of Medical Systems. 36(3): 1205-1222.

Kaplan, G., G. Bo-Linn, P. Carayon, P. J. Pronovost, W. B. Rouse, P. P. Reid, and R. Saunders. 2013. "Bringing a systems approach to health." Discussion paper. Institute of Medicine of the National Academies.

Landrigan, C. P., G. J. Parry, C. B. Bones, A. D. Hackbarth, D. A. Goldmann, and P. J. Sharek. 2010. "Temporal trends in rates of patient harm resulting from medical care." New England Journal of Medicine. 363(22): 2124-2134.

Litvak, E., and H. Fineberg. 2013. "Smoothing the way to High Quality, Safety, and Economy." New England Journal of Medicine. 369(17): 1581-1583.

Litvak, E., and M. Bisognano. 2011. "More patients, less payment: increasing hospital efficiency in the aftermath of health reform." Health Affairs. 30(1): 76-80.

Litvak, E. 2010. Managing patient flow in hospitals: strategies and solutions." (2nd ED.) Oak Brook: Joint Commission Resources.

Malangoni, M. A. 2006. "Assessing operating room efficiency and parallel processing." Ann. Surg. 243(1): 15-16.

Reid, P. P., Compton, W. D., Grossman, J. H., and G. Fanjiang. 2005. "Building a better delivery system: a new engineering/healthcare partnership." National Academies Press.

Ronen, B., J. S. Pliskin, and S. Pass. 2006. "Focused operations management for health services organizations. (1st ED.) Jossey-Bass.

Sevdalis, N., L. Hull, and D. J. Birnbach. 2012. "Improving patient safety in the operating theatre and perioperative care: obstacles, interventions, and priorities for accelerating progress." British Journal of Anaesthesia. 109(1): i3-i16.

CHAPTER 14

Emergency Department Benchmarking Alliance. 2014. Annual Report. www.edbenchmarkingalliance.com. Accessed September 21, 2014.

Hettrich C. M., R. C. Mather III, M. K. Sethi, R. M. Nunley, A. A. Jahangir, and the Washington Health Policy Fellows. 2013. "The costs of defensive medicine, Washington, D.C." American Academy of Orthopedic Surgeons.

Mayer, T. A., A. Morrison, S. Bersoff-Matcha, G. Drukenbrod, C. Murphy, J. Howell, D. Hanfling, R. Cates, D. Pauz, and J. Earls. "Inhalational Anthrax Due to Bioterrorism: Would Current Centers for Disease Control and Prevention Guidelines Have Identified the 11 Patients with Inhalational Anthrax from October through November 2001?" *Clinical Infectious Diseases.* 36(10): 1275-1283.

Zachariasova, M. 2009. "Justification of Medical Exposure in Diagnostic Imaging." Proceedings of an International Workshop. Brussels.

CHAPTER 15

Mayer, T. 2014. Teams and Teamwork." Presented to the American College of Emergency Physicians Emergency Department Directors Academy, Phase II. Dallas, Texas.

ADDITIONAL RESOURCES

About Studer Group:

Learn more about Studer Group by scanning the QR code with your mobile device or by visiting www.studergroup.com/about_studergroup/index. dot.

Our mission is simple: We want to make healthcare a better place for employees to work, physicians to practice medicine, and patients to receive care. You, the healthcare leaders of today, are integral to this mission. Your issues matter to us. Your outcomes are our priority. We succeed only when you succeed.

We equip organizations with proven tools, techniques, software, behaviors, and processes necessary for lasting, positive change that improves care delivery and, ultimately, saves lives. Through an evidence-based framework and innovative thinking, Studer Group is the authentic, energetic expert that provides organizations with the skills needed to transform. This structure and focus allows organizations to achieve higher accountability and transparency, and sustain consistency of operational, clinical, and experience results. Taking the highest calling to a higher level.

Working together, organizations are able to realize outcomes that matter most to physicians, employees, and most importantly, patients. We find that when we remain mission-focused in all that we do and teach, we are able to live out our purpose of making an undeniable difference in healthcare.

Studer Group Coaching:

Learn more about Studer Group coaching by scanning the QR code with your mobile device or by visiting www.studergroup.com/coaching.

Healthcare Organization Coaching

As value-based purchasing changes the healthcare landscape forever, organizations need to execute quickly and consistently, achieve better outcomes across the board, and sustain improvements year after year. Studer Group's team of performance experts has hands-on experience in all aspects of achieving breakthrough results. They provide the strategic thinking, the Evidence-Based Leadership framework, the practical tactics, and the ongoing support to help our partners excel in this high-pressure environment. Our performance experts work with a variety of organizations, from academic medical centers to large healthcare systems to small rural hospitals.

Emergency Department Coaching

With public reporting of data coming in the future, healthcare organizations can no longer accept crowded Emergency Departments and long patient wait times. Our team of ED coach experts will partner with you to implement best practices, proven tools, and tactics using our Evidence-Based Leadership approach to improve results in the Emergency Department that stretch or impact across the entire organization. Key deliverables include improving flow, decreasing staff turnover, increasing employee, physician, and patient satisfaction, decreasing door-to-doctor times, reducing left without being seen rates, increasing upfront cash collections, and increasing patient volumes and revenue.

<u>Physician Integration & Partnership Coaching</u>

Physician integration is critical to an organization's ability to run smoothly and efficiently. Studer Group coaches diagnose how aligned physicians are with your mission and goals, train you on how to effectively provide performance feedback, and help physicians develop the skills they need to prevent burnout. The goal is to help physicians become engaged, enthusiastic partners in the truest sense of the word—which optimizes HCAHPS results and creates a better continuum of high-quality patient care.

Books: categorized by audience

Explore the Fire Starter Publishing website by scanning the QR code with your mobile device or by visiting www.firestarterpublishing.com.

<u>Senior Leaders & Physicians</u>

Straight A Leadership: Alignment, Action, Accountability—A guide that will help you identify gaps in Alignment, Action, and Accountability, create a plan to fill them, and become a more resourceful, agile, high-performing organization, written by Quint Studer.

Engaging Physicians: A Manual to Physician Partnership—A tactical and passionate roadmap for physician collaboration to generate organizational high performance, written by Stephen C. Beeson, MD.

Excellence with an Edge: Practicing Medicine in a Competitive Environment—An insightful book that provides practical tools and techniques you need to know to have a solid grasp of the business side of making a living in healthcare, written by Michael T. Harris, MD.

Leadership and Medicine—A book that makes sense of the complex challenges of healthcare and offers a wealth of practical advice to future generations, written by Floyd D. Loop, MD, former chief executive of the Cleveland Clinic (1989-2004).

<u>Physicians</u>

Practicing Excellence: A Physician's Manual to Exceptional Health Care—This book, written by Stephen C. Beeson, MD, is a brilliant guide to implementing physician leadership and behaviors that will create a high-performance workplace.

<u>All Leaders</u>

A Culture of High Performance: Achieving Higher Quality at a Lower Cost—A must-have for any leader struggling to shore up margins while sustaining an organization that's a great place for employees to work, physicians to practice medicine, and patients to receive care.

The Great Employee Handbook: Making Work and Life Better—This book is a valuable resource for employees at all levels who want to learn how to handle tough workplace situations—skills that normally come only from a lifetime of experience. Wall Street Journal bestselling author Quint Studer has pulled together the best insights gained from working with thousands of employees during his career.

Hey Cupcake! We Are ALL Leaders—Author Liz Jazwiec explains that we'll all eventually be called on to lead someone, whether it's a department, a shift, a project team, or a new employee. In her trademark slightly sarcastic (and hilarious) voice, she provides learned-the-hardway insights that will benefit leaders in every industry and at every level.

The HCAHPS Handbook: Hardwire Your Hospital for Pay-for-Performance Success—A practical resource filled with actionable tips proven to help hospitals improve patient perception of care. Written by Quint Studer, Brian C. Robinson, and Karen Cook, RN.

Hardwiring Excellence—A BusinessWeek bestseller, this book is a road map to creating and sustaining a "Culture of Service and Operational Excellence" that drives bottom-line results. Written by Quint Studer.

Results That Last—A Wall Street Journal bestseller by Quint Studer that teaches leaders in every industry how to apply his tactics and strategies to their own organizations to build a corporate culture that consistently reaches and exceeds its goals.

Hardwiring Flow: Systems and Processes for Seamless Patient Care—Drs. Thom Mayer and Kirk Jensen delve into one of the most critical issues facing healthcare leaders today: patient flow.

Eat That Cookie!: Make Workplace Positivity Pay Off...For Individuals, Teams, and Organizations—Written by Liz Jazwiec, RN, this book is funny, inspiring, relatable, and is packed with realistic, down-to-earth tactics to infuse positivity into your culture.

"I'm Sorry to Hear That..." Real-Life Responses to Patients' 101 Most Common Complaints About Health Care—When you respond to a patient's complaint, you are responding to the patient's sense of helplessness and anxiety. The service recovery scripts offered in this book can help you recover a patient's confidence in you and your organization. Authored by Susan Keane Baker and Leslie Bank.

101 Answers to Questions Leaders Ask—By Quint Studer and Studer Group coaches, offers practical, prescriptive solutions to some of the many questions he's received from healthcare leaders around the country.

Over Our Heads: An Analogy on Healthcare, Good Intentions, and Unforeseen Consequences—This book, written by Rulon F. Stacey, PhD, FACHE, uses a grocery store analogy to illustrate how government intervention leads to economic crisis and eventually, collapse.

Oh No...Not More of That Fluffy Stuff! The Power of Engagement—Written by Rich Bluni, RN, this funny, heartfelt book explores what it takes to overcome obstacles and tap into the passion that fuels our best work. Its practical exercises help employees at all levels get happier, more excited, and more connected to the meaning in our daily lives.

Nurse Leaders and Nurses

The Nurse Leader Handbook: The Art and Science of Nurse Leadership—By Studer Group senior nursing and physician leaders from across the country, is filled with knowledge that provides nurse leaders with a solid foundation for success. It also serves as a reference they can revisit again and again when they have questions or need a quick refresher course in a particular area of the job.

Inspired Nurse and Inspired Journal—By Rich Bluni, RN, helps maintain and recapture the inspiration nurses felt at the start of their journey with action-oriented "spiritual stretches" and stories that illuminate those sacred moments we all experience.

Emergency Department Team

Advance Your Emergency Department: Leading in a New Era—As this critical book asserts, world-class Emergency Departments don't follow. They lead. Stephanie J. Baker, RN, CEN, MBA, Regina Shupe, RN, MSN, CEN, and Dan Smith, MD, FACEP, share high-impact strategies and tactics to help your ED get results more efficiently, effectively, and collaboratively. Master them and you'll improve quality, exceed patient expectations, and ultimately help the entire organization maintain and grow its profit margin.

Excellence in the Emergency Department—A book by Stephanie Baker, RN, CEN, MBA, is filled with proven, easy-to-implement, step-by-step instructions that will help you move your Emergency Department forward.

Studer Conferences:

Studer Conferences is a three-day interactive learning event designed to provide healthcare leaders with an authentic, practical learning experience.

Learn from innovative and inspiring keynotes with hands-on workshops and nuts-and-bolts sessions. The faculty at Studer Conferences go beyond PowerPoint slides and lectures to show you "what right looks like" with live-on-stage role playing and "how-to" sessions.

In 2015, Studer Group reformatted our conferences to bring you multiple conferences in one place to maximize your learning, reduce travel costs, and better utilize time away from your job.

Find out more and register for Studer Conferences at www.studergroup. com.

About the Authors

Thom A. Mayer, MD, FACEP, FAAP

Dr. Thom Mayer is the Chief Executive Officer of BestPractices, Inc., a National Executive Vice President of EmCare, and a medical director for Studer Group. He has been widely recognized as one of the nation's foremost experts in leadership, management, customer service, and flow in healthcare. He is also recognized as an expert in emergency medicine, pediatric emergency medicine, trauma, bioterrorism, and sports medicine.

Emergency Departments under his guidance have won prestigious awards from virtually every organization recognizing excellence in healthcare, including Press Ganey, PRC, Gallup, the Institute for Healthcare Improvement, the America College of Healthcare Executives, the Healthcare Advisory Board, and the Robert Wood Johnson Foundation. Recently, the Risk Free Emergency Department Patient Safety Program designed and implemented by Dr. Mayer and Dr. Jensen won the Urgent Matters Innovation Runner-up Award in 2014. Dr. Mayer also serves as the medical director of the NFL Players Association, where his leadership has revolutionized the care of injured athletes, especially in the crucial area of sports concussions.

Dr. Mayer has published over 100 articles and 120 book chapters, and has edited 20 textbooks. Most recently, Dr. Mayer has written *Strauss and Mayer's Emergency Department Management and Leadership for Great Customer Service: Satisfied Employees, Satisfied Patients 2nd Edition*, as well as *Leadership for Smooth Patient Flow*, written with Dr. Jensen and published by the American College of Healthcare Executives. The latter book was given the 2007 James A. Hamilton Award from the ACHE for the best book on healthcare leadership.

On September 11, 2001, Dr. Mayer served as one of the command physicians at the Pentagon Rescue Operation, coordinating medical assets at the site. The BestPractices physicians at Inova Fairfax Hospital were the first to successfully diagnose and treat inhalational anthrax victims during the fall 2001 anthrax crises, and Dr. Mayer has served the Department of Defense on Defense Science Board Task Forces on Bioterrorism, Homeland Security, and Consequences of Weapons of Mass Destruction.

Dr. Mayer's skill as a speaker is attested to by the fact that he has been the keynote speaker at numerous conferences, including the Press Ganey National Client Conference (twice), the PRC National Conference, and the Robert Wood Johnson Foundation Urgent Matters Conference, among others. He was named the American College of Emergency Physicians Speaker of the Year in the second year that award was given and has twice won the American College of Emergency Physicians Over-the-Top-Award for the highest scores among its speakers. Dr. Mayer was selected to present the most prestigious named lectureships for the American College of Emergency Physicians, the James Mills and Colin Rorrie lectures. Dr. Mayer has also spoken at Studer Group national conferences and regional conferences as well.

Dr. Mayer's academic appointments are as clinical professor of emergency medicine at the George Washington and University of Virginia Schools of Medicine and senior lecturing fellow, Duke University School of Medicine. Dr. Mayer's passion and energy in speaking about cutting-edge healthcare topics have resulted in valuable lessons for leaders and managers in healthcare, and he has received uniformly excellent reviews for his speeches.

Kirk B. Jensen, MD, MBA, FACEP

Dr. Kirk Jensen has spent over 20 years in emergency medicine management and clinical care. Board-certified in emergency medicine, he has been medical director for several Emergency Departments and is chief medical officer for Best-Practices and a medical director for Studer Group.

As a faculty member for the Institute for Healthcare Improvement (IHI), Dr. Jensen focuses on quality improvement, patient satisfaction, and patient flow both within the ED and throughout the hospital. He chaired two IHI Communities: Improving Flow through Acute Care Settings and Operational and Clinical Improvement in the Emergency Department. He currently leads the innovative seminar Cracking the Code to Hospital-Wide Patient Flow.

Dr. Jensen is a popular speaker and coach for EDs across the country. He is coauthor of the 2007 ACHE Hamilton Award-winning book, Leadership for Smooth Patient Flow. He is the recipient of the 2007-08 ACEP Honorable Mention Speaker of the Year Award. Dr Jensen presents on patient safety, patient flow, operations management, and change management at the ACEP Emergency Department Directors Academy. In addition, Dr. Jensen served on the expert panel and site examination team of Urgent Matters, a Robert Wood Johnson Foundation Initiative focusing on helping hospitals eliminate ED crowding and congestion as well as preserving the healthcare safety net.

Dr. Jensen holds a bachelor's degree in biology from the University of Illinois (Champaign) and a medical degree from the University of Illinois (Chicago). He completed a residency in emergency medicine at the University of Chicago and an MBA at the University of Tennessee.